Convergences

Inventories of the Present

Edward W. Said, General Editor

Off Center

Power and Culture Relations
between Japan and the United States

Masao Miyoshi

Harvard University Press
Cambridge, Massachusetts
London, England
1991

Library of Congress Cataloging-in-Publication Data

Miyoshi, Masao.
    Off center : power and culture relations between Japan and the
    United States   / Masao Miyoshi
    p.   cm. — (Convergences)
    Includes bibliographical references and index.
    ISBN 0-674-63175-7 (alk. paper)
    1. United States—Relations—Japan. 2. Japan—Relations—United States.
    3. Japanese fiction—20th century—History and criticism. 4. Literature,
    Comparative—Japanese and Western—History and criticism. 5. Literature,
    Comparative—Western and Japanese—History and criticism. I. Title.
    II. Series: Convergences.
    (Cambridge, Mass.)
    E183.8.J3M58 1991
    303.48'252073—dc20
    91-14420
    CIP

To Oe Kenzaburo

Contents

Note on Japanese Names and Terms

Japanese names throughout the book, except those of Japanese-Americans and Japanese-Europeans, are written in Japanese order, surname first. In the case of Tanizaki Junichiro, for example, Tanizaki is his family name or surname, and Junichiro his given name. Usually a Japanese has no middle name. Some writers are known in Japan by their surname and some by their given name: Tanizaki Junichiro is known as Tanizaki, while Natsume Soseki is known as Soseki. Usually—but not always—as writers achieve canonic status (often after death), they come to be known by their given names. This book follows the general usage.

All Japanese names are indexed under the surname. The names of Japanese nationals have no comma between the surname and the given name; the Japanese names of non-Japanese persons (such as Japanese-Americans) have a comma, indicating the conventional inversion of names for indexing: "Mishima Yukio" but "Ishiguro, Kazuo."

I have decided against the use of macrons to indicate long vowels in transliterated Japanese. Those who know the language will have no difficulty in differentiating the vowels, while to those without the language macrons are of little use.

Off Center

Introduction

Encounter with others is obviously a concern for everyone, no matter how reclusive. One always devises ways to meet, although the meeting takes different forms depending on the historical context. The understanding of particular modes and manners of encounter is crucial, and such knowledge produces disciplines from history and comparative literature to economics and psychology, from geography and sociology to political science and anthropology. Years ago I wrote a book in which I examined Japan's discovery of the West as the West forcibly reopened Japanese ports in the mid-nineteenth century. Through archival and textual studies, I sought to recover certain events and facts as well as the language in which they were recorded.

I seem to have been determined to see the event in neutral and symmetrical terms: the U.S. understanding of Japan versus Japan's understanding of the United States, their respective terms of demands and concessions, their interpretive frames, their polities, and so forth, as they were engaged in the act of encounter and confrontation. Japan's dispatch of an embassy in 1860 to Washington, D.C., was a particularly fitting event to examine because it was Japan's early tit-for-tat foreign-policy response to Commodore Perry's visit to Edo Bay, which threatened to force open the insular country. Of course, Japan's intention to stand equal with the United States was not recognized by the Americans of the time, nor even by most historians now. At any rate, I named the book *As We Saw Them,* with the belief that the ambiguity of "we" and "they" suggested both counterposed subject positions and symmetrical interchangeables.[1] *As We Saw Them: Japan's First Embassy to the United States (1860)*[2] senses the possibility of an alternative reading, recognizing a total power imbalance between the United States and Japan in the nineteenth century in most aspects of knowledge and practice. It does not, however, articulate this asymmetrical relationship. What is at stake is history in its material fullness, a view of the event before it is abstracted into the neutral terms of modern discourses.

I might of course return to a still earlier book, which examined modern Japanese fiction against the map and chronology of the modern novel. The book—*Accomplices of Silence: The Modern Japanese Novel*[3]—was sufficiently perturbed by the discrepancies between the Western novel and the Japanese prose narrative since the nineteenth century, and sought to do justice to the variant components—without, however, subjecting the Western novel to an equally rigorous test.

In both books, an imaginary symmetry was allowed to dominate and disguise historical asymmetry, as if the matter of accuracy and justice had nothing to do with power. These notions are products of binarism, itself no doubt a product of Cold-War ideology, before minorities criticism, feminist criticism, and the Frankfurt School theory in particular began to dislodge symmetry from the reading of always asymmetrical history, before, in short, cultural criticism began to emerge as a critical consciousness.

Off Center is thus an attempt to restore asymmetry in our perception. It tries to see Japan's encounter with the other not from a "neutral" or "objective" (meaning Eurocentric) viewpoint, but from an oppositionist perspective. It does not pretend to be universal, inasmuch as universalism at present cannot be other than a mask for concealment and forgetfulness. It seeks to be inclusivist and categorically rejects exclusivism. It not only discards Eurocentricity and ethnocentricity, but does its best to eschew ethnicity and nationalism as well as racism and statism so that history may be read in its fullness undisturbed by borders and boundaries that have been constructed as colonialism progressed.[4] In fact, if I were to find it necessary to revise this book someday, it might begin with the task of dismantling national and regional borders and boundaries such as those between Japan and the United States, or the East and the West, substituting economic, racial, and gender differences as they relate directly to problems and events in global history. The possible danger in such an enterprise at present, however, is an overabstraction that might encourage another kind of concealment and forgetfulness which haunts scientific and theoretical scholarship as it is practiced now.

This book takes off from literature. Although it aims eventually at the decomposition of "literature" as a historically constructed discourse, it makes use of it for now as a still dominant site of contestation. It takes liberties in criss-crossing disciplinary boundaries as it engages in cultural interaction and participates in cultural criticism. The book will not rest comfortable with the idea of culture, especially with the program of culturalism. Dispersal of culture, however, very much like decomposition of literature, has to await the passing of time, which will sooner or later redefine and revise the shapes of our speculation, toward which we with patience intend.

The book is in three parts. Part 1 (chapters 1 through 3) explores the perspective of inclusivism that works historically against colonialism and neocolonialism. The terms that have composed the critical discipline of literature are methodically considered and reconsidered. Thus the customary practice of examining exotic literatures and cultures from the centralist position is put to test. Chapter 1 argues against the practice of Eurocentric reading in Japanology, while Chapter 2 situates the Japanese prose narrative—and the Western novel—in the context of the world history of colonialism as well as literacy. In Chapter 3, the scope of argument is expanded to examine cultural assumptions as they operate in trade negotiations between the United States and Japan. The literary and the economical, the cultural and the industrial, are inseparable, of course. The usual formalized and abstracted arguments about literary and cultural problems must be reimmersed in the specific and concrete, in the everyday life of production and consumption, hegemony and acquiescence. This chapter reiterates a plea that cultural studies, as well as the social sciences, be directly engaged with issues that face everyone in the world now, and speak from that position.

Part 2 (chapters 4 through 6) makes use of literary and writerly texts to document the social conditions in Japan since the War. Writers—their works and lives—provide moments in which social practice and imaginary configuration clash. And the roles the West plays in these moments are examined and compared. Chapter 4 discusses writers of the immediate postwar period, who were compelled by the unprecedented foreign occupation to redefine their relationship to the dominant West. In their humiliation they sought consensus around the alien principles of individualism, freedom, and democracy, thus unwittingly reinforcing the serious self-contradictions that had been carried over since the prewar days. Chapter 5 offers a reading of Tanizaki Junichiro, a writer with a long history of negotiations with the West. Earlier, he had embraced what he imagined to be the West, and sought to discover it within Japan's social space itself. By the end of the war, Tanizaki remained undisturbed by the urgency of the Japan-West confrontation. His modus operandi may not work for everyone, but he was at ease with mixture, contradiction, and what's often thought of as vulgarity. Chapter 6 examines Mishima Yukio, who liked to see the global rift in the most violent terms. His construction of "Japan," "tradition," and "emperorism" reveals, in retrospect, a fatal attraction to the West as strong as that of any other colonized culturalist. What is interesting about Mishima is his strategy to politicize aesthetics, which indeed resulted in aestheticizing politics altogether and finally dissolving everything into "style." Mishima may be thought of as representing closure to the turbulence of the postwar era, and as a harbinger of the commodified style-only new Japan.

Part 3 deals more directly with Japan's own centralism. Chapter 7 examines the way Emperor Hirohito's death in 1989 was ritualized in the national will to agreement and centralism. The same centricity is then studied in relation to a film made by a purportedly progressive director, Oshima Nagisa, who nonetheless is inescapably encased in the Eurocentric frame of mind. While the emperor presides over Japan, the West dominates in the world, and Japan's place seems to be inscribed in the map of signification and power by such calculus of centrality. In Chapter 8, some signs of hope are detected among Japan's women and women writers. In their disappointment with their men and their challenge to patriarchy, some women are now following the brave examples of preceding generations and their sisters abroad. Still small voices, theirs are nonetheless the surest signs of the way for the Japanese out of the hierarchic order of control. In Chapter 9, conversationalism, the most conspicuous mode of critical and speculative exchange now in Japan, is studied. The intellectual and cultural scene after oppositionism was effectively erased around 1970 has not been a hopeful sight at all. In order to escape from the ideology of organizing and stultifying consensuality, it seems vital at this moment to examine the very form in which criticism and speculation, not to mention opposition, are systematically enfeebled. Throughout, it is hoped at the same time that the intellectual and moral blight in the West is not forgotten at any juncture in analyzing Japan.

Off Center, then, is a reading and at the same time a proposal—toward a world in which parts and margins are seen in their own terms, in their relations not to the center of power, but to a world that has no ordering center at all.

Perspectives

Against the Native Grain:
The Japanese Novel and
the "Postmodern" West

In Situ

The first item on our critical agenda is to situate the Japanese novel and ourselves as its First World readers in a discursive context. The "novel" will be contested thereafter against the *shosetsu* form, while the United States and Europe as seen from the perspectives of the Japanese will be kept in peripheral vision. My aim throughout is to locate critical positions and propose an alternative reading. I will begin with the examination of prose fiction, expanding the scope of reference gradually and whenever strategic.

Every experience of reading a marginal text is at least potentially upsetting. When a Third World text is read in the First World, the sense of unfamiliarity is often marked, and the reader's discomfort is proportionately acute. To restore the accustomed equilibrium, the reader either domesticates or neutralizes the exoticism of the text. The strategy for domestication is to exaggerate the familiar aspects of the text and thereby disperse its discreteness in the hegemonic sphere of First World literature. Thematic reductivism always helps. Once human nature is invoked, people everywhere are bound to prove alike; the reader may safely insist that men and women the world over are born, copulate, die, and write about this "universal" cycle. In this age of global interdependence and management, no geographical area is allowed to remain unabsorbed and unintegrated. Third World texts will be tamed, with the hegemony of the First World conferring the needed authority. Should a particular sample happen to be intransigent, it can always be rejected as an inferior product. The principle of canonicity never fails. The experience of reading a foreign text is nearly always transformed into an act of self-reaffirmation.[1]

Translation also intervenes. With the exception of "foreign natives"[2] in England such as Salman Rushdie, Kazuo Ishiguro, V. S. Naipaul, Timothy Mo, and Hanif Kureishi, or former colonials like C. L. R. James or Chinua Achebe, most non-Western writers need translation.[3] And yet skilled translators, even from Chinese, a language spoken by nearly one fifth of the world's population, are extremely rare. Thus Third World writers—even those deeply versed in Western history and literature such as Oe Kenzaburo or Lu Hsun—are not allowed free entry into the open market of world opinions. Translators and publishers of course make their own choices, depending on their own and their readers' "tastes," which are deeply embedded in their places in time and space. Furthermore, translation from non-Western languages is not a financially rewarding enterprise in most Western societies, which need few stimulants from the outside world, except as exotic curios. Thus even before reading itself begins, difficulties already abound for non-Western writers and their works.[4]

Neutralization also operates by distancing the menacing source. A strange text is acknowledged to be strange, and this tautology thrusts the text out of the reader's proximity. One opens a book in order to close it, as it were. Such pseudo-comments as "delicate," "lyrical," or "suggestive," if not "illogical," "impenetrable," or "incoherent," seek to conceal the absence of an encounter by cluttering up the field of reading and distracting the reader from the text. Most foreign texts thus remain more or less readerless, despite repeated attempts at their capture, appropriation, and representation at the hands of cultural administrators.

To come closer to our topic at hand, Japanese prose fiction in the last hundred years appears fairly well represented to English-language readers. As Japanese economic power rises, interest in the literary products of the nation, too, has grown a little. In the last forty years, a good number of its literary products have been made available in English, with male writers' prose fiction prominent among them until very recently. Hundreds of monographs have been written on Japanese literature, and more and more colleges and universities offer courses on the literature and culture as well as the language of the country. Despite such signs of increased familiarity, however, the First World reader continues to find Japanese fiction remote. In fact, many of the translations go quickly out of print as a result of poor sales, which obviously indicate the unpopularity of Japanese fiction among general readers. Correlative with this, Japanese fiction, unlike its French or German counterparts, seems to require the mediation of an expert's advice and commentary. There is no doubt, of course, that the social and historical distance between Japan and the West remains great. Either for this reason, or for others having to do with general Western ethnocentricity, a sort of proprietorship is maintained by some Japanologists, who impress outsiders with the difficulty of the Japanese language and the exceptionality of Japanese culture. It is also to be admitted that specialists in the United States often find themselves needing the cooperation of their Japanese colleagues, who in turn adhere to a system of export licensing. In these days of global cultural and economic exchange, then, the community of scholars is never free from the danger of becoming a multinational bureaucracy of learning that would keep the flow of traffic under careful control.

There is something very much like an official policy in the scholarship of Japanese literature in the United States, which seems consonant with a vague but definable "national interest." As geopolitical hegemony is to the state, so traditionalism is to its culture. The First World "tradition" is to be the universal norm and the inevitable future of every society in the world. There is also a generally accepted genealogy of knowledge that must be noted and dealt with by anyone engaged in this enterprise. The lineage of the Japanologists in America began with the religious and industrial missionaries who went to the Far East to civilize and democratize the barbarians. Then the imperial evangelists of civilization took over the role of teachers and advisors on their return home around the turn of the century. Their godsons, who had been dormant for a while, were mobilized into a cadre of interpreters and administrators during the Second World War and the postwar years. A noticeable advance in Japanology was made by this generation of Occupation-trained specialists, and their impact on scholarship remains both powerful and definitive. Because of the historical circumstances of missionary and conquest, this genealogy has no shortage of those uncritical (or even unaware) of their own ethnocentric and hegemonic impulses.[5] In addition, until very recently, the input from Japanese-Americans (*issei, nisei,* and *sansei*) was not conspicuous (in contrast to their European literature counterparts, for whom such infusion has provided an important and matter-of-fact propellent). Such an absence is cognate with the scarcity of oppositional readings of Japanese literature that might have provided a dialectic context for criticism. Area specialists in the Japan field are likely to be inbred and ghettoized, conversing only on rare occasions with scholars in other areas and disciplines. Of course, the blame for such isolation does not necessarily fall on the Japanologists themselves, but on those outsiders who are supremely indifferent to non-Western civilizations. The Japan field—like any other non-Western area-study field—has long been a sort of colony in the university, where extraterritoriality is still allowed to prevail.[6] Finally, the spectacular ascent of Japanese economy and industry in the last several years has given rise to suspicion and jealousy among some leaders in the First World, especially the United States. The Japanese have been extraordinarily sensitive to the negative responses commonly called "Japan bashing."[7] Hence, the Japanese government and businesses have sought aid and support from Japanologists in various formats. Most are bona fide scholarly projects funded by neutral agencies to pursue scholarly endeavors and to rectify errors and demagogies. Some, however, are covert operations funded by organizations and lobbyists, which seem to find recipients among specialists and institutions.[8]

Given this context, it should not be wholly unexpected to run into a remark like the following by an established academic translator of Japanese literature: "I do not believe Japan has produced a great literary corpus, or that it can boast a single undisputed literary masterpiece, or that very many works of classical Japanese literature can stand up to sustained, intensive literary criticism."[9] In contrast, a Third World–born professor of English who calls himself "American and unhyphenated" describes Japan as "a society with so few visible dysfunctions, so many visible achievements," indiscriminately labeling its literary productions "postmodern." The professor has been frequenting Asian countries for several years to enlighten them about American literature, and now he is explaining Japan for the benefit of the Japanese and Americans both.[10] Whatever such comments might suggest about the conditions of the Japanese literary field, one plainly sees here a discursive paradigm that is best called Orientalism. Whether dismissive or sycophantic, such remarks merely seek closure to prevent further examination and criticism. It seems appropriate, then, to reconsider the whole discourse of the modern Japanese novel as it is conducted in the United States, and to a lesser extent in Japan as well. We might begin by examining the words used to describe the body of prose narrative produced in Japan in the last two hundred years: modern, Japanese, and novel.

Premodern, Modern, Postmodern

The term "modern" is most commonly used among the Japan specialists as well as the generalists in their designation of the recent history and society of Japan. The adjective "modern," however, does not signify identically with its cognates such as "modernism," "modernity," or "modernization." All such terms seem embedded in different origins and contexts, which perhaps need careful discrimination. The modernization theory, still viewed as authoritative in the United States, is of course wide open to inquiries and challenges. Since historical transformation and continuity are obviously not synchronous throughout the world, the universal application of a historical periodization based on one historical system would be senseless as well as ethnocentric. Thus the modern period in the First World may or may not be "modern" in other parts of the world. Both in its referent (post-Renaissance, post-1800, post-1900, just now) and in its interpretant (capitalism, urbanization, individualism, alienation, secularization, industrialization, bureaucratization, and so on), the signifier "modern"—not to say "modernism," "modernity," and "modernization"—should be regarded as regional terms peculiar to the West.

The chronopolitical definition, however, is not always unilateral. Japanese historians and cultural theorists often choose to accept it. The majority who believe Japan to be a part of the First World agree with the Western modernization theorists and deploy the concept of *kindai,* a counterpart of modernity. On this supposedly universal chronology—often one of "development" and "progress"—some regard Japan as having already reached this advanced stage, while a few others believe the country to be still "premodern."

Those who believe Japan to be a modern society are not unanimous in their response to the diagnosis: there are those who approve progress and embrace Westernization, others who welcome progress but deplore Westernization, still others who are attached to traditionalism but accept a version of Westernization, and finally those who are both anti-progress and anti-West. Those who adhere to the view of Japan as premodern are similarly divided among pro- and anti-modernization. These different placements of Japan on the chronopolitical chart are no mere academic factionalisms in historiography. Although the intensity of disagreement has varied, the discord has exploded from time to time into a violent intellectual and political confrontation. In prewar Japan, this modernity with its implications of progress and Westernization was a crucial concept, closely enmeshed with traditionalism, nationalism, and Asianism, and profoundly dividing the ranks of intellectuals. In those years, the state forcibly intervened for the proper placement of Japan on the chart of progress as well as for the preservation of "cultural purity." Even in these post-postwar days, however, the disagreement persists. While a vast majority seems to accept that Japan has achieved modern status by now, Mishima Yukios and Maruyama Masaos insist on finding premodern elements in the fabric of Japanese society, although one rejoices at and the other laments such discovery. We can also recall the notorious conference on "Overcoming Modernity" held in 1942 among the leading wartime ideologues of Japan, whose geopolitical and chronopolitical analyses have been very much revived in recent years.[11]

While the presence of premodernity is still talked about, there has also been an increasing interest in the traits of "postmodernism."

First came the sense of the end of the postwar era. The urgent postwar programs for catching up with the West—economic recovery, political reorganization, and institutional rationalization, as well as atonement for war guilt—were felt to be sufficiently completed. And as the postwar democratization agenda was replaced by a far more aggressive economic expansionism, the targets of modernization that had loomed so remote only a few years ago began to appear in close range. The so-called decline of the West—the repeated political and military follies since the 1960s and the general loss of leadership and confidence—has contributed a great deal to Japan's rise. And as the West displayed revulsion at its own modern past and faced up to its postmodern possibilities, some Japanese intellectuals seem to have regained a quasi-prewar self-assurance. Far from being premodern, they are now postmodern! As a matter of fact, the description of postmodernism began to fit the Japanese conditions remarkably well, as if the term were coined specifically for Japanese society. The dispersal and demise of modern subjectivity, as announced by Barthes, Foucault, and many others, have long been evident in Japan, where intellectuals have chronically complained about the absence of selfhood. The postmodern erasure of historicity—on which Jean-François Lyotard reflects—is the stuff of Japanese nativist religion (Shinto), in which ritual bathing is meant to cleanse away not only the evil residuals of the past but the past itself. Anti-traditionalism has been a prominent counterforce to the official traditionalism, and parody and pastiche have constituted one of the two main cultural streams—together with imported "realism"—for the last two centuries.

For example, modularity has been conspicuous in Japan's architectural and literary productions. Visualization is the country's specialty, as evidenced in overabundant artworks, designs, and graphics. Japanese hostility to logic and rationalism have long been a clichéd source of embarrassment to the native philosophers (logocentricity appearing to be one crime Japan is scarcely guilty of)—so much so that Karatani Kojin and Asada Akira could boast to Jacques Derrida that there is no need for deconstruction in Japan as there has never been a construct.[12] Japan's packaging and image-making are world renowned, especially in these days of production and reproduction on the global scale. Even Baudrillard might find

Japan's devotion to simulacra a little frightening. Finally, its citizens, so desubjectified and decentralized, simply live—produce and consume, buy and sell—in late-stage capitalism, and politics (that is, a critical examination and intervention in interpersonal and intertypological relationships) has practically evaporated.[13]

This is a caricature, of course, but only to a certain degree. On the surface at least, these are indisputable traits of what is generally described as postmodern—with the notable absence of one crucial aspect of postmodernism, that is, feminism. The surface, furthermore, is hardly to be taken lightly in this context. Is postmodernism a historical period or a cultural system? In the context of Japanese society, it is clearly not a periodic term: these same traits seem to have been around much too long, under different economic and political circumstances. And if it is a cultural event, it should be localized and so treated, without essentializing it. Besides, these different assessments of today's Japan—premodern, modern, and postmodern—seem largely dependent on the end one wishes to serve. There is no neutral or innocent reading; nor does any particular reading hold ascendancy over others at present. Japan's "modern" novel, in this sense, should merely signify the body of prose fiction produced in Japan in the last two centuries without involving the customary referents or interpretants of the modern/postmodern West or the Western novel. Likewise, Japanese society as a whole needs to be discussed not in its singularity but in its particularity, *and* outside of the supposed "universal" norm of Western discourse.

Japan

As for the signifier "Japanese," the referent ought not to present any problem as far as territorial or linguistic definition is concerned (with the possible exceptions of Ainu, Okinawa, and other minority productions). The crucial question seems to be in the interpretant: whether recent Japanese prose fiction or its "culture" is singular and exceptional in the sense that it defies comparison with any other literature, or whether it is only a variant among many literatures and is unique only as any other literature is. *A priori* logic points to the latter, for exclusivism and essentialism are ethnocentric and fantastic, and as such both dangerous and groundless. If exclusivism and essentialism are merely forms asserting variance and particularity, then they should be so reformulated. Japanese literature, like any other national or regional product, is definable only in its relation to temporal and spatial constraints. It might be particularly and conspicuously "Japanese"; but there is nothing ontologically sacred or absolute in its makeup. It is as contaminated by other literatures and cultures as they are by their others. This aspect is important to keep in mind inasmuch as the need to deuniversalize and particularize the Western "norm" remains foremost on our new critical agenda. More generally, an alternative reading of the construct of "nation," as an "imagined community" as Benedict Anderson calls it, is indispensable to this book as an exercise in historical and social criticism, which will be dealt with more directly in the later sections.

The "Novel"

In this part of the book I take prose fiction as the central topos in discussion. Here too, however, a larger issue constantly looms in the background. Literature as a discipline is a historical product of European colonialism and nationalism. As religion began to prove unserviceable to the programs of the capitalist West, a nation's and region's social imaginary needed rearticulation. National literature filled this vacuum created by secularization of the "sanctity of a community." Thus texts and documents were grouped together in a category called "literature" toward the end of the eighteenth century, on the denuded horizon of the Enlightenment. A professionalized discipline called "literature" was formed around the mid-nineteenth century by cultural planners like Matthew Arnold—in the case of Britain—who, one recalls, became the first Professor of Poetry at Oxford to lecture in English. The job was for a while relegated to gentry, so-called men of letters; then it became a dead-serious business requiring the full service of specialists rather than amateurs. In the United States, the formation of national literature took place considerably later, just as its extracontinental colonialism commenced at a later date. In Japan, it was a program of the Ministry of Education that saw fit to establish the Department of National Literature at the Imperial University of Tokyo in the mid-1880s. Thus, it is not just the intraliterary categories, or genres, that need to be reimagined, but also the whole idea of literature itself, which is taken for granted only at great risk.

Lucien Goldmann's tripartite scheme in "The Revolt of Arts and Letters" might serve as a model for reading the history of the Japanese prose narrative form—so long as one refuses to surrender the particular to a universalist paradigm and remains wary about his concept of homology. He proposes the succession of classical capitalism, imperialism, and organizational capitalism.[14]

The lineage of Japan's modern prose fiction must be traced back at least to the Edo period (1603–1867). One does note toward the end of this age signs of a monetary economy and a rising bourgeoisie that might be characterized as constituting "a commercial revolution"[15] despite the central feudal regime of the shogunate. The city of Edo was the world's most populous city by 1800 and the administrative nerve center of the nation with a large bureaucracy and service industry. Rapid expansion, as well as the Tokugawa House's hostage system, produced a transient and migrant population alienated from its home villages. Transportation throughout Japan increased, and literacy spread across all classes. Publishing also grew, with an output readily comparable to that of contemporary Europe, accompanied by an expanded information network.[16] In short, there were several elements in the life of the Japanese that might be recognized as constituents of proto-capitalism.

Edo ur-capitalist feudalism found its literary forms in Kabuki drama and the prose *gesaku* (playful writing). *Gesaku* fiction is parodic, episodic, and self-referential. It is torn between the acceptance of formal restrictions and the energy for contesting them. There is an attempt to encompass an individual's mind and action within the framework of a biography, while the style and tone, ranging freely from the colloquial to the formulaic, from the ironic/parodic to the tragic/sentimental, and from the ordinary to the fantastic, prevent the construction of anecdotes and episodes into a narrative whole. The *gesaku* is engrossed in the thick texture of verbal surface, and thus it is inhospitable to characterization and emplotment. It refuses to be introspective or egalitarian and does not offer a discrete narrative outline to correspond to the contours of the gradually emerging individual. Likewise, it is organized by a chronometric sense of time that is aggregative rather than causal. If the earlier Edo prose (such as Ihara Saikaku's) celebrated the Tokugawa order that had finally arrived after a centuries-long chaos of civil wars, the *gesaku* seems to sense the coming end to the order, and it exhibits growing irritations at its realization of the conflict between feudal restriction and bourgeois liberality. *Gesaku,* often taken to be a literature of decadence, is at the same time an expression of resistance and criticism, however modest its scale and impact. Its playful sophistication contains at least potential traits of postmodernity.

The second stage in the history of prose fiction *(shosetsu)* is from the mid-Meiji era (around 1890) to the 1970s, including Japan's invasion of China and its war with the United States. At the beginning, Japan was about to regain its confidence after what had been a nearly colonial encounter with the West. Whatever political and economic success the Meiji restoration had produced was now to be tested abroad in the form of homegrown imperialism. At the end of this second stage, Japan was recovering from the death and destruction occasioned by its military defeat and from the humiliation of foreign occupation. During these turbulent years, Japan's state-controlled capitalism expanded steadily and survived the total annihilation of production systems. It even endured the massive leftist opposition of the 1950s and 1960s. In this age of nationalist capitalism, the individual was quite free to develop entrepreneurial skills. At the same time, state-imposed strictures were nearly absolute. The individual was expected to be cooperative and congruent with society and state, and though eccentricity was tolerated, neither defiance nor revolt was permitted.

The fiction of this period thus has some resemblance to Goldmann's "novel of the problematic character," though it is also distinct from it. Futabatei Shimei's *Ukigumo,* Natsume Soseki's *Kokoro,* or Dazai Osamu's *The Setting Sun* each presents a character in a claustrophobically confined space (in contrast to the panoramic expanse in which Edo fiction typically unfolds). The protagonist is a superfluous man, alienated and introspective. Further, unlike the hero in Edo fiction, the later hero is not just a name but an interior space that reflects on itself. The *shosetsu* comes close indeed to the modern novel here. Yet he is no Pip, Julien Sorel, or Oblomov. Bunzo, Sensei, or Naoji (respective heroes of the three works just mentioned) is always aware of the ensemble of his society in the sense that his problematic is one not so much of character as of role. Consistently, characterization is turned into an elaborate and refined social arbitration, as in a book of manners and morals. Preserving the traditional formal energy, the mode and style of narration range widely and freely in a given work. Transcending the boundaries of the individual's consciousness is the narrator, who is both inside and outside the character. This narrator, however, is not so much an omniscient god as an all-knowing paterfamilias. Such features correspond to the ambiguity surrounding the individual in state-dominated capitalism up to the very eve of the economic miracle of the 1960s.

In a long period such as this, there obviously will be more or less clearly identifiable subperiods. The *shosetsu* of the Meiji era, with Mori Ogai, Shimazaki Toson, and Soseki charting the course, received the direct "influence" of Western fiction, which means that Meiji writers acknowledged and valorized certain elements in Japan's narrative possibilities while ignoring and minimizing others. In their works, the problematic character is more pronounced at the center of the stage. Thus Ogai, Toson, and Soseki are the apologists—critical though they may be—for the Meiji bourgeoisie.

There were, on the other hand, a few who tried to present the life of the poor. In proletarian literature the wretched and the undifferentiated seemed to suggest a new possibility for characterization, a collective hero. The revolt, however, did not come from the lower depths of society. With the coming of the Asian and Pacific War, therefore, the resistance was easily neutralized and absorbed into the mainstream bourgeoisie, as individual writers underwent ritual conversions (*tenko*) whereby they abandoned their critical opposition and adapted themselves to the imperial programs. A very few who persisted in opposition—such as Miyamoto Yuriko or Kobayashi Takiji, were ruthlessly silenced by censorship, incarceration, or assassination. Some writers continued their passive noncooperation by remaining silent, while others collaborated actively.

Almost none was guiltless, since nearly all writers were at least acquiescent. None of them, however, was wholly guilty either, since they were all kept under coercion and most often in ignorance. In this gray mix of guilt and innocence, the contours of the individual were blurred into the background of the state totality.

This dialectic of the self and the other changed very little after the catastrophic defeat in 1945. As I discuss in Chapter 4, writers swiftly moved away from the rightist position of the war years, renaming themselves "humanists" and "modernists," "democrats" and "internationalists." There was an ironic repeat performance of conversion: in proclaiming their *shutaisei* (individuality) in unison, the writers were unwittingly reaffirming state collectivism. The oaths of readaptation were chorally orchestrated. In fact, as the Cold War commenced in the mid-1940s, it called for still another turning back, totaling three zigzag reversions for some writers: from the left to the right in the 1930s, from the right to the left after the war, and from the left back to the right in the 1950s. The Japanese state seems to have remained unaltered throughout these gyrations; with or without the emperor as its symbol, it has continually animated the people and loomed ever larger in the common mind.

Obviously the theme and mood of the *shosetsu* continued to change during this second period lasting three quarters of a century. Yet there are some formal constants that would justify this treatment of the duration as one period. In *Writing Degree Zero,* Roland Barthes suggests two features that characterize the type of novel that would correspond roughly to Goldmann's liberal capitalist novel of the problematic character: the preterite and the third person. According to Barthes, the preterite, or the historical past tense, signifies the "presence of Art" because the past tense abstracts a pure verbal act from the multiplicity of experiences. It connects one act with another, constructing a hierarchy in the realm of facts. "Allowing as it does an ambiguity between temporality and causality, it calls for a sequence of events, that is, for an intelligible narrative. This is why it is the ideal instrument for every construction of a world; it is the unreal time of cosmogonies, myths, History and Novels."[17] Barthes thus sees a "demiurge, a God, or a reciter" lurking behind the past tense. The deity is the author, the inaugurator, the creator present in the Western novel.

Now the Japanese language, which lacks a past tense and depends for temporal notation on the perfect and imperfect aspects, provides a possibility for art in a clearly different fashion. In the *shosetsu,* events occur without being conscripted into the unreal time of cosmogony. Unlike Barthes'—and Aristotle's—model, the *shosetsu* rejects the interpretive beginning, middle, and end. Doing away with the tension of a beginning that potentially and inherently contains the destination and closure of the narrative, it also rejects the acceleration of counterforce that will brake the narrative movement to the standstill of an ending. The *shosetsu* is more similar to the annals than to narrativized history.[18] Paratactic rather than syntactic, arithmetic rather than algebraic, the *shosetsu* is the expression not of order and suppression, as the novel is, but of space, decentralization, and dispersal. There is no creator; there is a shamanic priestess who articulates the tribal spirit by hearkening to it.

To put it another way, the modern novel expresses the problematic of the individual in the contradiction between formal constraints in emplotment and the ideological characterization of the individual as a free agent. The *shosetsu* is the reverse: while the character is always defined in the close texture of society, thus imparting to the character an approximation of a role, the plot is open-ended and spacious, as if one's true existence is irrelevant to the actual details of living, the acts and events of actuality. Politically and psychologically deprived of liberty and freedom, *shosetsu* characters seem to inhabit a space unbothered by life's constraints.

Barthes also points to the importance of the third person in the novel:

> The 'he' is a typical novelistic convention; like the narrative tense, it signifies and carries through the action of the novel; if the third person is absent, the novel is powerless to come into being, and even wills its own destruction. The 'he' is a formal manifestation of the myth, and we have just seen that, in the West at least, there is no art which does not point to its own mask. The third person, like the preterite, therefore performs this service for the art of the novel, and supplies its consumers with the security born of a credible fabrication which is yet constantly held up as false. (p. 35)

The third person is a mask the Western novel dons almost without exception. The convention demands the distance of the "he" *(sic)* from the author. As the "he" and the author gradually work up to be the third person, the "soliloquy becomes a novel" (pp. 36–37).

Against such a victory of the "he/she" over the "I" in the novel, the defeat of the "he/she" at the hands of the "I" characterizes the *shosetsu*. The *shosetsu* is so overwhelmingly marked by the dominance of the "I" form that the *shishosetsu* (I-fiction) is the orthodox convention. Instead of the "he/she" and the author attempting to transform themselves into the third person, they aim at discarding—or at least concealing—the narrator. The "he/she" will speak and write directly. He/she will not wear a mask but will insist on the first person even to the extent of aggressively reporting his/her own daily routine (thus excluding any formal and artistic intention) and presenting it as an emplottable event. It is the reverse of the novel: rather than a "credible fabrication which is yet constantly held up as false," the *shosetsu* is an incredible fabrication that is nonetheless constantly held up as truthful. Art is hidden, while honesty and sincerity are displayed. Distance is removed, while immediacy is ostensive. The rejection of individualism in Japan is thus compensated for by the dominance of the first person. What makes the *shosetsu* fascinating is this complex negotiation between the formal insistence on the "I" and the ideological suppression of the self. In other words, if "the preterite and the third person in the Novel are nothing but the fateful gesture with which the writer draws attention to the mask which he is wearing" (Barthes, p. 40), the aspects and the first person in the *shosetsu* are nothing but the fateful gesture with which the writer draws attention to his/her own naked face, which, whether he/she is aware or not, is no more than a mask.

The *shosetsu* is thus an art that refuses to acknowledge art. Signs of Western high modernist art are conspicuously absent. An author's will is directed to allowing order to emerge between the self, the work, and the reader, rather than within the work itself. The *shosetsu* refuses to abstract; it keeps the multiplicity of movement and experience concrete; and without organizing these into a shape, it lets the narrative run on. It disperses and decentralizes art so that the reader as well as the author may become aware of the space outside the work. It refuses to interrupt life with the willed discipline of art forged in the smithies of verbal form. Instead, it seeks to ignite flashes of beauty that lie unmarked at the rims of language. Thus the *shosetsu* is typically published in a serialized form. Unplanned at the beginning, the progression of the narrative is a coordinate of external time. As the narrative unfolds, its shape is constantly altered. There is no real conclusion until the author's death makes its ending unresumable. Relevance is always to the world outside the work, not to the work's autonomous unity.[19] In writing and reading a *shosetsu,* the individual is expected to merge with others, to hearken back to the voice of the tribe. Contextuality is all-important.

The third period in the *shosetsu's* history begins at the end of the unrest of the 1960s and the outset of Japan's unprecedented economic growth. The organization of this new Japan is incomparably powerful. The new Japan trains its citizens as well-adapted functionaries in its corporate program, mobilizing them far more efficiently than any militarist regime ever has. It is centrally planned and painlessly enforced. Of course, Japan's economic and technological advance is spectacular, and the pride and confidence the Japanese feel about it are understandable. Yet in this national celebration consumerism is pervasive, eating deeply into the fabric of life. The privatized experience that once was legitimate among intellectuals is now being emptied of self-contemplation. Thus critical opposition is now virtually nonexistent. Periodically, people may protest against rearmament, pollution, and political scandals, but such movements are both specific and sporadic. The overall sense of affluence dominates, and the occasional signs of unease about the harried pace of life and the surprisingly low quality of life for a leading industrial nation are put aside unacknowledged.

The mark of an individual is that person's purchases and possessions; as people labor they pass the time by daydreaming about advertised goods.[20] Books, too, are consumed; that is, they are bought, enjoyed, discarded, and forgotten. No longer authors, manufacturers of books dash off two or even three *shosetsu* a year, in addition to such lucrative media fragments as *kanso* (impressions), *rondan* (op-ed articles), assembly-line nonproducts such as *taidan* (dialogues) and *zadankai* (roundtable conversations).[21] Foreign books—including those by sophisticated theorists—are rapidly translated and even bought, but it is exceedingly rare to detect their traces in the ongoing critical discourse. Whether Foucault or

Lyotard, Said or Jameson, such theorists and critics are quickly Japanized, conspicuously consumed, briefly chatted about, and usually forgotten at once without affecting even slightly the shape and direction of Japanese intellectual discourse. The journals of opinion, once the arena of intellectual and ideological combats, are now congenial to those in the seat of power and authority. Many have simply disappeared, while few new ones have emerged. Hundreds of glossies appear every year with fancy titles like *Arera, Anthropos, Marie Claire,* or *Visio* and sell hundreds of thousands of copies. But most vanish within a year or two, having generated enough revenue through advertisements and/or tax losses.[22] Literary magazines are notoriously in decline. Books are promoted by large publishers by means of widely publicized awards and prizes that presumably certify quality and confer prestige but serve primarily to increase sales.[23] While more and more people are getting bored with printed words, literature has been redefined as a serious industry and a form of entertainment in which the writers' membership in the collective enterprise is taken for granted.[24] The three leading national newspapers in Japan have huge circulations—well over ten million copies—and compete in safe reporting and conformist analyses. Paralleling the holy alliance of capital, labor, and bureaucracy is a powerful consortium of writers *(sakka),* scholars *(gakusha),* reviewers/commentators *(hyoronka),* and publishers *(honya),* all supporting one another in a unified effort to advance their economic interests and power bases. Such a quadrilateral cooperative, often made closer by a shared college or publishing background, grows into an unchallenged monopoly. When several such alliances form a still larger cartel of literature and cultural industry, the nation's critical consciousness is ill served indeed.[25]

The *shosetsu* produced under such conditions is no longer characterized by the perfect/imperfect aspects and "I-ness." As a consumer, the "I" is even less distinguished from the others, while the sense of time, too, is robbed of its experiential discreteness. Thus the *shosetsu* that marked the beginning of this period is Tanaka Yasuo's *Nantonaku kurisutaru* (*Somehow Crystal,* 1980), which presents disembodied adolescent voices, or mildly erotic daydreams, whose only existential testimonies are store names, miscellaneous foreign words, and trade names that are carefully annotated in the book's 442 footnotes. Hardly gathered into sentences, nouns—especially names like Dior and Jaeger—echo in the hollows of dead narrative possibilities. Presented in a succession of slick commercials, these names are meant to guide the reader in the glamorous world of buying and consuming. *Nantonaku kurisutaru* tries to look ironic and sophisticated but barely manages to conceal its crude apologia for affluent kitsch. Through such disintegration of narrative art, high-tech Japan reduces human intercourse to a commercial transaction and human existence to a marketplace.

Under the circumstances, the literature of critical opposition is nearly invisible. There are a few determined modernists, of course. Oe Kenzaburo seems the most outstanding of those consistent intellectuals who continue their critical examination of self and society with unrelenting thoroughness. There are moments when it looks as though Japan's critical consciousness lives in Oe's work alone. But then, Oe could be said to be in search of lost time and dreams, building and rebuilding a mythical world of trees and woods, birds and beasts as well as men and women, assisted by his vast learning and memory of Japanese, Asian, and European history and literature. Thus he delivers himself from the grips of today's Japan. While his criticism is meticulous, it is distracted by compassion.

Several feminist writers—Kono Taeko, Tomioka Taeko, and Tsushima Yuko, for example—are also strikingly oppositional. One of the most fascinating works of these few exceptions is Inoue Hisashi's *Kirikirijin* (*The Kirikiri People,* 1981). A satiric utopian fantasy, this 834-page book traces the winning by a northern village of its independence from the state of Japan through a revolution lasting a mere forty hours from its happy beginning to its sad end. Narrating an event of forty hours' duration over more than eight hundred pages produces a dense surface and texture; as Inoue explains it, the book is also meant to be read in forty hours, with the reader—if he or she so wishes—matching the reading time hour by hour to the chronology of the revolution.[26]

In the tradition of the Edo *gesaku, Kirikirijin* is obsessed with the verbality of the text. The village revolutionaries insist on speaking in their local drawl, which happens to be the generally despised North-Eastern dialect. What is important is the work's rejection of standard bureaucratic Japanese that serves merely as a transmitter of messages. The marginal and deformational "zu-zu drawl" deflects the reader from the neutral flow of communication to the language of writing itself. The content must always be tested by the form.

The book's presence indeed looms in the criticism-erased Japan of today. Its exceptionality—even among Inoue's own works—also suggests, however, that Japan's economic miracle has finally neutralized the country's long-standing myth. In its single-minded devotion to mass production and consumerism, Japan is no longer distinct or isolated. As one of the most industrialized countries, Japan is in some ways comfortable with the so-called advanced nations. Fulfilling Fukuzawa Yukichi's slogan "Escape from Asia, and Join Europe," Japan seems now a full-fledged member of the global organizational capitalist alliance. As such, a significant part of its cultural life has merged with international mass phenomena. Does it make sense to call this situation postmodern? Possibly. Yet, as I have noted, Japan's "postmodern" traits were discernible earlier in history, thus denying its postmodernism a temporal specificity. In fact, there are rumors that the fashionable appellation *postomodanizumu,* has already lost its glamor, even its viability. Just like existentialism, phenomenology, poststructuralism, and the Frankfurt School, postmodernism, too, seems to be fast turning into a theoretical has-been. It has fulfilled its own prediction and has effectively self-destructed. At least the book market of Tokyo seems to have delivered the sentence with its customary incontrovertible authority.

Toward a Native Taxonomy

This examination of the Japanese prose narrative has been conducted within close proximity to the genealogy and context of the Western novel, within the larger West-generated category of "literature." This West-based procedure is unavoidable for two reasons. One, our concern is mainly with the reading of Japanese fiction in the United States, and hence references must be made to the native ground. Two, and perhaps more important, Japanese hermeneutics is such that critics and scholars in Japan are accustomed to regarding the *shosetsu*—erroneously, I believe—as a species of novel. With a few exceptions, most Japanese readers treat the form of *shosetsu* as a transparent container for a social and psychological record. The result is concurrence with and confirmation of the First World hegemonic interpretation, often accompanied by the Orientalist verdict that the Japanese novel is underdeveloped.

This strategy of situating the discourse in the context of First World literature is thus clearly unsatisfactory, and some other frame of reference is surely called for. Although this book is not intended to be a full exploration of an alternative methodology for reading the *shosetsu,* some suggestions must be made toward that end. Thus what follows is a description of a few forms that are indigenous to Japan and are not conformable to Western expectations. Genres, like most other things, are specific to history and geography. The *shosetsu* could be viewed as a confluence of narrative possibilities available to Edo and later writers whose perceptions and responses, dreams and realizations, were guided and defined by the constraints of their times. Just as the Western novel developed from an ensemble of epic, Renaissance drama, folklore, and ballad, so the *shosetsu* ranges over the *monogatari* and *utamonogatari, noh, nikki* and *tabinikki,* Buddhist sermons, *renga, kabuki,* and *kana zoshi.* We shall consider a few of these forms here as examples of the matrices of *shosetsu* components.

First, the tenth-century *Ise monogatari (Tales of Ise).* One of the earliest prose tales in Japan, or in the world for that matter, it is hardly narrativized. Its 125 sections taken together suggest the life of a historical Don Juan courtier whose poems had appeared in earlier anthologies. Despite the biographical drift, the man's name is seldom mentioned in *Ise.* If some sections refer to the events historically associated with his supposed career, there are many others that are irrelevant to it. *Ise's* sequence, in fact, only loosely resembles the chronology of a man's life. The modules follow one another paratactically, with the sole constant factor being the formulaic opening phrase in every section, "Long ago there was a man," or simply, "Long ago."

We have here, then, a narrative that is segmented into separate vignettes that together would hint at the vague outline of a man's life. The shadowy contours of a life—made barely visible by rejection of a tight syntax of motivations, causes, and consequences, and by adoption of a sequence of unrelated episodes—is a feature that we might well remember as we read Japanese narratives from later days.

Each of *Ise's* 125 sections has at least one *waka* (the standard 31-syllable poem). Out of the total of 200 poems, only about 30 are actually attributed to the central figure, the rest coming from various sources in the eighth, ninth, and tenth centuries. Some of these sections are no more than a poem plus a few introductory words on the circumstances of its composition, the whole passage often having been lifted verbatim from an earlier poetry collection. There are, however, many sections in which the preexisting poems are adopted into the narrative situation furnished by *Ise* as a whole. That is, a *waka* or group of *waka* seems to have encouraged the writer or writers to generate a narrative context around it: a poem extends to a narrative, which by continually referring back to its source poem makes a circular, reflexive movement between poetry and prose. We see here, then, a singular instance of generative cooperation and imaginative fusion between poetry and prose, *waka* poet and prose narrator, writer and reader, a historically identifiable person and a transparent referentially empty everyman (the man who lived "long ago"), all of them together composing this remarkably segmented and unplotted, and yet contiguous and interrelated, story. There is no single author, nor is there a discrete central persona. There is not even a fully integrated narrative that insists on representation. Further, the *waka* poems, the imaginative pivots of the narrative sections, are in no meaningful sense lyrical; they operate through the most intricate networks of conventions, both verbal and topical. Any expressive urge on the part of the poet is totally submerged in public conventions and practiced art. To a poetry that emerged within a perceptual scheme not yet sundered into subject and object, the term "lyric," which presupposes "the author's turning his back on his audience,"[27] simply does not apply.

Perhaps of more interest, all these sectionalized tales barely describe exterior events or episodes. Many are mere poetic commentaries. Even in more narrativized sections, the miniature tales relate the process and circumstance of poetic composition, as if an imitation of life were not as worthy as a reflection on art. The *waka* is generated by artifice, certainly not by the poet's "raw experience." Thus the poetry seems at least twice removed from reality or essence, and it would have no doubt invited Plato's contempt. Despite its famed closeness to nature, Japanese poetry is artificial, self-enclosed, and self-protective, just like the courtly life that produced it. The *Tales of Ise* thus seems to invite its reader to deconstruct the notions of biography, fiction, authorship, nature, lyric, originality, poetry, and prose all at once, and to tease the reader into this self-sealed dimension.

Now we move on to the fourteenth- and fifteenth-century *noh*. The noh is often called the noh *play* in English, which is quite inaccurate. Of course, the noh is staged, and is performed by those who talk, act, and dance; it has a chorus that chants with a small orchestra of flutes and drums; and it even has a few props. Yet the noh is not dramatic; neither tragic nor comic, neither mimetic nor symbolic, it is not even emplotted.

The typical noh opens with the entrance of an actor identifying himself in such vague terms as "I am a traveling priest called such and such" (no specific name is given). He says he is journeying for a purpose, say a visit to the grave of a fallen warrior or a poet. In a few sentences, and after taking a few steps, he declares that he has arrived at his destination. The noh space is obviously a poetic space not at all coextensive with any physical dimensions. The first actor then encounters the main actor (*shite*), who usually appears as a humble woodsman or fisherman. A short dialogue ensues in which the first actor repeats his intention, and the main actor supplies him with some information. The main actor disappears and then reenters, this time in the shape of the dead warrior or poet whom the initial actor seeks to mourn. The ghostly incarnation then reenacts a crucial scene, such as that of his death, in an emphatically stylized dance. All this time, the initial actor remains on stage, but midway his unmasked expression turns utterly blank, as if he were simply absent. On the noh stage, presence is not indicated by the appearance of a figure, nor absence by the disappearance of a figure.[28]

The story line, if there is a story line, varies from noh to noh, but the main interest of the noh is never in its unfolding of an unexpected event. Most of the events and characters are borrowed either from such well-known works as *Ise* or *Tale of Genji* or from public events via *The Tale of Heike,* and the audience is presumably familiar with them.

The performers, too, are not actors in the ordinary sense. The main actor sometimes performs two characters in one scene: In the case of a noh called *Tadanori,* the main actor impersonates both the defeated warrior-poet Tadanori and the person who kills him in the murder scene itself. This denial of a one-to-one correspondence between the actor and the character is even more conspicuously demonstrated by the chorus, which often speaks for one character and then for another, as if distinctions among characters were trivial. Unlike the Greek chorus, which sings in its own voice, the noh chorus presents several points of view, often even sharing a line with the main actor. Thus the noh seems indifferent to dramatic representation of human acts. It is set on presenting a being or doing, a "concrete abstraction,"[29] through a complex interrelationship of the actors, their masks and costumes (or the absence thereof), music, chorus, stage design, and theater space.

There are many other features that point to the radical differences between noh and Western theater, whether ancient, medieval, or bourgeois modern. The nature of the audience, the operation of the actors' companies, the mode of training and rehearsal, the masks and costumes, the visual and aural effects including elocution—all seem to minimize what Bertolt Brecht calls "hysteria" and to maximize his notion of the "alienation effect."[30] The audience are never deceived into believing that they are spying on a slice of life; theirs is an experience of sheer art, far removed from life. Noh has no dialectic of clashing agons. The protagonist/antagonist opposition, where such exists, is not resolved by one party accepting or vanquishing the other; rather, the barrier that has separated the warring parties is simply dissolved. Finally, the surface of the text is so dense with puns, associations, epithets, and allusions as to make it nearly impenetrable. In the case of *Tadanori,* verbal play among the warrior's name, the scene of a cherry tree in full bloom, and the name of the Lotus Sutra leads to the breathtaking last lines, "The flowers return to their roots" and "The flower is the master." This Yeatsian passage (I have in mind the closing stanza of "Among

School Children") asserts the sheer mastery of the flower, the central sign of the Buddhist Lotus Sutra principle and the noh principle enunciated by the fifteenth-century master Zeami. Like *Ise, Tadanori* is preoccupied with the nature of art. It is not about anything unless it is about art, about itself. The politics of noh is not in its narrative content at all but in its performative form.[31] Defying as it does the Western category of drama, the noh seems to require a different epistemology for its elucidation.

Linked poetry *(renga),* as practiced by Basho in the seventeenth century, continues the long tradition of poetic exchange that began as greetings and messages of love, among other things. Such art is typically created by more than one person. In Basho's case, the unit was likely a 36-line version that alternates between 5-7-5-syllable lines and 7-7-syllable lines. Usually four male poets participate in a session, composing their lines one at a time in a complex predetermined order. Certain rules obtain as to the thematic pattern. The motifs of season, love, journey, and religious devotion are also regulated; a vast number of objects and events are assigned to each of the seasons. The rules can be ignored, of course, as all rules are. Yet a tight nexus of rules paradoxically frees the poets from the restriction of their inner space. The participant poets seem to follow gladly the leadership of a master such as Basho, and they obey the rulings of the scribe-referee who decides on the propriety of each composition.

Of the thirty-six lines, each of which can be considered a whole poem, the opening poem is the only independent one; the poet who offers it is not bound by preceding compositions. At the same time, this freedom is not unlimited, for the opening poet must respond with sensitivity to the mood of the group, which in turn likely reflects the season, weather, time, place, and makeup of the session. The poets also watch their master as he sets the circle of poetic creators-transmitters in motion, assessing the potential his work will provide for them. The second poet takes over, often filling the empty space left by the first line. This second man is already a reader and a poet at the same time: he reads, that is, interprets and answers and shifts and continues, what is given (as well as what is *not* given) in the first verse. The brevity of each line must be maximally utilized to amplify the power of silence and clarify the contours of the "concrete abstractions" contained in the preceding line. The third poet typically transforms the context set by the second, and his shift may be dramatic. If the previous scene is set in contemporary life, in colloquial diction with a familiar object, the third poet might change it into a scene out of an ancient romance by adding an elegant and quaint phrase or an allusion. If an old man was suggested earlier, the third poet might magically transform him into a young woman by the subtlest qualification. Once the motion is set, the subsequent lines continue the process of metamorphosis, although the design of change itself must also be altered. Monotony must be avoided, and the principle of the three tempos—slow introduction, moderate development, and fast climax—that guides the movement of the Noh also operates in *renga*.

Renga, then, is first of all a miniature serialization in which what has already been composed is ineradicably present, determining what is to come and gradually narrowing the range of the future as the predetermined total length is approached. *Renga* also requires a joint effort. In Basho's *kasen,* four poets both complete and cooperate with one another. Obviously they all remember their *renga* as a whole, and yet the integrity of a work, as Western literature traditionally understands it, is totally irrelevant. Despite a certain discernible drift in the thirty-six lines as a whole, the main effect of linked poetry is that of a succession of metamorphoses that at the same time maintains a constant level of awareness about the possibilities and limits of the form.

The language of *renga* is once again characterized by polysemy, allusion, epithet, and association. Poems involve the whole corpus of literary precedents, which they both recall and parody. As a *renga* ranges over the various modes of humor, pathos, solemnity, intimacy, sentiment, eroticism, dramaticity, and contemplation, the language remains totally unsymbolic. The poetry prevents meaning from invading the image; it forbids interpretation to separate the form from the content. The meaning of *renga* is what it is. There is no separation between the signifier and the signified. *Renga* lines continue to remain empty of meaning as they shape images and echo sounds. None of these properties belongs to the speaker; as they manifest themselves, they enter the public domain of meaning that everyone—the poet and the reader or the poet-reader—shares with everyone else.

The modular line—the line that is a stanza that is a whole poem—thus depends on the sense of joint identity built around the revered master. The final poem, all thirty-six of these lines, is neither narrative nor lyrical, odic or ceremonial, occasional or accidental. The way of *renga* poets seems to harmonize with the other poets in the act of uttering words. As Beckett would say, and Michel Foucault would endorse, "What matter who's speaking?"

Finally, *renga* requires social networking that will enable individual local amateurs to form a poetic group from time to time. Basho's famed travelogues (such as *The Narrow Road to the Deep North* [*Oku no hosomichi*]) are not just purely poetic compositions. They do trace an aesthetic pilgrim's search for accumulated layers of poetic and mythical allusions to scattered places in Japan, which will serve to integrate a mythical community into an aesthetic form, as many critics both inside Japan and out would insist. But they are also by-products of a literary entrepreneur's peddling of his profession—the business of poetry—to the all-willing cultural consumers of seventeenth-century Japan. Quite obviously, this commercial program does not cancel the marvelous verbal achievements of these ever-fascinating poetic travelogues. Yet to see Basho's poetry as beyond the historical conditions of the time would be a greater mistake. Paradoxically, Basho's invention of what is known in the West as "haiku"—actually *hokku*, "opening verse," the first verse of a group-composed linked poem read in separation and detachment from the rest—indicates a step toward the mode of isolated individual poetic composition. In this sense, too, Basho's contributions to literary commercialism coincide with his role in the development of isolated poetic composition. Basho's practice in *renga*, in short, is a political exercise in commercial organization, community construction, and aesthetic "individualism" all in one stroke.

Ise, the noh, and linked poetry are not marginal elements in Japanese writing. In fact, their salient features are evident in such other genres as prose tales, essays, and diaries, and they are conspicuous in the *shosetsu* itself. Throughout, textuality is conceived of in terms not of autonomy but of interrelation. Authorship is seen as more public and communal than private and individual. The modality of art tends to be not representational and mimetic but presentational and linguistic; not "realistic" but reflexive. Less emphasis is placed on the acute sense of separation between the inside and outside, subjectivity and objectivity, artistic space and life space, than on the intense experience of the fusion and collapse of such isolations. Taxonomical perception, too, seems focused on the rejection of separation and discreteness rather than on the insistent detection of differences. As if guarding this literary space they inhabit, the art of these literary forms intently gazes at itself, determined to ignore the Other that will remain alien to this art.

Once born, Japanese forms tenaciously live on, in contrast to Western forms that typically evolve at a quicker pace. The thirty-one-syllable *waka* has remained virtually unchanged for twelve or thirteen centuries. In addition, older forms are adjacently or atavistically sighted in newly generated forms. If the emergence of the *shosetsu* is historically determined, the same historical forces keep these older forms very much alive in it. The *shosetsu* often tends toward preservationism and self-referentialism. To return to Goldmann's terms, our imminent task is to reexamine the historical circumstances that have allowed these forms of self-referentiality and parataxis, and of intertextuality and communality, to emerge and persist. The longevity of the forms is indisputable; the secrets of their survival are still untold.

We might also recall here the earlier assertion that Japanese literature does not conform to Western critical terms even though it is not ontologically exceptional. One must pursue this a step further: If Japanese literature is not an exception, in what context should it be placed? In what direction should the critic turn next? One might begin with the obvious, what lies closest to Japan's tradition—that is, Korean and Chinese literatures. Many qualities of Japanese prose fiction suggested here are recognizable in Korean and Chinese forms, and renewed efforts at formal reexaminations are bound to result in new discoveries. One might then turn to farther peripheries, the oral cultures of the Third World as suggested by many anthropologists and literary theorists. To call Japanese literature "oral" rather than "literate" might seem odd, but such Japanese forms as *monogatari, nikki,* noh, and *renga* as well as *shosetsu* could be best described as imbued with interiorized or residual orality. So considered, the *shosetsu* form might be more at home alongside the oral tales of the Third World than the Western novel. It is unwise not to remember the Western novel in the examination of the *shosetsu* form. But not to recognize the form's native visage and lineage might be an even worse blunder. One might find some consolation, however, in making these difficult efforts—of reading the *shosetsu* against the native grain in America—since one might be suggesting an alternative reading not only of Japanese fiction but more generally of fiction as a whole, for its reader of whatever origin. Finally, such an alternative reading might throw some light on the chronopolitical aspect of the postmodernism controversy.

The "Great Divide" Once Again:
Problematics of the Novel

Colonialism

First, a thumbnail sketch of history, with which all are acquainted in outline, though a good many might disagree with this particular version.

There were many empires before: Mesopotamia, Egypt, Greece, Rome, India, China, Islam, Mongol, Aztec, Inca, and others. Until 1500, however, every domination was—no matter how large—limited to a regional adventure. Beyond the knowable world there was always another world, elusive and immense. And the conquest and possession of those unbounded territories were never even imagined. The Spanish voyagers, on the other hand, were determined to reach the limits and discover the world elsewhere. In their search for Cathay, they planned to girth the globe. And as they encircled the world, they "found" lands which they at once proceeded to consider rightfully theirs. The discovery of the "Indies" and the "New World" by Columbus, Vasco da Gama, and Magellan was quickly followed by their conquest of Central America and western South America. The French, English, and Dutch began to settle the Atlantic coast of North America soon thereafter. Added to their ships and arms and munitions were the ravages of European diseases, and the destruction of the indigenous population was swift and vast. According to one count, the inhabitants of what is now known as Mexico were reduced by 96 percent between 1500 and 1600.[1] Wherever the Europeans went, native resistance was swept away as if the space they invaded had been vacant all along. And they did not hesitate to push further and further. Eastward they traveled beyond the Mediterranean Sea to the Near East and Far East. By 1700 practically the entire world—except for Australia—was exposed to the threat of the European empire.

What took place in these two centuries, however, is nothing compared with what was to follow in the succeeding three centuries. By 1700 Europe had completed the task of shedding most of the medieval paradigm of thought. Enlightenment reasoning, composed of secularism, rationalism, individualism, capitalism, universalism, and egalitarianism, prevailed. Cultural differences were now conceived of on the scale of progress and advance. The West's contact with the non-West occurred, in other words, just when Enlightenment ideas had provided the Westerners with a mission for progress, a self-proclaimed program to enlighten and civilize the uncivilized.[2] The Europeans found a powerful cause for the conquest of the world. The Moslem, Hindu, and Chinese territories that were still maintaining their traditional beliefs and institutions around 1700 were soon to be threatened seriously by the encroaching West with its ideas and forces. European domination steadily expanded as the Spanish hegemony was replaced by the British in the eighteenth century. Thus by 1850 the globe was not only unified and integrated but, paradoxically, sectioned and fragmented by European occupiers and settlers who claimed nearly every part of the world as theirs. They gave each fragment a new name, established it as a discrete colony, and incorporated it into the time and space of the West while erasing native geography and history.

This process was completed during the forty years between 1880 and 1920 in a mad scramble to expropriate the leftover territories, Africa in particular. At the height of this era of imperialism, nearly 85 percent of the earth was ruled by Europeans, a mere 10 percent of the total human population.

Western adventurism was unique among all the empires in being truly global. Despite serious conflict and competition among themselves, Western nations were in unison in identifying themselves as white and civilized while calling all others colored and uncivilized. They were also united—though involved in varying degrees—in trying to extend further the boundaries of their collective ecumene. In fact, the intra-European rivalries which erupted from time to time resulted in intensifying the imperialist aspiration of the West as a whole.

The aspects in which these European nations resembled each other were far more conspicuous and significant than the aspects in which they differed. Thus it was a European racial empire, dividing the world into the West and the rest. Each European nation needed also to unify and centralize itself. The nobility and independent cities were incorporated into the nation-state, which was thereby enabled to guide and direct colonial and imperialist undertakings by merchants, soldiers, and priests. Thus while Europe continued to conquer the world, its individual nations carefully constructed the myths of national tradition and culture, all the while promoting the citizens' loyalty to their nation-state. The history of global European colonialism is identical with the history of nationalism.

The political geography of the colonized world was somewhat like a specular image of its "motherland." Each colony was seeded with a quasi-identity: its language, customs, polity, and culture were all affected by the nationalistic European master state. Colonial borders were often drawn arbitrarily, cutting across tribal habitats and ignoring geographic markers. Thus civil and regional wars were inscribed into the colonial landscape. To take just one example, as the Arabs freed themselves in the early twentieth century from the Ottoman Empire under the "protection" of the Western powers, the Middle East was broken into the smithereens of Palestine, Jordan, Lebanon, Syria, Iraq, Egypt, Saudi Arabia, and many others, each endowed with bits of British and French traits and quasi-national colonial identities. As geography and history were warped into the political design of the West, these "nations" were bound to face a long, painful process of conflict and adjustment, as we have witnessed ever since. Although the people were often derided as irrational, unstable, and violent, the complex annals of their struggles were direct consequences and calculated effects of the Western division and occupation. Such a jigsaw puzzle of colonial borders is replicated in every other region of the world, from Africa, the Near East, Central Asia, the Far East, and the Pacific Islands, to the Caribbean and Central and South America.

Like the region of Europe, the colonized territory—today's Third World—also shares certain aspects, despite its regional variations. With few exceptions, the non-Western nations were confronted by a profound crisis of identity. Their separate traditions—histories and geographies, as well as moral and religious systems—had to face the choice (in actuality, hardly a choice) between surrender to the all-consuming Western "universalism" and resistance to it at the risk of forcible conquest. China of the eighteenth and nineteenth centuries, for one, decided to ignore Western technology and science until it was forced to cede to humiliating Western demands. Sooner or later, every part of the non-Western world was opened up by the powerful alien civilization. In other words, metropolitan management of remote peripheries was unprecedentedly efficient and complete. The West's incomparable technology could be made productive or destructive at will, or so it was thought until very recent times. Nor did the modern Western empire ever doubt the legitimacy of its universal and objective knowledge and high altruistic moral mission. The European empire was the center and norm of humanity, and the imperialists were convinced of their exclusive authority. More important, this metropolitan authority was generally respected and accepted by the colonial elites employed as mediators between the administrators and the native subjects. Thus Western arts and mores also assumed universal status throughout the world.

As the Western integration of the globe neared completion, there were attempts at colonialism from non-European sources. Settlers of Western origin and descent moved on to establish their own colonies, as in the case of the United States on the North American continent, in the Caribbean, and in the Philippines, or the European settlers in South Africa advancing into neighboring territories. Among such programs of secondary colonialism, the instance of Japan requires special attention.

First of all, Japan is the earliest non-Western case of modern imperialist aggression. At least at the ideological level, however, this aggression also contained a nativist program of fighting back against the Western conquest. Although the struggle was almost from the very beginning contaminated with a homegrown version of imperialism that meant to duplicate and improve on the Western design of domination and exploitation,[3] and although it was rapidly overwhelmed by brute militarism, it is not impossible to discern in the struggle signs of reactive, counter-contestational will and energy. Second, whether Japan's "anti-colonialism" was fundamentally a thin pretext for a later "Greater Asian Co-Prosperity Sphere" (meaning merely Japan's prosperity), the fact remains that Japan defeated the Russian czarist army and navy in 1905, one of the mightiest of the European imperial forces. In this limited sense, Japan became a model for other independence-movement leaders. Sun Yat-sen of China, Ho Chi Minh of Vietnam, and Gamal Abdel Nasser of Egypt were at least conscious of Japan's precedent in both its potentials and actualities, its achievements and disasters. Japan and East Asia were not likely to have been in the minds of Frantz Fanon, Jomo Kenyatta, or Mahatma Gandhi, but the problems they faced are not entirely different from those with which some of the Japanese intellectuals grappled in the years before, during, and after the Second World War. In this sense, too, the cultural productions of Japan in the twentieth century have been inextricably enmeshed with the developments of Western colonialism and non-Western nativism.

Worlds

Between the First World and the Third any representation is treacherous. The term "Third World" implies a space apart; a fissure among the three worlds is assumed. What is exactly meant by such recognition, however, is not at all clear. The acknowledgment of a First-Third binarism as a part of the Cold War strategies to absorb and control the nonaligned nations into the capitalist bloc can itself point to a number of attitudes.[4] For example, it can be a racist reaffirmation of the First World with its essentialized characteristics; it can likewise celebrate placement of the First World at a more advanced stage on a supposed scale of progress and modernization. Conversely, it can signify a reactive nativist valorization of Third World communality or spirituality; it can also congratulate Third World traditionalism, proposing permanence as an absolute.

As long as one persists in seeing the two worlds in terms of the future versus the past, or modernization encumbered by alienation versus traditionalism ridden with stagnation, one is trapped in an amalgam of misguided arguments: that social development is internal and autonomous; that the historical continuity of a society is "either an evolutionary progress or gradual decline"; and that all the institutions of a society are expressions of a primary essence.[5] Underlying all such developmental misreadings is a pervasive ethnocentricity of which Hegel, who foresaw an ending to history, is patently guilty, and with which Marx, who saw no end in history, is complicit. The First and Third Worlds are irrevocably implicated. Any historical event in one affects the other; or, any situation in one has an adjacent factor in the other—although the absolute asymmetry in power between the two worlds is extremely unlikely to change for the foreseeable future. Regardless of the fracture between the two worlds, global contextualization and integration are by now irreversible.

Before I proceed any further with this argument, three obvious points need to be reasserted. One, to see problematics against the background of a contiguous global scene is not to suggest that the world is seamless or that humanity is one. There is no such society, nor is there likely to be one, ever. As power operates, it separates. As late capitalism penetrates into the peripheries, the gap in wealth grows greater—with predictable consequences. The global human family, together with the theology of humanism, is inescapably—and perhaps irremediably—shattered.

Two, neither the First World nor the Third is a homogenous entity; each is further fractured along the axes of race, class, and gender. Not just white and black, rich and poor, men and women; but rich men and poor women, or rich black women and poor white men, or even poor yellow women living in the First World and rich white men inhabiting the Third World. Any discourse in colonialism is accompanied by serious qualifications and complications concerning internal colonization. The poor and powerless of the First World are mobilized to serve as the actual agents of colonialism—often at the expense of their compatriots in poverty. Foreign occupation gives birth to native elites, who then begin to speak on behalf of their colonizers and become in turn the colonizers of their compatriots. Within each colony, the reinforcement of patriarchy, too, is a frequent complication as a function of the presence of foreign aggressors. Centrifugal segmentation continues, intensifying the pattern of differences and the dynamics of oppositions. Political and economic refugees and exiles further complicate the borders.

Three, the logical symmetry in the relations of the two worlds is deceptive. Just as white racism cannot be balanced by reverse racism, Orientalism cannot be equated with nativism. They are equally ugly perhaps, but one has power, the other does not. One has far greater access to certain types of information and knowledge—thus the ability to persuade and manipulate—than the other. Cultural contaminations are never reciprocal; power always imbalances the relationship. Take, for instance, role reversal in the theater of difference. Third World intellectuals with almost no exceptions embrace some aspects of a Western Enlightenment ideology. In so doing they are likely to place their own society at a lower position on the evolutionary scale while identifying themselves with what they perceive to be First World intellectuals. Capitalism is cosmopolitan by definition and is adept at setting aside an alluring transnational space for educated Third Worlders. Protobourgeois bureaucracy—increasingly a full-blown phenomenon everywhere, from Kenya to India, from Indonesia to Mexico—absorbs alienated natives, who in turn generate ideologies enticing to the neophytes. The tragedy here is that assimilation is a sham possibility. The West these converts have turned to does not reciprocate; it is indifferent, if not outright contemptuous, toward them. Identification and transference are merely wishful, and this knowledge eats into their self-perception, as best described in Frantz Fanon's *Black Skin, White Masks*. To the extent that the concept of nationhood is a product of Western hegemony, nativism is also its by-product, one hardly capable of combating Western internationalism and universalism. And the colonial intellectuals' return home, to their own nativism, is full of hazards as well.

To this, it is important to note, a white equivalent simply does not exist. The whites may indeed empathize with the predicament of the Third World, adore its exoticism, and even go native. But they do not face the wall of indifference; they are typically welcomed. While a Man Friday (in *Robinson Crusoe*) receives only patronizing condescension in London, a Lord Jim meets respect bordering on awe from both his Patusan friends and his author. Mr. Kurtz, we all know, is not an analogue of Caliban. The psychological asymmetry exactly replicates the political one-sidedness of colonial oppression.

Such configurations of power between the West and the Third World are indispensable to our consideration of the differences in the literary products of the two worlds. For the purpose of comparison, the novel, or the prose narrative, might prove more useful than poetry or drama. The latter forms historically have more in common throughout the world, inasmuch as their emergence and development date back to the remote past preceding the Renaissance and the Enlightenment that began to integrate the globe and at the same time rend it farther apart into the conquerors and the conquered. At least at the earlier stages, poetry and drama seem to constitute communal activities in separate spheres, whereas the novel, or the printed prose narrative, late in its birth, is from the very beginning destined to be discriminatory and alienating. To this modern literary form we now turn.

The prose narrative, that is, colloquial fiction of some length written and printed for mass consumption, is of course not homogeneous the world over. The Western novel that begins in the eighteenth century as a function of the Enlightenment is culture-specific, and one needs to propose countermodels with dissimilar genealogies and topologies. To take a few examples, African prose narratives, mostly written in the oppressors' languages and printed by their technology, have different relations to the indigenous myths and tales from those of Western literatures. In China, prose fiction goes back to the Sung dynasty and beyond, but the so-called modern novel is considerably divergent from its "classic" precedents as well as from the modern Western novel.[6] Arabic colloquial fiction, sharply distinct from both aristocratic poetry and folktales, has at the same time inextricable relations to them in its relatively short history.[7] South American fiction has a closer tie to European literature via the centuries-long exposure to Spanish works, and Jorge Luis Borges or Julio Cortazar are hardly out of place in any European literary scene. But even that development is counterbalanced by more self-consciously native writers like Juan Rulfo and Gabriel García Márquez.[8] Every national/regional prose narrative has a good deal to do with Western hegemony and colonialism in general and the Western novel in particular, and yet it refuses to be subsumed by English, French, German, Spanish, or Russian literary history. If the dominant Western novel continually threatens to become the universal norm in the mind of both Western and native readers, some Third World writers struggle to locate forms of their own against it. Dostoyevsky and Flaubert appear to belong to the "universal" canon, and Lu Hsun and Mori Ogai do not.[9] Questions are being raised, however, from many directions today regarding the motivations and consequences of canonicity itself.[10] Instead of thrashing around in the vast territory of world literature, however, let me concentrate my discussion on one non-Western model, the Japanese, and refer to others whenever such a maneuver looks sensible.

The *Shosetsu:* Formal Features

In Chapter 1, I cited the Japanese narrative as an alternative form to the novel. The aim was to situate the reading of the foreign narrative form side by side with our own in order to learn the way of seeing the other against the native—that is, our own—grain. In that chapter, I briefly proposed a genealogy, history, and taxonomy of the *shosetsu,* concentrating on emplotment and characterization. Throughout, I glanced in the direction of the hegemonic concepts and categories that would not apply to the Japanese form in its history. Here let me fill in other features of the later Japanese prose narrative, so that its comparison with the modern Western novel's traits may yield a different kind of insight into the position as well as the condition of the *shosetsu*—and by extension, the Japanese social imaginary—in today's world. Of course, at the same time, the project of decentering our own practice is firmly on my agenda.

As in other Third World histories, the development of narrative in Japan was disrupted at the point when the West forcibly imposed itself on the unwilling country. As in many societies overwhelmed by the Western powers, the early Japanese response was to learn how to modernize, that is, Westernize.[11] In the process the Japanese were urged to stress the discontinuity of the present from the past. Thus the indigenous prose narrative *(gesaku),* prevalent during Japan's isolation from the world, was put aside so that a new international form might take hold. Authority over this imported fiction was invested in the elite writers and journalists *(bundan),* and not in the universities (to which the preservation of classic tradition was consigned). Thus the *shosetsu* tended to be "progressive," which meant in this case pro-Western and anti-traditional. Critical orthodoxy has frequently emphasized the breakdown of tradition that took place at the encroachment of the West. Of course, there have been those who resisted such a "cosmopolitan" enterprise—especially during the turbulent half-century after the 1890s when the production of a national tradition was on the state agenda. They believed in the superiority of the older form that best embodied the uncontaminated "essence" of Japanism. What is important here is that despite their contrasting views, the progressives and preservationists concurred in acknowledging the seriousness of discontinuity, that is, diagnosing the postdisruption *shosetsu* as intrinsically Western and modern. Their only difference was in valorizing either the older or the newer *shosetsu.* The choice was framed—again, as in many Third World countries—in the form of *either* modern Westernization *or* traditional nativism.[12]

In fundamental aspects of form, however, the older and newer forms of Japanese fiction seem to share a great deal more than is usually assumed. There are certain undeniable changes such as the setting aside of literary language and the adoption—or virtually the invention—of a new "colloquial" written language.[13] Nevertheless, both versions are sharply distinct from the Western model. In fact, if the older *shosetsu* appears non-Western and the newer version seems to conform to the specifications of the Western novel, it is mainly because they are both read as transparent records of social scenery, in markedly different new and old versions—with their narrative grammar and textuality largely ignored. Thus it is crucial here to look into formal characteristics of the *shosetsu* that have more or less persisted for the last three hundred years, both before and after the opening of Japan to the West.

One, there is no apparent attempt at formal coherence—as understood in the West—in the *shosetsu.* Often there is not even a central event; instead the work consists of separate episodes and anecdotes. Underlying the disparate actions might be some consistent tone or mood, but what is important is the definite indifference to the formation of a center and structure. Often a work opens without a discernible beginning, and ends without a bang. No preparation is made toward a climax or denouement. Quite obviously the Judeo-Christian belief in Genesis and Judgment is not an operative morphology here. Events succeed events, just as seconds and minutes and hours follow in an indeterminable flow—often not even in a cyclic rhythm. The borders of the text seem minimally evident.

Two, the plot is of course sequential, but hardly consequential. That is, the events are not syntactically cumulative but paratactically aggregative. Causality that operates to rule over moral failures and social successes is not a focus of concern, nor is psychological observation or analysis a major interest. Suspense and resolution are not strategically significant. In the Japanese grammar of motives, association and juxtaposition on the surface of the text determine the direction of events and actions, not the intersection of privacies and transcendences at the depth, nor the Burkean pentad of scene, act, agent, agency, and purpose.[14] Related to this is the fundamental structure of temporal markers, as has already been touched on. Sequentiality is left ambiguous because of the mixture of the complete and incomplete aspects (which are often misunderstood as the present and past tenses). Discursive priority and temporal priority are freely mixed, thus confusing/liberating the totality of "meaning."

Three, its characters are largely types or names. What tortures and pleases an individual out of a type or a name into a separate character, the interiorized and privatized sense of the self, is indisputably absent. In an earlier tale such as Ihara Saikaku's *An Amorous Man* (1682), the central character is no more than a name arbitrarily applied to the agents of all the actions—without the slightest self-consciousness as to the reasons for such attributions. Even when an alienated modern man or woman is the predominant figure in a more recent work, the individual is usually worried about his or her relationship to groups and models, and the worrying self is subsumed by the preponderance of the collective consciousness. Fitness is the principal anguish into which the unfit are tracelessly absorbed.

Four, the narrative point of view is hardly ever fixed. Far more freely than in a typical nineteenth-century European novel, points of view keep shifting and merging. This means an entirely different epistemology and psychology: everyone is assumed to know everybody else so well that the separation between individuals is negligible. In Chapter 1 I discussed the difference between the *shosetsu* and the novel, using Barthes' terms, in the issues surrounding tense/aspect and first-/third-person narrative voice. To capitulate the points in slightly different terms, it is true that the first person is predominant in the *shosetsu:* the orthodoxy of Japanese fiction is "I-fiction" that records the life of the author. And yet, paradoxically, it is not egocentric. Quite unlike the autobiographical novel (whether in first or third person) such as *David Copperfield, The House of the Dead,* or *Sons and Lovers* that fashions a critically selected persona, the *shishosetsu* is a form of documentary chronology that supposedly exemplifies the normative life of a member of the collective. The writer can be eccentric, but in his or her difference the reader merely sees the limits of homogeneity. Supposedly, I-fiction is always honest and factual, and it rejects fictionality and mediation. Thus it cannot come to a true end, for instance, until the author comes to the end of his life. Writers like Dazai Osamu, Mishima Yukio, and Kawabata Yasunari consequently had to commit suicide in order to bring their diaries to completion.

Five, the *shosetsu* texture is often dense, rhetorical, and formulaic. It depends heavily on the common stock of poetry and poeticity. As the prose of *The Tale of Genji* is nearly always on the verge of turning into poetry, the *shosetsu* style is always conscious of its own performance in disjunction with the drift of the narrated events. Transparent description is unexpectedly absent and would be out of place.

Six, the length is extremely variable. The material extension of a novel has formal significance. In order to do the job it intends to do, the novel needs an ample space in which a series of events are to be introduced, interwoven, and braked to a halt. The length also consolidates the textual desire for autonomy; the novel thus longs to transform itself into a "world." However, the term *shosetsu* (literally, "small talk," or gossip) is indiscriminately used whether a story is long or short. The difference in the nature of narrativity between a short story in three pages and a three-hundred-page romance is simply ignored. The indifference is understandable in view of the anecdotal aggregativeness of the *shosetsu* form. It also points to the readerly desire for a sequence of affects, rather than a cumulative construction of a structure and textuality. At any rate, this *shosetsu* idiosyncrasy is as noteworthy as the other features, and yet it is hardly ever taken note of by Japanese or foreign readers.

The list can go on to include many more features such as the mode of production and consumption,[15] the role of authorship, and the politics of literary associations and connections, which are markedly different from the Western counterparts. But for now this ought to suffice, since the point here is simply to find terms for comparison, rather than fully describe the ecology of the *shosetsu* form. Now, how does one explain this form that is indifferent to coherence, strings together episodes and anecdotes, has few interiorized characters, has radically undifferentiated points of view, and has a verbose surface, and yet is adamant in insisting on honesty? How does it remain attractive to the Japanese reader?

Let me explain as a First World reader. First, as I have already mentioned, the hegemonic bracketing of perception is such that these formal characteristics are largely unobserved. Second, when they are noticed, they are likely to be explained away as a matter of exotic or essentialist aberrations, either positively or negatively. Third, and more important, the indigenous vocabulary concerning form has not yet been fully investigated either inside or outside Japan. By this I do not mean tonal qualities such as *wabi, sabi,* and *iki,* which have at least been taken seriously by consumer designers and cultural merchants like the airline companies or department stores—although real notice can perhaps be taken of them.[16] I mean instead a principle of beginning, middle, and end that seems completely irrelevant to the causal or even consequential connections of events, the *jo-ha-kyu* (introduction-transformation-acceleration) or the *ki-sho-ten-ketsu* (beginning-succession-change-conclusion) notion, often cited by Japanese critics and aestheticians as rooted in the sense of pace and proportion. They are usually temporal concepts, as in poetry and music, but they can also be spatial, as in architecture. In fact, the principles of pacing are believed to be operable in a temporal-spatial complex such as drama, or even in military strategy.[17] What such an immensely generalized abstract principle of form can mean in relation to the formal features of the *shosetsu* is as of now totally unclear. Is it a generalization mobilized to serve as the model of the totalized *idea* of "Japanese culture"? Or is it some still-to-be-articulated aesthetic and constructional principle? Or is it merely an instrument for obfuscatory evocation of cultural nostalgia? The only thing that can be asserted here is that the *shosetsu* form seems as saturated with a formal consciousness as the novel is, but that our own—or I should say, my own—hermeneutic short circuit does not allow me to recognize its contours.

Finally, to turn from what the *shosetsu* is not to what it is, the *shosetsu* is a verbal flow concerned with contiguous variations in pace, which seeks to decentralize discursive space, fragmenting the dominant narrative focus into segments and sections. The *shosetsu* prefers external movements and groupings of collective members to interiorized drama of individuals, and attracts the reader's attention to its own presence and artificiality. Here one recalls Fujiwara no Teika, a medieval poet-editor-critic, who compared Japanese literature to "singing" *(uta);* or the fifteenth-century practice of group composition of serial poems *(renga);* or an eighteenth-century critic-linguist, Motoori Norinaga, who thought of Japanese literature as essentially *con*-textual. Singing, collective authorship, contextuality, and paratactic rather than syntactic emplotment are oral, or vocal, features. And the formal difference that persists between the *shosetsu* and the novel can now be explained as that between choral performance and isolated speculation, or more generally, between orality and literacy. It is on this point that the *shosetsu* is found to share many features with the modern narrative forms not only of Korea, China, and the rest of Asia, but also of the Third World as a whole. The advantage of such generalization is twofold. One, the novel/*shosetsu* comparison can now be shifted to a larger comparison of the Western as against the Third World narrative forms that can in turn be placed in the hegemonic historical context. Two, so placed in the general scheme, the discourse can be freed of the provincial essentialism that has long obsessed the practitioners of Japanology.

Orality/Literacy and Speech/Writing

The underlying proposal here is that between Western and Third World literatures there is a general area of difference that might be usefully explained in terms of orality and literacy. Such a generalization, however, must be at once severely qualified by an awareness that, of all binarisms, this particular example is fraught with great hazards. Developmentalism, the underpinning of post-Enlightenment ethnocentricity, is accustomed to dividing the world along the line of logic and literacy. In this view civilization evolves from orality to literacy, as a child does to adulthood. At the height of Western imperialism, Lucien Lévy-Bruhl proclaimed the creed of the "Great Divide" in *Les fonctions mentales dans les sociétés inférieures* (1910), which was translated into English in 1926, and reprinted in 1985, under the somewhat more moderate title *How Natives Think*.[18] Lévy-Bruhl argues that the divide that runs between the civilized and the primitive is cognitive and structural, whether it be essential (genetic) or developmental (maturational). The civilized are logical and rational, while the primitive—meaning all non-Western peoples—are prelogical and irrational. After such blatant racism was generally discredited, the orality/literacy binarism took its place as a new shelter for ethnocentricity.

A good example is Jack Goody and Ian Watt's "The Consequences of Literacy." Written in 1963, the article argues that the rejection of the dualism between "mythopoetic" and "logoempirical" modes of thought "has been pushed too far: diffuse relativism and sentimental egalitarianism combine to turn a blind eye on some of the most basic problems of human history."[19] Goody and Watt believe that the division along the Lévy-Bruhl line still exists, although for them the separation does not occur exactly between literacy and nonliteracy. Their great divide is between ancient Greek civilization, which is "really literate" (p. 42) with its fully phonetic alphabets, and all other literate and nonliterate societies ranging from oral cultures to civilizations that merely invented pictographs, logograms, syllabaries, or phonetic alphabets (like Hebrew's) that lack letters for vowels. The Greek model, as they see it, is truly phonetic in the sense that each letter represents a sound, an abstraction, and every sound is represented in a letter, unlike all other models where representation is still deeply embedded in concrete objects. The syllabaries and phonetic signs without vowels are also unsatisfactory because they do not attain to the degree of analysis and abstraction that the Greek alphabets did. This is the reason, according to Goody and Watt, for the greatness of ancient Greek civilization, which no other race had achieved anywhere else. Thus humanity is in debt to the Greeks for their "historically unique" (p. 52) contributions in the development of epistemology and taxonomy. Their alphabets were so efficient and capable that they enabled the wide spread of literacy; other writing media merely produced proto-literacy and oligo-literacy (p. 36). For Goody and Watt, the alphabetically literate Europeans alone are also capable of history, taxonomy, logic, creativity, individualism, and democracy. Such marks of civilization are all "consequences" of the phonetic literacy that developed in Greece at the time of Plato and Aristotle and more recently in the post-Enlightenment West. All non-Western societies including India and China are cognitively mythical, pre-logical, and irrational as well as collective, theocratic, and undemocratic, that is, anterior to full maturity as a civilization.

What are the implied effects of alphabetical literacy on the novel? Goody and Watt argue that in light of the "general contrast between oral and alphabetically literate culture," "a certain identity between the spirit of the Platonic dialogues and of the novel" becomes manifest:

> This general kinship between Plato and the characteristic art form of literate culture, the novel, suggests a further contrast between oral and literate societies: in contrast to the homeostatic transmission of the cultural tradition among non-literate peoples, literate society leaves more to its members; less homogeneous in its cultural tradition, it gives more free play to the individual, and particularly to the intellectual, the literate specialist himself; it does so by sacrificing a single, ready-made orientation to life. And, in so far as an individual participates in the literate, as distinct from the oral, culture, such coherence as a person achieves is very largely the result of his personal selection, adjustment and elimination of items from a highly differentiated cultural repertoire; he is, of course, influenced by all the various social pressures, but they are so numerous that the pattern finally comes out as an individual one.   (p. 63)

From this Goody and Watt proceed to valorize the novel with its individualism and democracy over all other narrative forms. And this form is characterized as unique to "alphabetically literate culture," the West, alone.

The views advanced by Goody and Watt display a profound ethnocentricity as well as a self-serving advocacy of free "alphabetically literate" intellectuals. They also ignore all historical circumstances surrounding the question of writing, such as social formations and economic and political conditions. When the article was republished in 1968 in book form together with a dozen responses by regional anthropologists, however, no respondent commented on these self-centered doctrines. Instead, they more or less served to support and elaborate the theory of the great divide between the cognitively superior Western civilization and the non-West.[20] Alphabetic literacy, their ground for the division, was not seriously discussed. Goody has continued since to pursue the matter in his numerous anthropological studies of Africa, whereas Watt has returned to his accustomed literary criticism. Watt has not abandoned comparative cultural studies, however, but merely redirected his interest to a lasting project of reading Joseph Conrad. It is to be noted that Ian Watt, the author of *The Rise of the Novel,* one of the most widely respected studies in the United States and Britain from its publication in 1957 to around 1970, has been consistent in arguing for the preservation of the Great Divide theory and the disengagement of Conrad from colonial discourse, while his objective is proclaimed to be to maintain "neutrality" and "artistic excellence."[21]

A view opposite from Goody and Watt's hostility to the non-West is that of Claude Lévi-Strauss in *Tristes Tropiques*. Lévi-Strauss would see writing as an instrument of violence. The prelapsarian tribe of Nambikiwara Indians had lived a mythopoetic idyllic life until writing implements arrived. In a story recounting his stay with the tribe, he romanticizes his experience of witnessing the visible change brought about among the tribesmen who saw him write. At once strife commenced, unraveling the traditional fabric of a closely woven oral society. "If my hypothesis is correct, the primary function of writing, as a means of communication, is to facilitate the enslavement of other human beings. The use of writing for disinterested ends, and with a view to satisfactions of the mind in the fields either of science or the arts, is a secondary result of its invention—and may even be no more than a way of reinforcing, justifying, or dissimulating its primary function."[22] Lévi-Strauss privileges the Nambikiwara Indians as uncontaminated by literacy. What is important to us is his insistence on the division between the literate

Westerners he himself represents and the innocent tribesmen, which is as decisive as Goody and Watt's.

Whether in Goody and Watt's Eurocentricity or in Lévi-Strauss's Rousseauesque nostalgia, the orality/literacy opposition between cultures is held to be a stable feature. And the invention of literacy, as they argue, produces by itself a decisive cognitive change, the consequences of which are—again for both groups of comparativists—simply immense. As they see it, a given society is either oral or literate, and the great divide between the civilized and the primitive is as unbridgeable as was believed a generation ago. In the meantime, social formations and relations, in both the tribal and external contexts, are largely ignored in these ethnological observations and descriptions.

Such reinforcement of the ethnocentric division is not unique to Goody, Watt, and Lévi-Strauss. Goody's own *Domestication of the Savage Mind* (1977), *The Logic of Writing and the Organization of Society* (1986), and *The Interface between the Written and the Oral* (1987) revise and elaborate a few points but more or less continue along the same line, together with the works of other anthropologists and comparativists. There have been numerous literary historians and critics such as Albert Lord, Marshall McLuhan, Walter Ong, and Eric Havelock, each contributing to the intensification of separateness of the self and the Other from a variety of West-centered perspectives.[23]

There have been attempts, on the other hand, to revamp the distinction altogether. Targeting on what he calls an "ethnocentrism *thinking itself* as anti-ethnocentrism," Jacques Derrida fiercely assaults Lévi-Strauss in *Of Grammatology*.[24] According to Derrida, the spoken word is as abstract as the written. Thus for him there is no "leap" (p. 120) between speech and writing, for language is "always already a writing" (p. 106). Literacy penetrates into language itself, and the idea of pure orality is a sheer illusion based on deep-rooted ethnocentricity. While Derrida's objection is characteristically conducted on a highly abstract level of epistemology, Brian Street's 1985 book *Literacy: Theory and Practice* is a practitioner's exercise over various positions on the issue. His principal opponent is Goody, whose insistence on the consequences of literacy is, in Street's view, both ungrounded and biased.[25] Much of what Goody attributes to literacy, according to Street, is in fact a consequence of social forces that may or may not be related to the emergence of literacy. Thus for Street, literacy is an ideological production, depending for its various effects on the complex nexus of historical factors. This, I think, is significant in deflating the exaggerated evaluation of literacy and disclosing the persistent racist program behind it. Finally, Roger Chartier, in *The Cultural Use of Print in Early Modern France,* subtly analyzes the gray areas between orality and literacy, stressing that "writing was present at the very heart of an illiterate culture."[26]

There are, however, at least two grounds on which Derrida's and Street's corrective proposal must be challenged. First, as they make clear, there are literacies and literacies, as there are oralities and oralities. Some societies have long been lettered (early China and India, for instance), yet literacy has been restricted to a segment of society because of economic and political patterns. Likewise, written texts have varying relationships to orality. Now that hardly any society is completely oral—or literate, for that matter—sharp division of the world into oral and literate groups is even less meaningful. However, recognition of the coexistence of orality and literacy in a given society does not mean that oral and literate activities are identical either in operation or in consequence. Speech enables certain social and psychological experiences, while writing enables others. If orality and literacy blur in certain written documents, it is not because speech and writing, the two modes of communication, are finally identical, but because orality is better preserved in some than in others. Derrida and Street seem to allow some specific differences between the two, and yet they are too eager to demolish the ethnocentricity of Lévi-Strauss, Goody, and others to accept the full significance of such differences.[27]

Second, Derrida's and Street's denial of the binarism collapses the social variables into a single model of oral and literate mix, thereby licensing—clearly against their intent—the universalist reading of cultures and societies. If one is to take their unitarist theses at face value, they seem to be proposing that every society in the world more or less uniformly exercises speech and writing. Obviously this is not true, in the sense that the industrialized societies are far more dependent on literacy—or a version of literacy—

than the unindustrialized. More important, the unitarist view would encourage indifference to the vast inequity between the rich nations and the poor. Despite his indisputable anti-racism, Street's unitarism on this matter is bound to present itself as a version of universalism like the "family of man" that has been invented to ignore the facts of segregation and inequality in the world.[28] Derrida's "language is always already a writing" could easily be lampooned as "economy is always already wealth." His stand on apartheid comes perilously close to a Kantian precision that has very little to do with the actual oppression and suffering in the Republic of South Africa.[29] After clear perception of injustice and inequity, one can and must begin a program for active speculation that alone legitimates scholarship and criticism. Derrida's and Street's contributions are obvious, and yet their universalism could give support to the hegemonic appropriation of Third World varieties—for instance, on the matter of narrativity.

Literacy is not a cause for a cognitive transformation of a culture. It may not even be a cause for historical events. It is unquestionable, however, that literacy is adjacent to serious social and cultural changes. It is present at urbanization, bureaucratization, industrialization, individualism, capitalism, nationalism, and colonialism.[30] Although precise terms that will link these historical transformations to each other are not easy to establish—cause, enabling factor, necessary reason, sufficient reason, homology, or else metaphor, metonymy, analogy—they are neither crucial nor even necessary at this point. And I might add to this list of co-present historical trends the topic at hand here: the Western prose narrative form, the novel. Without widespread literacy and printing, there would have been no novel; and literacy, printing, and the novel were produced only in certain societies deeply engaged in expansionism and colonialism.

The Western Novel

The Western novel had its birth soon after European expansionism began in earnest. The adventurism received a powerful celebration in Shakespeare's *Tempest*.[31] As the novel form became established in Britain by the marked advances in literacy, printing, and colonialism, expansionist energy resurfaced in Defoe's *Robinson*

Crusoe, where voyage, self-discovery, domination, expropriation, and accumulation equally occupy its narrative space. The voyager from England's lower middle class sailed into an "empty" space and became its governor and its ruler, just as a novelist charts a story on blank pages, with no agreed-on rules guiding the advance. Crusoe's island is a colonialist's utopia, just as the novel as a printed narrative form is a colonial utopian space in which the subject meets the objects in a struggle for mastery. The emergence at this time of the novel, with its huge length, free-wheeling advance, and eventual organizational control, is certainly no accident of history. The growing need for understanding of and cooperation with the colonial enterprise had to produce the energy that could be propelled only into this particular form of narrative. One might likewise note the nearly total absence of the female in the novel. Crusoe's wife occupies less than a sentence, which only announces her death—an absence displaced by disappearance.

Crusoe and the reader are both dislocated loners. In this sense, too, Robinson Crusoe is Prospero's descendant, and *Crusoe* the novel continues the colonialist discourse of *The Tempest* the play. The discourse, however, is now conducted in a significantly different mode—to fit the aggressive operation to extend the dominion of European nations. The novel, despite its preoccupation with social relations, is a lonesome form indeed. Take, for instance, Crusoe's diary. The rhetorical and narrative device of a journal inside a tale is in itself nothing new. But the one in *Robinson Crusoe* is particularly gratuitous in the sense that much of the experience recorded in it is already told in the outside narrative. Thus some events, such as the storm and the shipwreck, are repeated twice or more. The journal's tone and texture are not clearly distinguishable from those of the main narrative either. What is effected between the main text and the journal, then, is not so much a dialectic tension as a simple distance between the narrating Crusoe and the narrated Crusoe, or Crusoe the reflector/observer and Crusoe the experiencer/observed. As the Crusoe outside the journal reexamines the Crusoe inside, the physical text of the journal with its materiality transforms Crusoe's conscious being into a subject and an object, twice. In this moment of self-fragmentation was born the self-consciousness that characterizes the novel form.[32] And this birth is inconceivable outside the context of colonial adventurism where man faces alone the elements to be conquered.

Historical colonialism continued steadily throughout the eighteenth and nineteenth centuries until the imperialist climax around the turn of the twentieth century. A curious thing in the history of the novel is that there are so few works that directly confront this Western domination during much of the nineteenth century. Colonial life is constantly referred to in most novels, and the motif of sailing out is often employed thematically as a device for closure, as if the departure from home is—together with death and wedding—the end (that is, a beginning) of everyday life.[33] But seldom is a full representation given.[34] This shyness before the age of Kipling, Haggard, Stevenson, and Conrad may be an indication of some unacknowledged yet felt unease about colonial domination that needed to be concealed from the unwitting participants in the national program.

If outright disclosure of expansionism was avoided in the novel, however, the narrative form itself reveals a number of crucial features with close bearings on global adventurism. Take the initial formal perception of the novel as the "comic epic in prose," for instance. "Comic," meaning "anti-heroic," guarantees that the circle of novelistic characters remains ordinary bourgeois just like the author and his or her readers. Untoward encounters with alien savages and natives are to be avoided, except when they are portrayed as lower, funny figures. The novel is essentially an exclusivist form, making sure the European middle class will have an autonomous and complete sphere of being. The residual feature of "epic" that is expressed as "picaresque" and then as "bildungsroman"—as the spatial advance is turned into the temporal—defines the novel as a story of departure, voyage, struggle, self-discovery, settlement, and return. Distance in journey is precisely commensurate with degree of maturation. As industrialization and urbanization continue, the city-country contrast begins to loom, as Raymond Williams has shown. Of course the urban-rural dualism always suggests a similar structural pair of homeland metropolis and colonial peripheries, even if the latter opposition is not frankly acknowledged. Finally, the "prose" of the definition seems to indicate that the novel is free from historic prosodic and other formalist restrictions, very much as colonial space nearly always meant an unmapped, unordered, untouched territory. The native geography was simply ignored, just as the native population was considered absent or invisible. The novel is an aggressively utopian form that the author populates *ex nihilo* with characters generated in a godlike act of creation. The writer's authority becomes increasingly unchallengeable. The rise in the prestige of the novel is a measure of the social control expected of and exercised by the novel form itself. As to the establishment of authorial control and authority, however, one might better return to the property of literacy.

The novel as a long printed tale is always read at a distance from its author. The distance is both physical and metaphorical. In opposition to the situation of the oral tale, which is recited and heard in proximity, the author and the reader do not share the same space or time. The novel is more isolated in composition and autonomous in reception. The author can always trace back at any moment, adjusting parts to parts and beginning to ending (except for those works published in serialization). The reader, too, can open, close, and reopen a book at will. The possibility of repeated readings—though not identical experiences—transforms a novel from a temporal production to a more spatial object, a commodity. And the spatial contours of a book provide the reader with a greater variety of relationships with it. Once a novel is written, printed, and distributed, it is ineradicable and presumably available to an infinite number of future readers. A writer can address a novel to any imaginable readership; likewise, a reader has, theoretically at least, an infinite selection of books to read, as against the severely limited availability of oral recitations. Contextuality is replaced by textuality.

Greater freedom necessarily means at the same time greater alienation. The reader is left with his or her own interpretation, since interrupting to question the author would be impossible. Different booklists for individuals mean the absence of common knowledge and shared information (homeostasis), which presumably are more easily attainable in an oral culture. The written and printed text of a book thus asserts itself, making the communicative linkage of the author and the reader (the speaker and the listener) much less attainable and definable. An oral recitation can be interrupted, approved or disapproved, cheered or booed; the audience reception is at once returned to the reciter, allowing him or her to steer the performance to a desired effect. A printed book is far more remote; an author finds out how a work is being received only through reviews, sales, or chance conversation. Very much like a privatized character in a bourgeois novel, the reader, too, trudges alone in search of meaning without a comrade. Social divisions make a common bibliography unimaginable, while this impossibility of common information and interest makes social divisions even more acute. Thus the importance of lit. crit. and other humanities courses, where society—through the use of its professors (i.e., institutional employees or secular priests)—tries to set up and enforce a canon, disseminate acceptable interpretations, and quietly guide the emancipated leadership back into a safe sanctity of agreements.

No society has ever been free from tribal control. Goody and Watt might celebrate the freedom and democracy resulting from literacy, but they leave out the darker side. Bourgeois society gives freedom to its citizens and takes it back in a complex, sophisticated fashion. Commodities may be abundant, but the benefits of the great choice in selection are canceled by the denial of the choice of not buying. Interpretations are free, perhaps; but from early school days students, that is, readers, are trained to respond in certain directions, as the cultural experts (Stanley Fish's "interpretive community") see fit to recommend.[35] While an oral tale exerts undisguised control over the audience, the novel manipulates through its sophisticated and mediated structure, distant narrator, interiorized characters, and supposedly unrhetorical style. A colonial counterpart might be the members of a Western society mobilized to leave their homeland, discover a virgin forest, build settlements, give a new geography and history to the new land, and then be expected to return home. If they do not go home in person, their ties to the old country are kept intact nonetheless. The clichéd image of the British colonialists grotesquely hanging on to their English habits and habiliments in the middle of a jungle is of course no caricature. To this very day, neocolonialists cling to their homeland identities. For the distinction from the natives must be kept absolute, whenever the natives cannot be obliterated and their existence needs to be acknowledged. This, it seems to me, is what is practiced in numerous classrooms in the humanities in Western universities, both at home and abroad. One remembers that when the principle of indoctrination was most vigorously denied several decades ago, the nearly universally held motto was Archibald MacLeish's line, "A poem should not mean / But be." Theology is most effective when its absence is displayed.

Very much embedded in the oral context of communicative exchange, Third World narratives retain their characteristic features even when written and printed. The narrative forms that impress ethnocentric Westerners as naive and unformed are crafted to different demands and expectations. In fact, once alerted, one realizes that it is the Western novel that is unique and exceptional, and not exotic non-Western tales and romances. Produced in a historical circumstance that is at once enlightened, aggressive, and expansive, the Western narrative form attends to the modern Westerner's necessity for privatized inner space. Its epistemology and hermeneutics are similarly inscribed with the historical objectives of the adventurist West. On the other side of the Great Divide, Third World narratives are testimonials to the history of suffering at the hand of colonial oppressors. So viewed, the episodic, decentralized, aggregative, dialogic, multivocal, public narratives of Asia, Africa, the Middle East, and the Americas are restored to their proper place among the expressions of peoples. And the *shosetsu* takes its place right among them.

Quite obviously, the Third World is not exclusively peaceful and nonviolent. The history of Japan as the one Third World nation that has succeeded in absorbing and reproducing imperialism has already been cited. Having joined the ranks of the Western colonizers, Japan has produced a narrative form that is very much like the Western model. Some of the works in the late Meiji through early Showa eras (1900–1970) are privatized and autonomized—though not necessarily interiorized. Japan's most recent leap in production and consumption (since 1970) seems to have positioned Japan in the economic and social conditions that are best called late capitalist and characterized by symptoms common in global hegemonic societies. But even now the residual oral traits almost always persist in various aspects. How this historical development relates to the narrative formation is intriguingly uncertain.

Bashers and Bashing
in the World

If cultural assumptions are deeply imbued with economic and political motives and conditions, political economy is conversely shaped by cultural assumptions and productions. Such a proposition is indisputable, even trite. And yet in the practice of literary and cultural criticism, seldom does one see an attempt to link specific trade and industrial policy and development directly with cultural imaginaries. Seeking to cross over, if not clear away, the boundaries that apparently lie between the economical and the cultural in many critics' minds, I now turn to one of the most virulent issues between Japan and the United States. Friction and negotiations over trade between the two nations reveal a core of cultural solipsism and misapprehension and entail deliberate misrepresentations and concealments.

Japan's emergence as an economic superstate is by now a given. It is very much talked about—often negatively, with fear and resentment. This "bashing" is a constant topic in both the United States and Japan. In this chapter I will examine bashing as a form of cultural criticism, contextualizing trade in social practice and tracing the "open-door" policy to the history of the West, just as in the previous chapters the reading of the novel and the *shosetsu* was related to the history of Western hegemonism.

Japan Bashing

When did Japan bashing begin in the United States? At the demise of textile or steel mills? On the desertion of shipyards? With the closing of television and consumer electronics factories? After the decline of Detroit? Or with the increasing threat to Silicon Valley? We began to see those pictures of laid-off mill hands and assembly-line workers furiously smashing up goods marked "Made in Japan." Occasionally, members of Congress, senators, and, inevitably, pres-idential candidates issued statements, but they were routine and most Americans paid little heed. Then in 1982, unemployed Detroit workers beat a young Chinese-American to death, mistaking him for a Japanese. A man and his son-in-law were fined and received suspended sentences—without spending a single day in jail. Asian-Americans were outraged, forming an alliance in protest for the first time in history. But the American majority ignored the incident, which was after all a local, blue-collar, minority affair.

Bashing became full-blown with Theodore White's article "The Danger from Japan," published on July 28, 1985, in the *New York Times Magazine*. White is unremittingly rancorous as he portrays the Japanese as they "go about dismantling American industry" (p. 22). Comparing the German trade surplus with the Japanese, he has this to say: "The Germans, somehow, evoke little American bitterness because we understand their culture. . . . The Japanese provoke American wrath because they are a locked and closed civilization that reciprocates our hushed fear with veiled contempt" (p. 38). The essay closes with a dire prophecy as if another war were about to break out: "The superlative execution of their trade tactics may provoke an incalculable reaction—as the Japanese might well remember of the course that ran from Pearl Harbor to the deck of the U.S.S. Missouri in Tokyo Bay just 40 years ago" (p. 59). White was on the *Missouri* on that glorious day with General MacArthur. Vying with nostalgia, anger and fear are now palpable even in the central establishment of American society. Japan's challenge is se-rious, and bashing is spilling over from the economy to other areas of the U.S.-Japan relationship.

I am not interested here in the specific signs of Japan's recent trade hegemonism. One sees them everyday on television and in periodicals. Some of the most eye-catching items: The trade imbalance stands at 50 billion dollars annually in Japan's favor; Japan's per capita income is higher than that of the United States; eight of the world's ten largest banks are Japanese; a single Japanese corporation, Nippon Telegraph and Telephone, is worth more than IBM, AT&T, General Motors, General Electric, and Exxon combined; nearly a third of the U.S. budget deficit is now shouldered by Japanese investors;[1] we all know about Mitsubishi's acquisition of a major share in the Rockefeller Trust, and American annoyance and irritation have been so alarming that Japan's Foreign Ministry and the Ministry of International Trade and Industry have repeatedly warned Japanese investors to take a "low posture"—without visible effect;[2] the total real estate value of Japan is twice that of the United States, which is twenty-five times its size;[3] the Tokyo Stock Exchange trades in the largest value in the world, exceeding by far the New York or London exchange; the profits of Nomura Securities Co., the world's largest securities company, are larger than the profits of all the U.S. securities companies combined; Japan's share in the global financial and capital market stands at 40 percent; Japan's capital investment in the Dover Tunnel enterprise is over 30 percent;[4] in 1983 U.S. manufacturers of semiconductor-making equipment held a 69 percent share of the world market, compared with 25 percent for the Japanese, while by 1993 the Japanese are expected to command a 55 percent hold on the market, compared with 32 percent for U.S. manufacturers;[5] finally, the *Economic Daily News (Nihon Keizai shimbun)* predicts that Japan's net foreign assets, which were 11.5 billion dollars in 1980 and 180 billion dollars in 1986, will climb to 853 billion dollars in 1995. And "Japan by 1999 will have a capital surplus big enough to buy the equivalent of several European countries."[6]

Theoretical economists reassure us that that economy has so many variables that any prediction is foolish and unreliable. Also, unanticipated events can upset the geopolitical balance, abruptly altering the economic conditions—as in Eastern Europe and the Middle East in 1989 and 1990. Japan's economic expansion obviously will not last forever.[7] Since economists began to voice such skepticism several years ago, however, Japan's industrial and trade statistics have continued to mushroom. Some of the prognoses of

Japanese economic expansion have been proved right, and others are bound to be, despite many likely setbacks. Japan's reentry in the near future into the military and commercial aeronautic industry, for instance, is an ominous prospect for U.S. competitors. All of this seems to mean, as *Business Week* remarked in November 1987, that Japan is for now "the banker . . . landlord and employer" of many Americans and will be so of many more by the mid-1990s.

Things are not all rosy for the Japanese, however. The higher per capita income is due in large part to the favorable exchange rate of the yen with the dollar. Japan's general quality of life is far poorer for most of its citizens than that of the United States.[8] The housing situation is worse than in several developing nations;[9] Japan has by far the highest consumer prices; it also has the greatest proportion of unpaved roads among the industrial nations; and parks and other public facilities are quite meager. Above all, vital areas of cultural and critical life are sorely deficient amidst the general prosperity of the country.[10]

Japan bashers thus seem to have good reasons for their concern, anxiety, and resentment. But who are the bashers? Only a little while ago the word meant to cudgel, beat, and smash—violent acts intent on destruction—as it still does in British usage (such as "Paki-bash"). In the United States it has come to refer more loosely to condemnation, stricture, or simply negative criticism. Thus, although the word sounds crisp and no-nonsense, it is too inclusive of various types and classes to be specific. A basher can be informed or uninformed, analytic or irrational, honest or deceptive; in short, anyone who is less than encouraging, enthusiastic, or euphoric about Japan seems to qualify as one.

The question of who sets up the standard, who decides on a basher or nonbasher designation, however, is rather curious. The Japanese, who for decades have been extremely sensitive to and defensive about international responses, might be expected to be the ones to group all negative critics together as bashers, regardless of the substance of their arguments. And they indeed do in Japan. But the judges in the United States are Americans, who anticipate and preempt Japanese paranoia. (Hence there is an element of irony in the American use of the term, and also in my continued use here despite its inexactitude.) The October 9, 1989, issue of *Newsweek,* occasioned by Sony's buy-up of Columbia Pictures (featuring on its cover a geisha replacing the Statue of Liberty in the Columbia logo), contains a list of twenty names divided into two columns: one lists the leading bashers, and the other the apologists. Here the focus is on trade, and the criterion is whether or not the person holds to the modernization theory. Those who believe that Japan is trying in good faith to follow the open market rules like any other capitalist country and needs no discriminatory treatment are apologists. The bashers, on the other hand, are those "revisionists" who hold that Japan's trade performance is so different from any other country's that the conventional rules of free trade should be replaced with protectionist measures.

The bashers include Congressman Richard Gephardt, Senator John Danforth, and scholars and journalists like Chalmers Johnson, Clyde Prestowitz, Karel van Wolferen, and James Fallows. The apologists are headed by former Ambassador Mike Mansfield, followed by current administration officials such as James Baker, Richard Cheney, and Richard Darman as well as scholars like the late Edwin Reischauer and Ezra Vogel. Both groups are mixed bags. The best I can make out, with some hesitation, is that by and large current administration officials and established Japan experts at orthodox universities tend to be apologists, whereas "outsiders"—former trade negotiators and non-Japanologists—tend to be bashers. Many apologists such as Reischauer and Vogel speak and read Japanese, whereas most bashers—like Fallows and van Wolferen—do not (with the exception of Johnson, who is thoroughly comfortable with the language).

What can we see in this? First, the apologists have a good deal to lose by severely condemning Japan before the U.S. public. Aside from their complex relations with the "best ally of the United States," officials in the Bush administration cannot risk the ire of the Japanese investors on whom they depend for financing their budget deficit. Having invested time and energy and having gained powerful influence in Japan itself as well as in the Japan field in this country, the expert scholars, too, cannot stand off at a critical distance. Japan has accepted them as its guides and teachers, and they now owe to their Japan at least a sympathetic representation.[11]

Thus the more administratively responsible and the more established in Japanology, the more pro-Japanese they are likely to be. Conversely, the less centrally placed in Washington and the less involved in the academic establishment, the freer they are to be critical of the Japanese. Politics and scholarship are both vulnerable to allurements, and the immediate conjunction of self-interest and judgment is hazardous, whether in the direction of apology or bashing. This is especially important in these days when the academic disciplines are increasingly unembarrassed in their affiliation with funding sources, just as politics seems to be incorporating self-interest into congressional, executive, and even judiciary, not to say partisan, structures. With its resources Japan can exert powerful influence. About 80 percent of the money for U.S. academic research on Japan, *Business Week* reports, comes from Japanese sources.[12]

Second, scholarly apologists have had less of interest to say about Japan in recent years. They tend to see Japan still in terms that have been in stable use since around 1950: as an exemplar of modernization theory in the context of the Cold War, a country that has pulled itself out of its premodern stage of development through learning from the West. They are blind to the Orientalism that is implied by such a view. The apologists have commented very little on the changes that have been taking place in Japan's intellectual and cultural life alongside its economic prosperity since around 1970. For many of them Japan remains a capitalist haven, where the process of modernization has been unaccompanied by the usual ills such as violence, strife, or radical reform.

To say this about the apologists, however, is not to seek a membership among the bashers. Too many bashers present disturbingly perverse views as they discuss the U.S.-Japan relationship and interpret Japanese society along the way. Some of them are perilously unaware of their Eurocentricity, bordering on racism. As the Detroit murder case and Theodore White's portentous warning suggest, the potential dangers are enormous, and the anger could explode into an ugly altercation that will prove mutually destructive. Those few whose criticism of Japan's economic and industrial practice seems to offer sharp insight are those who have been observing the negotiating table or the negotiators around it.

We could begin with Chalmers Johnson, who has been called the

"Godfather" of revisionists and bashers. Johnson's analysis of the Ministry of International Trade and Industry (published in 1982) was groundbreaking in interpreting Japanese institutions in their own terms rather than placing them in Western categories. His descriptions and analyses are clear and precise. His concern since writing *MITI and the Japanese Miracle* has been with Japan's trade practice, scrupulously refraining from cultural generalization. He has advised the Japanese to work toward greater separation of bureaucracy, business, and party, and his proposals, in admirably plain and original terms, for programs ranging from strengthening bourgeois politics to improving trade equity are increasingly urgent and exacting as well as specific and cogent.

Johnson's consistent recommendation to the United States for the establishment of a Department of International Trade and Industry (DITI) in addition to the formation of an articulate and coherent industrial policy seems quite sensible in view of the general disarray of U.S economic and industrial priorities. In this respect, Johnson is as much a basher of the United States as of Japan, and he lucidly explains the U.S. misconception of its own patronizing and self-defeating role vis-à-vis Japan. Although the United States is unlikely to accept much of his advice outright against its long-vaunted creed of anti-protectionism, nor is Japan, because of its long-established state corporatism, such rejections will be only at their own risks.

I cannot agree with Johnson, however, about the idea of national defense generally and the defense of Japan in particular. A number of questions I would raise are: Who needs the U.S. troops in Japan—Japan or the U.S.? If both, how much should each pay for them? Should Japan pay more than 40 percent ($2.5 billion) as it does now?[13] How much more? More fundamentally, against whom is this defense? Finally, shouldn't Japan's economic and military future be scrutinized in the contexts of East Asia, the Pacific, and the world? To pressure Japan toward rearmament, or further armament (its military spending already ranks third in the world), involves risks too high to be justifiable in view of its history. Aside from the fear of Japan in the rest of Asia, many Japanese are themselves still gripped by the fearful memory of the Second World War. The Japanese may not be eager to express their regret over their past conduct abroad, but they do remember the damages done to themselves. Nor can they forget how the process of militarization irresistibly dragged them into a total war. Those days still haunt many Japanese as a nightmare, and Chapter 2, Article 9, of the U.S.-initiated Constitution has taken deep root.[14] It is quite unlikely for Japan to tolerate massive rebuilding of armed forces, not to say creation of a nuclear arsenal, in the foreseeable future. Japan as an economic superpower should be pressured to exert its responsibility and leadership in the form of genuine economic and industrial assistance to the countries in need, not in the form of an army, even one that belongs to "international peace-keeping forces."[15]

Johnson's MITI analysis was put to use recently by three writers: Clyde Prestowitz, James Fallows, and Karel van Wolferen. Each is widely read among not only policy makers and industrialists but also general readers. Of recent publications by these three, Clyde Prestowitz's *Trading Places,* like Johnson's recent works, mostly focuses on trade issues. He too is rigorous in criticizing the U.S. confusion and folly in spending—two trillion dollars on defense during the last six years (p. 7), for instance, while Japan has been steadily building an economic and industrial base with its earnings and savings. As he sees it, the United States is looking more and more like a developing country (pp. 306–307). Like Johnson, he proposes a balanced budget, the establishment of a DITI, a restructuring of regulatory agencies, a clear and long-term trade and defense policy, and other measures to restore reciprocity in the flow of trade and technology with Japan.

As for his prescription for Japan's future, he believes the key to the desired reciprocity lies in Japan's improvement of the material standard of living of its citizens. He urges also a second land reform so that Japan's notorious land and housing prices can be normalized. Japan must help its consumers to become a major international market. And finally, Prestowitz holds that Japan must abandon its myth of uniqueness as well as its cultural essentialism. These are perfectly sensible suggestions, except for his Johnsonian insistence on an increase in Japan's share of defense efforts, which in his version comes to an annual contribution of $100 billion "toward the public costs of maintaining the free-world system."[16]

Generally meticulous as they are, both Johnson and Prestowitz take for granted that unilateral expansion, be it economic or military, is unjust and unacceptable. They are of course right. At the same time, they are uninterested in recalling that the West's domination lasted for more than two centuries, and during that time, trade imbalance—exploitation and expropriation, to be more accurate—was also taken for granted. It was assumed in fact that colonization was for the good of humanity—even by reformers like Marx, not to say advocates of "open market" and "free trade" (which meant in actuality nothing less than the colonizers' rights of free entry and penetration into their colonies).

And Prestowitz persists in such assumptions even now. Take, for instance, his discussion of Commodore Perry's arrival in Edo Bay in the 1850s. As he explains it, Perry was a fair open-door trader, while the Japanese were, like their twentieth-century descendants, unfair and unreliable negotiators (p. 77). But Prestowitz surely cannot be ignorant of the far more widely accepted view: Perry's enterprise is usually known as "gunboat diplomacy," a part of Western adventurism, which is by any measure not a fair or recip-rocal relationship.[17] Or, for that matter, how about all those years when the balance of trade was in the United States' favor? Did the United States ever propose to amend the inequity? Are those years to be balanced off against the period after 1945 when U.S. aid alone let Japan survive and recover? But wasn't the postwar aid—like the Marshall Plan for Europe—also a part of the U.S. strategy for its own economic health and for the Cold War, thus at least in part a self-serving program? Only when a non-Western nation dared to copy the practice and use it against the mightiest Western country, and indeed caught up with it, did economic "colonization" become an unfair and immoral transgression. Certainly the reference to past injustice on one side cannot justify current malpractice on the other. At the same time, this historical imbalance is as glaring as the trade inequity that the West now protests. The Japanese, rightly or wrongly, are fully mindful of the West's historical mercantilism and imperialism when they engage in what look like blatant examples of them to Americans in the last decade of the twentieth century.

Compared with Johnson and Prestowitz, most other bashers are imprecise and undisciplined. Among them Daniel Burstein is the worst. A New York–based journalist, he scornfully describes the Japanese nouveau riche buying up brand-name consumer goods in

Western metropolitan centers. Tokyo is full of BMWs, Porsches, and Ferraris. Ostentatious goods from Dunhill, Gucci, and Jaeger are everywhere. "A random check of the Tokyo subways showed an average of $10,000 worth of Vuitton paraphernalia visible in every rush-hour car."[18] "From Hawaii's beaches to Vermont's bed and breakfast inns, Japanese tourists poured into the United States, delighted to discover how 'cheap' everything was" (p. 67). This writer's most bitter complaint, however, is reserved for Japan's uncontrolled accumulation of dollars in Japan. Damned if they buy; damned if they don't. He continues:

> Rich countries of the modern world—notably Britain and the United States—have historically been Christian countries. The political expression of their wealth has been accompanied by a Judeo-Christian-influenced moral agenda, albeit often hypocritical, on questions ranging from charity for poor nations to human rights. As wealth passes to Japan, a different kind of moral values is coming to the fore, lacking both the impulse to global charity as well as the attendant hypocrisy characteristic of the American order of things. In a culture whose ethical basis does not assume that we are all God's children, and whose interest in brotherhood falls within its own borders rather than the world's, the primacy of national self-interest is a virtue, not a vice. (p. 251)

In the penultimate chapter of *Yen!* titled "Money, Power, and Guns: The Birth of the Japanese Empire," Burstein is contemptuous toward Japan for having no requisite proper style for imperialism (pp. 280–283), yet at the same time he warns his countrymen against "the twenty-first-century possibility of an ultimate, final showdown" with the Japanese empire (p. 292). Contradictions simply vanish before Burstein's incensed paranoia.

There is perhaps no point in quoting such rant. And yet one ought to take into sober account how little anti-racist efforts have accomplished in the United States in all these years since the 1960s. For Burstein and his ilk, "Judeo-Christian" morality and the "American order of things" still serve as the norm of social and international behavior. Exclusivist ethnocentricity persists as if the last three decades had been completely erased. Are all civil rights reforms being forgotten? Is there no reflection on marginality? Has racism come back to life? In fact, one remarkable feature of the current bashing, on both sides, is a surprisingly tenacious essentialist current. A society, a culture, and a nation are all identified and defined as a pure abstract absolute that is sterilized from any interaction with other elements and forces in history. No speculation on how the idea of a nation or culture has been constructed ever bothers the mind of a combatant. Japan is; the Japanese are.

James Fallows, too, displays such essentialism. In a widely read *Atlantic* article, "Containing Japan," he locates the sources of trade friction in Japan's unbalanced practice.[19] Although he gives "technical and even moral credit" (p. 44) to Japan, Fallows deplores its economic performance, which results in a worse trade imbalance every year. His explanation for such a development is "the one-sidedness of Japan's ambitions" (p. 48). According to Fallows, this rejection of reciprocity is due to "the weakness of 'universal principles' in Japan." Japanese life is "based on highly personal loyalties" and not on "such abstract principles as charity, democracy, world brotherhood, and so on" (p. 48). It is difficult to remain within the specifically defined scope of the trade problem without immediately translating it into broad cultural terms. Fallows's reference to the "universal principle," however, is indeed unfortunate. Such a principle has never been practiced, in the West or anywhere else. As cultural critics have been arguing in recent years, the Enlightenment notion of universality is a function of a particular self-interest of the West that is deeply complicit with its economic and military expansionism. Japan's neo-mercantilism needs to be combatted, but for different reasons; it also needs an explanation other than lack of the universalist principle. For Fallows to assert it now—very much like other bashers who insist on reciprocity on moral grounds—is historically lame and intellectually remiss. Fallows does make several insightful observations in the article, such as the Japanese need of "outside pressure" (*gaiatsu,* p. 52) for initiating a change, which has a great deal to do with the Japanese lack of confidence (or *shutaisei*) in the past centuries, especially in the postwar years. He leaps to a hasty and easy essentialist conclusion, however, revealing at the same time his own unexamined Eurocentricity.

Fallows's *More Like Us: Making America Great Again* finally urges Americans to recover their "uniqueness" (Chapter 1, "The

Importance of Being Abnormal").[20] His association with Japanese who often take pride in being unique has apparently taught him to use the same rhetoric with Americans. The myth of uniqueness, however, never works, for the Japanese, the Nazi Germans, or for the Americans. Are the Americans one unified group under one flag, in one social, economic, religious group? An impossible fantasy. The "us" in the title looks like those who have already been successfully homogenized, leaving out those who have so far been disallowed or unable to join them. Don't imitate Japan, Fallows says to America; be true to yourself; the Japanese are for obedience and conformity, while the Americans are for freedom and individualism—as if the antonyms could explain the two societies. Under the thin layer of pluralism and egalitarianism, Fallows's argument is as exclusivist and essentialist as he accuses the Japanese of being.

The sharp outline that is visible in Johnson's argument is lost in Fallows's case, which makes a facile link between Japan's economic practice and its culture. The reason for this confusion might well be found in his Japanese opponents, who make it a habit and strategy to rely on culturalism in their defense of neo-mercantilism. Trade and culture are obviously related: they are two different but partially overlapping perspectives on the same activities. In order to talk specifically about the terms of trade negotiation, however, it does seem better at first to keep clear of the murky territories between them. The problem is that issues too general to belong specifically to economic and trade practice are always on the verge of intrusion; trade talks inevitably entail larger cultural and historical issues, which could be kept out only by willfully ignoring them. In order to discover how culture and trade intersect, we might do well to turn to the official documents produced in June 1990 by the Working Group of the U.S. and Japanese governments during the Structural Impediments Initiative (SII) talks.[21]

Structural Impediments Initiative

These documents are in the form of a joint report on both countries' achievements and future plans in designated areas, rather than observations and recommendations or demands by two adversarial parties, thus muting the severity of frustration and clouding the likelihood of reform in both countries. Still, even a cursory glance at the "initiatives that address the issues" reveals that they hardly provide specific plans for trade and economic problems. The trade representatives have read the bashers' hit lists with care; the agendas on both sides are vast and wide-ranging, from Japan's need for greater spending to the U.S. need for greater saving, from Japan's necessity for a better housing situation to the U.S. crisis in the budget deficit. These are urgent items, and they are eventually conducive to reducing the trade imbalance. But how directly relevant are they? And what are the chances of implementing such agendas in the reasonable future?

To take one of the most heatedly discussed issues from the Japanese side of the list, the report recognizes a need to amend the Large-Scale Retail Store Law, which was devised to protect small retailers. The law serves to prevent the sales of imported goods because the mom-and-pop stores are usually organized "vertically," receiving goods from manufacturers and thus shutting out the distribution of imported goods.[22] The law in question is targeted against large chain stores, such as Daiei and K Mart, that might be expected to carry U.S.-made merchandise. It requires large-scale stores to obtain consent from all local shopkeepers before MITI permits the chain to open an outlet. This coordination process makes it virtually impossible for large chain stores to open outlets even when they can compete with generally lower prices and more abundant goods. It goes without saying that the conservative Liberal Democratic Party (LDP) in power depends heavily on small retailers for support. A collusion exists, as is well known, among manufacturers, retailers, the Liberal Democratic Party, and the government to strictly control the distribution network and market expansion, with the resultant rejection of U.S.-made merchandise. Should the law therefore be repealed for the purpose of reducing the trade surplus? SII does not support any radical measure of the kind but promises relaxation of rules such as the "shortening of coordination processing period for opening stores" to "less than one and a half years," "exceptional measures concerning floor space for import sales" (for an increase of up to 100 square meters, roughly 1000 square feet), and other trivial changes, which in all likelihood will alter little or nothing.

The U.S. Trade Representative obviously retreated—for now—in the face of determined resistance on the Japan side. There are two questions to be raised here on behalf of the mom-and-pop stores. First, the small shops are still very much alive in Japan, unlike in the United States or in England, serving their neighborhoods as an informal center of communication not only in country communities but even in the middle of a metropolitan area like Tokyo or Osaka. To replace the small, personal (though not necessarily friendly) neighborhood institution with large corporate retail chains cannot be called an unqualified improvement. Second, whether desirable or not, the vertical organization from manufacturers to retailers has been in effect for generations. While the structure has allowed retail prices to remain unconscionably high for the consumers, it has served social purposes such as stability, security, and community preservation. Although Japanese manufacturers are far more powerful and self-interested than their American counterparts—even to the extent of being able to sacrifice both retailers' and consumers' immediate interest—the price, it is possible to argue, has been willingly paid for the preservation of social relations, not just at the instigation of the manufacturers. Small stores are inefficient in distribution, unfair to the consumers, and counterproductive for balancing the trade payments. And yet the social arrangement of retail stores is historically rooted and socially accepted. Until the exorbitant pricing begins finally to weigh more heavily on the consumers than they can bear, and until the huge number of Japanese travelers abroad (now annually one tenth of the whole population) return home with the knowledge and experience of buying at far lower prices—even Japanese-made goods!—and begin to demand a similar retailing system in Japan, nothing is likely to happen to the current mode of distribution. I would further argue that parts of the practice are not without merit: in fact, urban dwellers and geographical scholars such as Lewis Mumford, Jane Jacobs, and Maeda Ai might count the disappearance of neighborhood stores among the lamentable blights of corporate living.[23]

Finally, should large-scale retailers be allowed to operate freely in neighborhoods, they are likely to be not American but Japanese stores, because of the high land costs that discourage foreign purchases. And in the process the goal of increasing U.S. outlets as intended by SII will be entirely unfulfilled.

I do not mean by this that the status quo ought to be preserved. The SII report is another Japanese attempt at stalling and trivialization, and the United States is willing to go along with it. The real ills will remain unremedied. The collusion should be broken, the vertical organization reformed, and foreign-made goods freely distributed by small stores—not for the sake of binational reciprocity, but on behalf of Japanese consumers. Such demands will not be met by the displacement of neighborhood stores alone.

On the U.S. side, the Japanese raised the issue of work-force education and training. To heighten America's competitiveness, its work force needs to be better prepared. The report cites various initiatives already taken by U.S. officials and agencies in education. The connection between educational improvement and trade imbalance is certainly comprehensible. But the goals mentioned by the U.S. delegation, such as "a high school graduation rate of 90 percent or more," "preeminence in the world in math and science scholastic achievement," "full adult literacy," or "several years of foreign language training" in the high school core curriculum, are no more than idle dreams without fundamental social reform. U.S. Trade Representative Carla Hills could not have been serious when she cited President Bush's agreement with the U.S. governors to achieve these objectives by the year 2000.[24]

A question that might arise is why this issue was raised at all by the Japanese Work Group. Were they just stalling? Did they earnestly believe that educational improvement would reduce the U.S. trade deficit and that the U.S. government could promise and achieve such goals? Or did they know all along that these were idle dreams and empty promises but decided nevertheless to include them, as preemptive bargaining chips, so that the U.S. failure to keep its promises might excuse their own failures in the future?[25]

The point I would like to make is that both Japanese neighborhood stores and U.S. general education are not in themselves vital structural impediments to trade balance but parts of larger social and cultural contexts that provided the negotiators with items to haggle over. Washington's 240 items for Japan and Tokyo's 80 for America are not "structural impediments" that could be readily removed by the two governments, even if they wielded great power and authority over their respective peoples. If the reduction of Japan's trade surplus is the real objective, the governments must take measures that fall within their mandate and ability. Everything else would be a futile exercise in tokenism and gesticulation.[26]

This brings up an obvious question regarding the different relationships Japan and the United States have to the trade negotiations. Although in the long run both countries have a great deal to lose by trade imbalance, the immediate situation is quite otherwise: the United States will experience a crisis before long if the current trend continues, while Japan will merely become richer. The United States wants to redress inequity; Japan does not. While the United States acutely needs the removal of impediments, Japan is by and large indifferent, and there is very little the United States can do about it. SII in this sense is an entirely futile attempt on the part of the United States, and Japan is fully cognizant of its impotence. If changes are to be made in Japan, they will have to come from the Japanese themselves—many of whom, it should be noted, agree with the U.S. Trade Representative that consumer sacrifice on behalf of manufacturers and megacorporations must be halted.

In a recent article, Chalmers Johnson observes: "The idea of a level playing field means that people should play by the same rules. But since the Japanese play by different rules, and since we seem to have had little success in agreeing on what a new set of common rules might look like, we must learn to match rather than imitate them." It sounds fair enough—at first. Upon second thought, however, this idea of game-playing looks inadequate. As Johnson would be the first to admit, the United States and Japan are at present engaged not in play but in something akin to combat, a conflict at least—although it is far from, and one hopes will never become, military combat. Conflict arises because no agreement can be reached on rules. When Commodore Perry arrived in Edo Bay in the mid-nineteenth century, the United States took no heed of the rules Japan was following. When Cortés met Montezuma, the Spaniards and the Aztecs had rather few rules in common. To take more recent examples, the West and oil-producing colonial Arabs did not agree on rules, free trade or otherwise. Nor do the United States and Japan.

Johnson concludes: "The challenge for American national and corporate economic policy is to recognize our differences from

Japan and to begin to formulate strategies for managing them. It is also the indispensable first step toward avoiding another national collision." I heartily agree. The realization of the different rules itself will constitute a context that the two opposed parties will begin to share in time. One realizes at the same time how difficult it is for the United States to match Japan's unified economic front. The Japanese social organization allows the state-corporate alliance to flourish, even to the extent of collusion and conspiracy. A version of the relationship is certainly not absent in the United States—as long as the corporate interest coincides with the state's. But when they diverge? Can the City of Los Angeles be closed to American real estate sellers as well as to Japanese buyers? Can U.S. manufacturers be forced to decline the infusion of Japanese capital surplus? Even Lee Iacocca, the great Japan basher (who nonetheless accepted a joint venture with Mitsubishi Automobile), would flatly turn down such a regulation.

To retrace history a little, at the end of the Second World War the United States was faced with a devastated world market while it had a hugely expanded industrial capacity. In order to prevent the violent collapse of its own productive structure and to save the world from poverty and starvation, the United States established—in addition to its own Marshall Plan for Europe—three agencies in the United Nations that would coordinate global trade relations: the International Monetary Fund (IMF), the World Bank, and the General Agreement on Tariffs and Trade (GATT). Their objectives were to remove nontariff barriers, reduce tariffs, expand the U.S. "open market," and enlarge world trade. The scheme was successful, and throughout the 1950s U.S. corporations dominated in the gradually recovering world. For example, the profits of General Motors in the mid-1960s ($25 billion), were larger than the GNP of any of 130 independent nations.[27] The United States expanded its industrial operation throughout the world, taking advantage of the "open door" policy guaranteed by the World Bank, IMF, and GATT. "Within fifteen years," Walter LaFeber says, "sixty-three nations controlling 80 percent of world trade belonged to GATT. Using the Marshall Plan and GATT as tools, U.S. officials created a new, vast market place."[28]

The GATT and IMF that had helped the U.S. economy dominate

began to work against it, however, once the trade balance was reversed and the double deficits of trade and budget turned the United States into a debtor nation in 1985. But even earlier, as the tide of exports from Japan and the Asian Newly Industrialized Economies (NIEs) overflooded the United States, the so-called principles of fair trade and open market ceased to make sense to many, especially since these countries practice the "premodern" economic mode of control and restriction. Arrangements outside of and in violation of GATT had to be devised to cope with the new situation: the annual Summit meeting, the secret annual meeting of finance ministers and heads of the central banks of industrial nations (so-called G5 and later G7), or the Omnibus Trade Act, whose Super Article 301 allowed the United States to levy a 100 percent tariff on specific products deemed unfairly exported. At this point, the principle of free and unrestricted trade was no longer credible.

In September 1985, G5 met at the Plaza Hotel in New York City to raise the value strength of the yen against the dollar. The meetings of the finance officers of leading industrial countries had been kept secret for ten years, but this one was made public, as if the extra-GATT arrangements were to be taken for granted. The rate of ¥242 to $1 was abruptly revised, and at the end of the year it stood at ¥199 to $1. The yen rose further, to the neighborhood of ¥120–150 to $1 in 1990. The purpose of weakening the dollar was to make U.S. export easier to Japan and other nations. For a brief period, it looked as if the measure was a success; soon, however, Japan's export regained its strength, and the U.S. trade deficit remained unchanged. Further, with the aid of the strong yen, Japanese traders aggressively entered the investment and capital transfer market, buying up corporations, bonds, and real estate properties and thus achieving the global domination of Japanese money. The United States needed something more drastic to end its double deficits. Hence the SII talks and thus the threats of Super 301—so far with no effect. The integration of the European Community in 1992, now including the reunified Germany, and the steadily rising challenge of the Asian NIEs add more gloom to the prospect. In order to fight back, the United States is trying to establish several free trade agreements with Canada, the EC, and APEC (Asian Pacific Economic Cooperation) outside of GATT. Under the circumstances, the "principles" of free trade, open market, and reciprocity are even less persuasive than before.

Conflicts abound in history, and in retrospect they are always placed in a shared context—the rulers and the ruled in a revolution, or the North and the South in the Civil War. The discovery of a shared context of conflict is the process of historical interpretation. The current trade conflict is no exception. What we need is historical understanding as to why what look like Japan's deceptions to the Americans are rooted in history, or why—if it must be so phrased—a "deception" is perpetrated, or how differences have come about in the manner of achieving the same goals, why individuals are motivated differently in different societies, or even why a nation can be so self-enclosed. In short, what historical forces shape a given society into a different organization with a different imaginary and a different articulation? Trade negotiations must be deeply inscribed with historical understanding.

Cultural Difference

In search of historical context for friction between the two countries, I will shift the focus from trade to culture, specifically to the work of three writers who have recently published books on Japan's cultural situation. Ian Buruma, Peter Dale, and Karel van Wolferen all view it from an adversarial perspective; van Wolferen is usually concerned with political economy, but his systematic comprehensiveness places him more properly among cultural critics.

First Ian Buruma, who writes regularly for the *New York Times* and the *New York Review of Books* on Japan and other parts of Asia. His book, *Behind the Mask: On Sexual Demons, Sacred Mothers, Transvestites, Gangsters, and Other Japanese Cultural Heroes* (New York: Pantheon, 1984), traces the genealogy of such charming cultural heroes to the characters who appear in Japan's genesis myth. A clever book, it tries to unmask the lovely clichéd image of Japanese culture, and it does that well. As Buruma constructs his history, however, the Japanese cannot escape from predetermination. By this principle of "temporalizing of the essence," all Japanese are inescapably trapped into the pit of demons. Just as he blames the Japanese for being insular, nationalist, and essentialist, however, he himself is inescapably caught in collective stereotyping. Buruma traverses many borders in his projects of cultural criticism. His article on Hirohito's war responsibility in the *New York Review of Books,* for example, curiously exonerates the emperor from war responsibility by a similar logic of essentialism: as he compares the emperor with Hitler, he explains that Hitler is "unique"; thus no one else, by definition, can be like Hitler; therefore, Hirohito is not guilty. Likewise, since the Holocaust is unique, the Japanese war atrocities cannot be compared to them; therefore, the Japanese war record is not that bad.[29]

Buruma has written on numerous topics in connection with Japan in recent years, including the country's new nationalism, and reviewed books by Edwin Reischauer, the former ambassador; Edward Seidensticker, who has translated many Japanese literary works; Morita Akio, the chairman of Sony; and Tanizaki Junichiro, among others. He is always deft and agile, but when one reads his works together as a group, a curious mannerism becomes noticeable. Fluent in Japanese, Buruma uses his personal interviews and conversations in support of his argument, and he does it with impressive skill. The problem is, however, as *Behind the Mask* deploys a demonology as an all-pervasive backdrop, Buruma's articles, too, keep a stable of villains, who consist of business executives unused to critical thought, second-rate professors, and nondescript politicians who appear and reappear repeatedly. He likes to quote and make fun of them. He has a good reason for being contemptuous: they are by and large uninformed, inarticulate, and unacquainted with serious ideas. But the question remains, why does Buruma always choose these particular lightweights in his analysis of Japan and always find them to be foolish and comical? Should Japan be represented by Watanabe Shoichi, an incoherent professor of English who has manufactured so far one hundred twenty books for chauvinistic businessmen; Fujio Masayuki, an uneducated former minister of education who was fired by his prime minister for insulting the Koreans; Umehara Takeshi, a confused philosophy professor and best-selling author who was appointed by Prime Minister Nakasone to direct the International Research Center for Japanese Studies, a notorious think tank so far mainly staffed by mediocre neo-nationalist writers or worse? Since they are not interesting, nor even funny—except for the initial shock effects they provide by their obtuseness and perversity—Buruma's frequent use of them is both incomprehensible and inexcusable.

An article titled "Behind the Garden Walls" is intended to take Japanese intellectuals "seriously." "They should be drawn into the international discourse, just as German intellectuals are, or Polish, or Mexican, or Chinese."[30] Agreed. But who are the Japanese intellectuals Buruma wants to invite out to an international forum? He chooses a middlebrow magazine, Shokun [Gentlemen], read by exhausted executives and bureaucrats, for his august undertaking, zeroing in on a relaxed roundtable discussion[31] among shabby writers and professors. Mediocre thinkers speak as one would expect. A Japanese-Canadian professor of Japanese literature proclaims that opening up the country to foreigners would "dilute the loyalty of the Japanese people." Japan should not, therefore, open up "because that would seriously affect the nation's essence and way of life . . . What we really need to do is to educate more Japanese who can be spokesmen for Japan on a world stage." Buruma bristles: "intellectuals, traditionally in the West, but in many other parts of the world as well, are precisely so-called because they are not spokesmen, but individuals with independent minds in pursuit of truths." Buruma likes inanities. But why doesn't he discuss real minds? What is disconcerting about this article is that he actually drops a few names—Kato Shuichi, Karatani Kojin, Inoue Hisashi, and Oe Kenzaburo—but at once evades them on the ground that they have been "mute" lately or that one is "very much a personage of 1968, a former leader of the leftist student movement." In truth Buruma is maddeningly addicted to easy reads, shunning any writer who requires more than a cursory glance. He cannot possibly be ignorant of these writers' recent works. To call Oe, Inoue, or Kato a writer of the 1960s is absurd. His neglect of women writers, too, is puzzling.

Buruma's persistent concentration on mediocrities, which in this article includes a Foreign Ministry bureaucrat whose Harvard doctoral thesis many years ago apparently impresses Buruma, cannot be accidental or erroneous. He does not think deeply about history, nor does he try to understand the past. His discussion in another article on the Kyoto philosophers such as Nishida Kitaro and Watsuji Tetsuro is so reductive that the only explanation of his misrepresentation is that he has never read their work. (Their texts are as obscure as Husserl's or Heidegger's, which they discuss with ease and familiarity.) Nishida and Watsuji were far more sophisticated than the recent vulgar nationalists in their understanding of European philosophy, although they indeed searched for the ground of Japanism and in the process committed themselves to essentialism. Buruma disregards real thinkers such as these and deliberately chooses muddled, wrongheaded, and uninteresting men from today's Japan so that he arrives at the conclusion that he set out to reach. Buruma's recent book, *God's Dust: A Modern Asian Journey* (New York: Farrar, Strauss, Giroux, 1989), says little that is new. His quick wit and knowledge of the language cannot compensate for glibness and prejudgment, which barely conceal his fundamental ignorance and contempt. He should do his homework, or at least reflect on the reason for his prejudice.

We have been hearing more and more about the Japanese myth of uniqueness lately from Japan's right-wing ideologues and, increasingly, from popular writers of middle-of-the-road political leanings. Peter N. Dale rightly directs his attention to this aspect of Japanese myth-making.[32] He is intelligent and insightful as he points out what amounts to Japan's exceptionalist and essentialist posture of mystification. The Japanese are anxious and defensive about themselves, and this fear of inferiority—perhaps nurtured over many centuries through their geographical proximity to the civilizations of China, India, and Korea—manifests itself as an aggressive assertion of their difference from any other people. Dale is obviously right; no one is unique *and* everyone is unique.

As one reads Dale's criticism of Tanizaki Junichiro's discussion of the Japanese language (which the Japanese writer calls "unique"), one begins to wonder if in the years before World War II, to which he freely makes reference as he discusses Japan's singularity complex, people anywhere in the world were free from the conviction of uniqueness and superiority. The White Man's burden? White Australia? Did the Europeans ever doubt their absolute superiority, not to say uniqueness, before the gradual dissolution of empires forced them to modify their Eurocentric modernist views? Before postmodernism? There is serious historical asymmetry in Dale's reading of Japanese people. He does not seem to question the assumption of uniqueness that has been sustained in the West until recently. One ought to ask if the cultural anthropologists, linguistic comparativists, or philosophers of the prewar days were quite aware of the dangers of essentialism and the uniqueness myth, as Dale seems to imply. How about Paul Valéry's "The Crisis of the Mind" (1919)? Edmund Husserl's "The Crisis of European Man," written in the 1930s?[33] Or Ian Watt's and Jack Goody's "Literacy in Traditional Societies" in which (as I discussed in Chapter 2) the two writers claim that the ancient Greek and modern European languages are the only languages capable of rational discourse and democracy—written as late as 1963? And Goody at least is still widely respected as a central authority on literacy and orality as well as on African patriarchic practice. Why, then, does Dale single out the Japanese?

If all peoples, nations, and cultures before, say, 1945 thought they were unique and this history is by now widely recognized, how does Dale explain his characterization of Japan as *uniquely* unique? He is in fact making double errors: one, in forgetting the globally ubiquitous ethnocentricity of the time, and two, in choosing Japan as the one unique group encumbered with a singular self-centeredness. Dale—as well as Buruma—would do well to ponder the hidden reason for his choice of this particular country at this particular moment in history.

I might add that Dale did not read Tanizaki's other works, in which he shows a totally different attitude toward the West. I will be saying more about this writer in Chapter 5, but here I would like to refer to his *Nyozetsuroku,* in which he attacks Tagore's privileging of the Orient. Far from the naive chauvinist Dale thinks he is, Tanizaki is a sophisticated cultural critic, albeit with occasional lapses.[34] Finally, I might also mention that Tosaka Jun rejected all notions of Japanese uniqueness in *Nihon ideorogii ron,* which was written as early as 1935.[35]

The last cultural basher I would like to talk about is Karel van Wolferen, whose *The Enigma of Japanese Power* (New York: Knopf, 1989) is the most massive, best researched, but no less wrongheaded of all the bashing exercises. He opens the book this way: "Japan perplexes the world. It has become a major world power, yet it does not behave the way most of the world expects a world power to behave; sometimes it even gives the impression of not wanting to belong to the world at all." Its nearly five hundred pages are devoted to proving this point. He almost succeeds; in fact, he almost did with me—when I read a few chapters selected at random. Van Wolferen carefully examines what others have often taken for granted. Thus Japanese education, praised usually as a great success story, is rigorously analyzed as unintellectual, uncreative, and numbingly unexciting and unserious. The media and information distribution are similarly criticized. Van Wolferen's account of the disappearance of intellectual criticism from Japanese daily life is brilliantly to the point. His characterization of the role played by Japanese intellectuals as "servants of the System," too, is quite accurate. So is his treatment of the general participation in the making of the myth of homogeneity, which is exclusive and racist. His analysis of the Japanese devotion to the erasure of difference and disagreement is also shrewd. I was deeply impressed for several hours, unable to put the book down, until I was fatigued by the monotony of his relentless negativism. Gradually, it dawned on me that much of what he says in the book is awfully familiar; it is not just a feeling of *déjà vu,* but something that I see, hear, and experience every day—here in the United States.

Much of what he describes is no different from any industrialized, managed society, just like ours. Van Wolferen is criticizing the life of the modern world with great frustration and discontent. Aren't American universities "subservient to the state"? Aren't American press and media all too willing collaborators of the state? Isn't this what Edward S. Herman and Noam Chomsky argue in their recent *Manufacturing Consent: The Political Economy of the Mass Media* (New York: Pantheon, 1988) and Chomsky in *Necessary Illusions: Thought Control in Democratic Societies* (Boston: South End Press, 1989) as well as in his earlier books? Hasn't Edward Said been pointing this out also? Even van Wolferen's central metaphor, "The System"—which is a vague assembly of power sources that seem to operate in Japan in separation from the state apparatus—is reminiscent of our own vocabulary in the sixties and seventies when rebels tried to pinpoint their enemy and could not. In other words, van

Wolferen seems to have given no serious thought to Europe and the United States, not to mention his own relationship to them. Did he put them out of his mind as he lived in and looked down on Japan? He did not learn the language, which seems to have severely isolated him from his environment. His work is a nostalgic, homesick, colonialist book, which no doubt has a powerful appeal to a great many Americans who know nothing about Japan and do not wish to think seriously about the United States or Europe; and that is exactly what makes it more dangerous than the others.

The Enigma of Japanese Power, however, cannot be dismissed simply. It has detailed analyses of cultural and social features as well as economic and political operations. And actual failures of Japanese society are shrewdly pointed out: its exclusiveness, its racism, its acceptance of hierarchy and authority, its dissolution of intellectual criticism (increasingly noticeable), its persistent sexism, its rejection of the basic rights of the individual. Yet van Wolferen does not place them in the context of the history of Japan or of the world. Thus the most crucial problematic in cultural criticism, the line between cultural variant and cultural failure, social idiosyncrasy and social deficiency, is never adequately discussed. Nor is he even aware of the problematic of the seer and the seen, the subject and the object. If the Japanese are groupy and collective, they immediately invite van Wolferen's scorn; if he sees in the Japanese a decided absence of independence and autonomy, he compares it at once to the Western development of individualism. Van Wolferen is pursuing a nostalgic imaginary, while completely ignoring the failures of the modern West. His argument betrays no awareness of postmodern discourse in which errors of the Enlightenment and modernism are being confronted. For van Wolferen, Europe (or his Netherlands) is the height of human progress—despite its ongoing class bias, sexism, and racism—compared with which Japan, or any other non-Western country, can never be other than a paltry sham. He has stayed too long out of Europe to remember even the history of Dutch Indonesia.

Nor are the specifics of history clearly explained. Japan's racism against other Asians is not identical in its ideological makeup with its alleged racism against Westerners. They may operate similarly, but they are embedded in totally different historical contexts. One is in contempt, while the other is in fear. Of course, fear and contempt may be ultimately cognate, but their destructiveness differs qualitatively. Japan has been a brutal colonizer in Asia for the last 150 years, once militarily and now economically; it was, however, once almost a victim of economic and even military colonialism of the West. Moreover, Japan is a victim of Western cultural colonialism even today. So many of the perplexing problems between Japan and the West are generated precisely at this juncture between cultural passivity and economic aggressiveness. This imbalance will continue for the foreseeable future to upset those interested in the question of Japan. To ignore this asymmetry would have important consequences for our vision of the world in the twenty-first century. Van Wolferen, like Buruma, is engaged in the wrong battle. It is not whether the West or Japan is now morally right, but in what relationships history has placed the West and Japan, and how the world as a whole is going to be affected by them in the coming century.

There is a disappointing nonparticipation by the experts in general cultural criticism. Of course, the area of anthropology has been in disarray since the appearance of Foucault's and Said's works shaking the basis of the discipline. Johannes Fabian's theoretical attack on the discipline of anthropology from inside is an important contribution in this respect, although the book has nothing to do directly with the studies of Japan. Clifford Geertz's *Works and Lives: The Anthropologist as Author* (Stanford: Stanford University Press, 1988) is a call to the fieldworkers to return home. According to his remarkable *New York Times* interview following the book's publication, the Western fieldworker proves never to have encountered the natives.[36] Besides, Geertz thinks that what is important is the audience at home to whom the ethnographer has to tell his or her stories. This is an admission of defeat, nearly acknowledging the absence of a discipline.

Geertz discusses Ruth Benedict's *The Chrysanthemum and the Sword* in his book as one of the four exemplars of anthropological approaches. Benedict, too, is a student of the Other who realizes at the end that she has been all along gazing at no one but herself. There are other fundamental faults in her assumptions. Still, she tried to reach out and find the Japanese at the time of war—a bold enough feat no anthropologist seems eager to repeat today. The time does seem ripe now to challenge Benedict in locating anthropology once again in the middle of history. The more theory-conscious younger scholars like James Clifford and George Marcus are too introspective to engage in the battle of bashings, even between two better-matched combatants. We will not be receiving any help from these experts as we bloody ourselves in our cultural criticism exercise. Even less will help come from anthropologists in the Japan field, who are by and large reluctant to enter an ephemeral arena muddied by politics, preferring to remain neutral social scientists untouched by either bashers or apologists.

America Bashing

Japan had no reason to complain much about the United States as long as binational trade ran smoothly. Once friction became perceptible across the Pacific, however, it did not take long for Japan's suspicion and insecurity to flare up. Numerous reports had circulated about the United States: its educational failures, violence in the streets, the drug war, the homeless, urban dilapidation, and all such bleak events and scenes that are not difficult for anyone half familiar with American life to pick up. The Japanese media began to publish stories about U.S. protectionism, American arrogance, and U.S. decline in economy and productivity. The Japanese are now feeling both pity and superiority about these developments, totally undreamed of only a few years earlier.

America bashing has two themes: Japan's superiority and America's inferiority. The Japanese who like to think of themselves as "we Japanese" continually repeat and reinforce the myth of homogeneity and uniqueness: "we Japanese are united," "we Japanese love simplicity," "we are harmonious in Japan," "rice is our soul (not soul food)," "we work harder in Japan," "we Japanese are moral," or even "Japanese cuisine is the best in the world." Such innocuous-sounding statements are gathered together to construct an exclusivist myth of Japanese culture, changeless and pure. Obviously this essentialism provides an effective instrument in formulating a protectionist policy. The other side of such self-concern is dyslogistic characterization of what is Other to them: there are numerous anti-American, anti-Semitic, anti-Western, anti-Asian, and anti-African books being written in Japan. A typical contention is that the United States is a mongrel society, hopelessly fragmented into contending groups. These tracts may not pose a serious threat in themselves as yet, but the disappearance of criticism in today's Japan makes them potentially disastrous because there is little that would engage and contest them. Unrestrained, they could gather power as they did in the prewar years.

The *Asahi* newspaper published a series of thirty-five interviews on the matter of bashing. Called "The Deep Truth of Japan Bashing: American Views of Japan" ("Nihon tataki no shinso: Amerikajin no Nihon kan"), it collects impressions and comments from Japan-trade experts in the United States. *Chuo koron,* a middlebrow monthly that supposedly remains middle-of-the-road (but actually leans to the right), continues to publish analyses of views emanating from the familiar revisionists as well as the apologists from both countries. So far, however, not one full-scale monograph on the subject that can counter the revisionists' comprehensive and coherent analyses has appeared in Japan. The editor of the *Asahi* series commented in the last installment, titled "Let's Argue Calmly: Japan Has No Theoretical Armament" ("Reisei na ronso shiyo: Riron buso o kaku Nihon"), that "the views of Japan as the Other [*Tasha to shiteno Nihon*] and as the prime menace in the United States have an organized and consistent theoretical foundation as an assault weapon devised by certain scholars, journalists, and bureaucrats. Japan's greatest weakness at present is in having no such intellectual and theoretical weapon with which to resist and respond to these Americans."[37] Although her combat metaphor is unfortunate, she is accurate. Typical of the current discursive erosion in Japan, most rebuttals are brief, fragmentary, episodic, undocumented, and un-systematic. Numerous comments have been printed, but they have little to offer in the way of information or insight, and any substantial apologies for Japan seem to come from U.S. apologists. Here, too, there is a peculiar dependence on foreign scholars for support, as if cultural colonialism continues even in these aspects. Such absence of complete analyses and reports encourages rumors and intensifies fears. The two countries are said to be on a collision course.

Edward Seidensticker, one of the best-known translators of Japanese literature, was quoted by van Wolferen as saying "The key to understanding Japanese society is to understand that [the] Japanese have not been taught to say No!" (with an exclamation mark).[38] As many people know, a book called "The Japan That Can Say No!" (*Noo to ieru Nihon!* with an exclamation mark) was published in Japan in January 1989, cowritten by Morita Akio and Ishihara Shintaro, an ex-novelist turned Diet and cabinet member (who happened to be one of the three candidates for prime minister in 1989). The book, a million-copy bestseller in Japan, was translated into English by an agency in the Pentagon, and the unauthorized translation was copied and circulated extensively in the United States. No doubt an America-bashing book, it is nonetheless neither an intellectual formulation nor a sensational polemic. It is a collection of occasional speeches by the two men, unstructured in theme or substance. The two have different opinions and emphases, though they are equally casual and slovenly. *The Japan That Can Say No!* is as uncritical and self-centered as any work by a Western writer. The one thing that distinguishes it from its Western counterparts is a lack of matter-of-fact contempt for the opponents. Of course, the authors are smug and at times gloating. But arrogant and racist they are not, as far as their remarks about Americans are concerned. Ishihara says that if Japan should decide to sell semiconductor chips to the Soviet Union rather than to the United States, it will change the balance of military power: "Some Americans say that if Japan were thinking of doing that, it would be occupied. Certainly this is an age [when] things could come to that."[39] It is a silly and irresponsible remark, but as has been pointed out in Japan, it is irresponsible in relation to the Japanese manufacturers, not the American policy makers. The authors' bad-mouthing of America's well-paid executives may have infuriated Lee Iacocca; I find them reasonable, not being Mr. Iacocca. The brief comments they make about American business are in fact shrewd: should they come from the mouth of an American, they wouldn't offend anyone, even people in business. The sensitivity American readers seem to feel is exactly the oversensitivity of those who did not expect the Japanese to say "No!"—like Professor Seidensticker.

Compared with Ishihara, Morita says little that is new or offensive to the American reader. Those who have read his *Made in Japan: Akio Morita and Sony* (New York: E. P. Dutton, 1986) or heard his numerous lectures in the United States know that his points are by and large harmless and at times even humorous. For example, he refers to the contradiction between the federal government that wants the flow of Japanese capital to be stopped and the state governments that want it to continue; or he points out the hypocrisy of the Big Three auto makers, who bash their Japanese counterparts while buying Japanese engines, transmissions, and even finished products (which they sell under their own brand names). Morita is frequently inaccurate and simplistic regarding the trade imbalance or Japan's lifetime employment practice (which is true only of large corporations, a small portion of the Japanese employers). But his contributions are at worst foolish rather than malicious or arrogant.

Ishihara is far more aggressive and confrontational. His fault, however, is not so much unrestrained hostility as overstatement and inexactitude. His charge against Americans as racist is too inclusive, and his charge against the use of atom bombs in Hiroshima and Nagasaki as racist and inhuman needs further qualifications. As long as he is making reference to the West's historical expansionism and colonialism, however, he is not amiss. His inexcusable moral and intellectual failure is his erasure of and obliviousness to Japan's own racist record and performance, which allow him to proclaim an absurd and dangerous policy of its political leadership in Asia now. Similarly, his claim that Japan improves on everything that it imports from other civilizations, from Buddhism to technology, is simply ignorant and infantile.

But Ishihara is not all incendiary. He criticizes Japan's defense policy, especially the U.S. control of the Self-Defense Force that was built entirely in conformity to U.S. specifications.[40] Ishihara explains the need for a fundamental adjustment now that the Cold War binarism no longer exists. Insofar as he is committed solely to Japan's defense, excluding even the dispatch of a peacekeeping force abroad, Ishihara is far more sensible than his American opponents: "I do not oppose cooperation with the United States and even the maintenance of American forces on Japanese soil. But to the extent that the strategic mission of U.S. forces is beyond direct Japanese interests, they should not be based here rent-free. To the extent that they help defend Japan, our own forces must be capable of defending the U.S. bases."[41] Likewise, his acceptance of the U.S. Trade Representative's demand to streamline Japan's distribution system and to dismantle the bureaucrats' intervention is sensible enough. Ishihara's anti-Eurocentricity needs no apology, as long as it is concentrated on the decentralization of its hegemonic power. The danger of Ishihara's challenge is that his anti-Eurocentricity is always on the verge of being transformed into a perverse program of alternative hegemonism, proposing Japan's leadership in Asia.[42] That is why as a spokesman for the next generation of Japan's politicians he requires careful scrutiny in the years to come.

Homma Nagayo's brief article in the *Diplomatic Forum (Gaiko Foramu)* is representative of Japan's liberals, who are very much pro-America and pro-West, although deeply disturbed by what they perceive as constraints on Japan. On behalf of the "mutual friendship" of the two countries, he reflects on the revisionists, placing them in the genealogy of Orientalists descending from Percival Lowell down to Theodore White and Gore Vidal. Focusing on van Wolferen, he rejects his idea of "the System," without, however, providing much counterargument. I am including Homma here because even a moderate conservative like him is in virtual agreement with Ishihara and many others about the changed international relations so many Americans refuse to accept. "Whether or not Japan belongs to a world whose standard was first established by the West—Europe and the United States, to view the world from such a perspective is itself anachronistic. . . . Whether or not Japan belongs to the world is no longer an issue; to think about today's world as a club in which Japan is among the powerful regular members and officers is the natural course of things." Having said this, Homma suddenly resumes an apologetic posture, recalling, "Of course, Japan has many problems to reflect on."[43] At this point, perhaps there is no one in Japan—except among the fossilized Foreign Ministry bureaucrats and LDP officials—who is in any mood to agree with the revisionists about the trade or foreign policy of Japan vis-à-vis the United States. Japan has indeed entered a new era.

There are a great host of practitioners of the science of Japanism *(Nihonjin-ron)*. Insecure in their relationship to the outside world, the Japanese have long been preoccupied with their self-identity. For centuries, Japanism was directed to continental Asia, to the West from the nineteenth century on, and after 1945 more specifically to the United States. Wavering violently between self-hatred and self-infatuation, the Japanese identify themselves with and distinguish

themselves from the Americans. Throughout, they think of themselves as one group and as unchanging, trying all the time to define
its core and essence in moral and aesthetic terms. Sometimes they
even try to define themselves by physical features like brain structures, finding sympathizers among respectable American scholars.[44]
These are all tiresome and only occasionally amusing absurdities.
Many writers and professors seem dead serious about them, however, and a vast number follow them in earnest. As an exercise in
cultural criticism, these accounts are obviously worthless; as an
object of study, they may be significant inasmuch as they have been
prevalent at all times, but are practically epidemic in recent years.
They are also not to be taken lightly since they might yet cause
mischief if the United States–Japan relationship becomes more
strained in the years to come.

Free Trade

Let me briefly go over the familiar metanarrative. A while ago the
European Enlightenment imagined itself to be universal, as it offered
the promise of progress. In fact, "progress" as an imaginary was a
brilliantly effective instrument for the justification of a global mission
of expansion, which offered civilization, meaning conquest. Geopolitics was thus always legitimated by chronopolitics. And even history, not to say ethnology and anthropology, was complicit, as it
wrote itself in a West-centered chronology. To the extent that the
Enlightenment was a regional, self-serving project of the West, and
to the extent that modernism constituted an exclusionist metropolitan position in the nineteenth- and twentieth-century world, the
scrutiny of modernism was unavoidable after economic, industrial,
and environmental globalism at last *geographically* integrated the
world. Acid rain kills trees everywhere; the destruction of rain
forests affects everyone; ozone depletion is a worldwide crisis.
Universalism was tested not among ideas alone but among people
and peoples.

When universal citizenship was proclaimed by the Enlightenment,
with the guarantee of freedom and equality, the individual citizen
turned out to be simply a man.[45] But this is not inclusive enough.
The individual with guaranteed freedom and equality was of course

not just a man, but a *white* man, a white *heterosexual* man, a white *propertied* man—excluding all the rest, the virtual entirety of humanity, the female, black, brown, red, yellow, gay, and poor. The status of free autonomous subject was granted only to the smallest proportion of humanity. Modernism was bound to be replaced, or at least radically qualified, by something more inclusive, more particularized, and more decentralized.

The idea of free trade in an open market is firmly foregrounded in the Enlightenment notions of universal citizenship, civil society, and the modernist ideology of democracy. For Adam Smith the growth of commerce is firmly associated with the growth of liberty. From the beginnings of the Industrial Revolution he learned that division of labor and growth of markets were crucial to the accumulation of wealth. Such ideas were readily applicable to world trade. Unhindered, the individual's pursuit of self-interest would lead to the promotion of the collective interest; similarly, free trade, left alone, would result in the progress and prosperity of all nations. Whenever the universalist merchants went abroad to trade, they were convinced that they were there to civilize and benefit those they encountered. The flow was to be in one direction only. They could not have imagined that someday the direction might be reversed.

It was reversed. Not just Japan, but also the Asian NIEs are now engaged in trade that is not "fair" or "reciprocal," just as the West was for centuries. They come to sell and buy while their own markets still stagnate in "premodern" conditions. The Western demand for fairness and reciprocity is both desperate and understandable, but it must be acknowledged once and for all that there has never been fair trade or an open market. And if they are going to exist now and in the future, it is because the meaning of geopolitics and chronopolitics is radically changing on this enclosed and endangered globe. Should Japan replace the West as the world's hegemon, it would not escape the same fate that is now visited on the West. No nation can escape any longer from the condition of the entire earth, which is reeling now under the waste created by the production and consumption of presumably fair-trade and free-market nations.

Writers

Who Decides, and Who Speaks?
Shutaisei and the West
in Postwar Japan

My point of departure is where I am situated now: as a citizen and resident of the United States, still haunted by the memories of two past wars, and ever rankled by unceasing global crises. I try to teach, and know. My first war experience was as a Japanese subject with little knowledge of the unfolding history around me. My second, the war in Vietnam, was as a naturalized U.S. citizen acutely aware of my earlier ignorance during what is known in Japan as the Fifteen-Year War. This time, I promised myself, I would learn and act—resist the State, if necessary. Did I?

As I teach, I try to be neither nostalgic about my own past nor utopian about the world. To see what constitutes the world and to describe it without allegorization is nearly impossible, but such an impossibility is what all of us are conscribed to inhabit.

Shutaisei, according to Kenkyusha's *New Japanese-English Dictionary,* is "subjectivity; subjecthood; independence; identity." All four words are pertinent, but none of them exactly corresponds to the Japanese term. The absence of an English equivalent underscores that *shutaisei* is a native invention. Initially coined by the Kyoto philosophes,[1] it is a word widely used after 1945 to fill a perceived gap in the Japanese language. The Japanese thought they saw the concept they named *shutaisei* everywhere in Western intellectual discourse: individualism, democracy, liberalism, libertarianism, subject, subjectship, subjectivism, and libertinism flourished without bound. A compound of *shu* (subject, subjective, sovereign, main), *tai* (body, substance, situation), and *sei* (quality, feature), the word means inclusively the agent of action, the subject of speculation or speech act, the identity of existence, and the rule of individualism.[2]

Dealing with the idea of *shutaisei* as it was deployed comprehensively in the immediate postwar years in political and institutional programs, in intellectual exchanges, and in literary works, this chapter will examine the role played by the West in the form either of the ruling Allied Powers or of a generalized intellectual and cultural model. Throughout, self-definition in terms of the individual or the nation as a whole is its concern. The context is specific as to time and place; the argument, however, which concerns power, knowledge, and art, is obviously not localized.

Supreme Commander

No Japanese knew what to expect in the summer of 1945. The fate of the vanquished is in the victor's hand; the victor knows it, the vanquished does not. The Potsdam Declaration merely suggested the general outline of Japan's future. The innermost circle of the ruling class who participated in the surrender proceedings expected and hoped for the best, that is, that the status quo would be maintained. They believed the coming changes to be only minor adjustments.[3] Ordinary people, on the other hand, were anxious, and retribution was taken for granted.

Not that the Japanese were wholly ignorant of the outside world. Newspaper and news-agency correspondents were stationed in neutral and friendly cities such as Stockholm, Zurich, Berlin, and Lisbon, and some diplomats in Moscow and Bern were trying to communicate and negotiate with the Allied Powers.[4] Thus they knew a little about the intentions of the Allies and even about the early signs of strain in U.S.-Soviet relations before the spring of 1945. Still, the continual quarrels among the war leaders in Japan made analysis of news and reports extremely difficult and their transmission to the public nearly impossible. In addition to the harshest information control, there was a shortage of paper, limiting the daily newspapers to two pages, with minimal tidbits of hard news and proportionately ample propaganda.[5] People were of course told of the latest lost battles but were repeatedly assured of the final victory; and they tried their best to believe the unbelievable. 256533

The initial conflict between the Japanese rulers' hope for continuity and the conquerors' zeal for fundamental alteration of the enemy state was easy to understand. What no one knew then and what we could see only retrospectively was the great freedom with which the Occupation policy was formulated and executed at the early stage by General Douglas MacArthur, the Supreme Commander of the Allied Powers (SCAP). How was one officer allowed such latitude in decision making? And what constrained him later?

First, the basic documents setting forth the U.S. occupation policy—several working papers issued by the State-War-Navy Coordinating Committee after December 1944, the Potsdam Declaration, and the Basic Initial Post-Surrender Directive of August 29, 1945—were all written in too general and broad terms to serve as adequate guidelines for SCAP's particular problems. While the August 29, 1945, Directive cautioned that it was "not the responsibility of the Allied Powers to impose upon Japan any form of government not supported by the freely expressed will of the people,"[6] it stipulated nonetheless a number of principles on matters such as freedom of religion, democratization, and various reforms (Part III, Section 3). Literally interpreted, the document could have permitted the overthrow of the Japanese government with no interference from the Occupation authorities. Second, the highest office in the Occupation structure was to be the Far Eastern Commission in Washington, D.C., which would be represented in Tokyo by the Allied Council for Japan. Because of the deteriorating relationship between the United States and the Soviet Union, however, the Commission, composed of the fifteen nations that had warred with Japan, was not established until later, and even then was never allowed to function fully by the United States. China was too weak to be considered seriously as a great power; the influence of Great Britain was being phased out of the Pacific region; France's participation in the war with Japan had been minimal; and the Soviet Union was to be the target of containment. As far as the United States was concerned, the Occupation was, unlike in Germany, "allied" in name only, and the actual administration was solely in the hands of the Supreme Commander's headquarters. General MacArthur, for instance, virtually ignored the Allied Council meeting. Third, the General's relationship with his home government was hardly cordial. Of course, no war hero is expected to conform to the rules meant for ordinary bureaucrats. MacArthur was not even an ordinary hero; he was a living myth aspiring to become a living god, replacing the emperor himself. Under the circumstances, he was apt to ignore communications emanating from the likes of President Truman or Secretary of State George Marshall. George Kennan, one of several State Department officials dispatched to Japan to investigate the General's intentions and activities in 1948, later recalled his mission as "nothing more than that of an envoy charged with opening up communications and arranging the establishment of diplomatic relations with a hostile and suspicious foreign government."[7]

Perhaps more fundamentally, however, there was the marked degeneration in U.S.-Soviet relations. Even before the Yalta Conference, there had been ominous exchanges.[8] In subsequent texts such as Churchill's Fulton speech in March 1946, Truman's joint Congress speech in March 1947, Marshall's June 1947 Harvard speech, and Kennan's "X" article in July 1947, one sees the unmistakable steps of acceleration in rhetoric and intensification of measures in the name of national security. There were internal critics like Henry Wallace and Walter Lippmann, but the Truman administration steadily worked to maintain the global hegemony of the United States bequeathed by Great Britain at the demise of its empire. Henceforth, any regional conflict and local problem had to be assessed in terms of the grand scheme of "world peace." There is a startlingly blunt statement made by George Kennan, widely hailed as one of the most lucid and humane of the Washington policy makers, that

> we have about 50% of the world's wealth, but only 6.3% of its population. . . . In this situation, we cannot fail to be the object of envy and resentment. Our real task in the coming period is to devise a pattern of relationships which will permit us to maintain this posi-

tion of disparity without positive detriment to our national security. To do so, we will have to dispense with all sentimentality and day-dreaming; and our attention will have to be concentrated everywhere on our immediate national objectives. We need not deceive ourselves that we can afford today the luxury of altruism and world-benefac-tion. . . . We should cease to talk about vague and—for the Far East—unreal objectives such as human rights, the raising of the living standards, and democratization. The day is not far off when we are going to have to deal in straight power concepts. The less we are then hampered by idealistic slogans, the better.[9]

The Soviet Union responded in kind, and paranoia became a settled condition of world diplomacy.

MacArthur's policy changes reflected this widening global rift. At first the Government Section of the General Staff, composed of former New Dealers impatient to democratize the Japanese state, was in ascendancy, initiating a rapid series of sweeping reforms ranging from full-scale revision of the Constitution to land redistri-bution, dissolution of trust and combines, revamping of the educa-tional system, purging of over 200,000 war leaders and functionaries, establishment of labor unions and organizations, the establishment of individual civil rights, the guarantee of free speech, free press, and academic freedom, a step toward equal rights for men and women, and the redistribution of wealth through taxation. Even the war-fatigued apathetic Japanese were astonished by the radicalism of such reforms. Communist Party leaders hailed the American Occupation troops as the liberators of Japan. The news reached Washington and began to trouble the policy makers as they pondered the economic and industrial potential of Japan in the context of the Cold War. As Washington now saw it, Japan ought to be incorpo-rated with the Western alliance rather than being left in isolation in abject defeat. MacArthur's experimentation must be halted, and his reformers must be restrained. Before the end of 1946, the Intelli-gence Section of the General Staff, headed by a German-born gen-eral (a Franco admirer who "looked like, and sometimes thought like, Hermann Göring"),[10] led the management of the Occupation. By the summer of 1948 MacArthur's initial dream of converting Japan into a Switzerland was over; Japan was now a friend of the United States, an ally in arms if at all possible, as suggested first by

Secretary of War Kenneth C. Royall in January 1948 and spelled out in the National Security Council resolution 13–2 of October 1948.[11] The MacArthur-dictated Constitution had to be either rewritten or reinterpreted to enable such a transformation.

What is significant in this barest summary of the Occupation is, first, the irrelevance of MacArthur's basic policy to Japan's own interest, and, second, the absence of events and actions initiated by the Japanese in these immediate postwar years. It should at once be admitted that the military occupation of a defeated nation in a total war inevitably leads to its integration with the victor nation's own political and economic objectives. In such a situation very little can be institutionally carried out by the defeated nation. In Japan's case, exhaustion after a fifteen-year war and inexperience in defeat—among other things—drove people into an acute spell of dejection. In response to each of these reform proposals or orders, Japanese officials were passive and dependent, and citizens were uncritical and docile. Inertia indeed engulfed the whole population.

Even under the most adverse circumstances, however, people do survive, and survival requires maneuvering. They needed food, shelter, and clothing; and they had to get used to the imposed changes. In the process they learned what they had not learned before and would not have learned had they won the war: domestic privacy. The newly found privacy in Japan was not part of the integrated whole, as it might be in an established liberal bourgeois society. It constituted a dialectic opposition to the all-invading, hitherto largely unchallenged state. For the first time the Japanese encountered a space outside collective existence. This autonomy of the private might be expected to grow into a full political consciousness with individual rights guaranteed by the state, but Japanese political history is more circuitous. The discovery of privacy was effectively incorporated into the economic pattern of production and consumption with the dazzling economic success of the sixties, bypassing political individualism. At any rate, the phenomenon was not recognized for what it was even when the postwar writers were engrossed with the existential problems involving *shutaisei*.

Several developments in the public sphere demonstrated all was not prostration and acceptance. The labor movement gathered momentum far exceeding SCAP's encouragement or expectation. As-sisted by the intensifying food and employment crisis throughout 1946 and spearheaded by Korean and other non-Japanese residents, unions were organized on an immense scale and prepared a united front for a general strike in February 1947. Although it began with SCAP's blessing and ended with SCAP's alarmed intervention, still it was as close as Japan ever came to a worker's revolution. A second development was the performance of Prime Minister Yoshida Shigeru. Unlike the previous three prime ministers, Yoshida, a con-servative/liberal prewar diplomat, was not intimidated by either MacArthur or his lieutenants. He was aware of the U.S.-Soviet disharmony and sensitive to schisms at the headquarters, which he manipulated so that he, a conservative, might stem the tide of reformism. After his third administration especially, Yoshida was skillful enough not only to stall American zeal but at times even to slow the "reverse course" of American policy to the advantage of Japan as he saw it.[12] When John Foster Dulles tried to force Japan to rearm in the face of Mao Zedong's victory, for example, Yoshida was adamant in resisting the pressure. Disliked by the intelligentsia, Yoshida was no doubt committed to the interests of power and money, and his contributions to the reconstruction of Japan are far from indisputable. In view of the other Japanese leaders over-whelmed by the conqueror, however, Yoshida's insight into the Cold War and his use of such knowledge stand out as marks of indepen-dence and autonomy. Does this mean that MacArthur and Yoshida, who were portrayed together in Richard Nixon's *Leaders,*[13] recog-nized each other, a megalomaniac American warrior meeting an autocratic Japanese conservative to play the game of remaking a country? Hardly. Yet the Second World War was perhaps the last war in which one could entertain a romance of oversized heroes. Multinational corporatism thereafter would enmesh the world too closely to allow room for the invention of heroism. Yoshida was one such personage it was Japan's turn to produce.

Finally, one must mention the enormous activity in literature and in ideological discourse that burst onto the scene soon after the end of the war. As if to make up for lost time during the preceding fifteen years or more, writers expressed and exchanged views that had been anathema. The texts published then are interesting in themselves; in context of *shutaisei,* they also illuminate the nature of Japanese political thought.

Critics and Intellectuals

Beginning in the winter of 1945–46, numerous journals and periodicals were inaugurated, and others were resurrected. Older luminaries were awakened from hibernation, and new talents were recruited. Those crudely printed and bound publications—under titles such as *Sekai* (World), *Ningen* (Humanity), *Chisei* (Intellect), *Tembo* (Prospect), *Shinsei* (New Birth), *Kindai Bungaku* (Modern Literature), and *Shin Nihon Bungaku* (New Japanese Literature)—were full of desperate hopes mixed with gnawing uncertainties. They were exuberant over the suspension of censorship and "thought control," although the relief was far from unqualified, as SCAP at once initiated a censorship system of its own.[14] Quite naturally, liberation by foreigners from the long oppression by native leaders made writers question what had brought them to where they were. The agonized reassessment of the past history, the present situation, and the future course engaged every intellectual who had lived through the hostilities since the thirties.

One circumstance may have helped to focus such questions on the issue of war responsibility: Prince Higashikuni Naruhiko, who was the first prime minister after the surrender, emphasized the need for "general penitence on the part of the entire population" *(zen kokumin so zange)*[15] as the first step in the reconstruction of Japan. Although the recommended wholesale penitence was for losing the war rather than for waging it, his intention was clearly to preempt the inquiry into war responsibilities and to diffuse it, as if such a strategy might satisfy the Potsdam Declaration provisions concerning war crime retribution. Higashikuni was swiftly disabused of his self-serving interpretation of history. SCAP ordered the arrest of principal wartime leaders soon thereafter.

As the novel idea of war crime gradually sank into the minds of the Japanese, several writers began to express their own views about the writers' involvement in the war. It is ironic that the whole issue

of *shutaisei*—encompassing responsibility, autonomy, independence, individuality, and self-identity—emerged at least partly as a
response to the American demand that war criminals be named and
punished.

A series of interrelated questions was raised. Why was Japan
defeated? What went wrong? The questions surrounding the destruction of the empire were at once replaced by those regarding the
commencement of hostilities. Why did the Japanese invade China
and attack Pearl Harbor? At whose instigation? Didn't they, people
and rulers alike, know that Japan's resources were extremely
meager? If not, what blinded them to this and other obvious facts?
Such questions in turn led to those about the political makeup of the
country. What made people accept the decisions of their leaders?
Who were these leaders? How did Japan's decision-making process
systematically exclude the populace at large? Or did the people
participate? If yes, was the entire population to blame after all? Was
the Japanese form of governance intrinsically inoperable and iniqui-
tous? And, finally, is there something uniquely wrong about Japan?
What are the "essential" features of the Japanese people?

These are all enormous questions, none of which were readily
answerable. In nearly every article published in these postwar journals, however, the discussion inevitably touched on *shutaisei,*
whether it began as an inquiry into Marxist historiography, into the
junction of ideology and literature, or into the development of sci-
entism in Japan. The Japanese were surrounded by curious eyes;
they had to know themselves. The war years were now presented
as a period of general stupor during which people followed orders
and suggestions like automatons. How to regain or, more precisely,
to nurture *shutaisei* was a principal topic of Japanese intellectuals
as they exchanged views and opinions in these bleak months.

In the March 1946 issue of *Ningen* magazine, Shiina Rinzo begins
his "Significance of Postwar Literature": "Postwar literature has
revealed the individual's determination to take responsibility for
being human. . . . In postwar literature what is not true in the
individual's own terms is no longer seriously considered, and one
stakes oneself on the subjective truth. To be strongly subjective is
what differentiates today's literature from that of the past years."[16]
But what is individuality? As Shiina sees it, suffering alone is unique

to an individual, and thus suffering confirms individuality. Suffering, however, must not be allowed to become self-sufficient, nor should it be permitted to degenerate into nihilism. How does one prevent such degeneration? Shiina seems entirely satisfied with setting forth his answer in moral and psychological terms. One ought to suffer, one ought to try the impossible, one ought to love humanity, one ought to seek happiness. . . . Shiina's advocacy of *shutaisei* is just that, an advocacy. How does one, or Japan as a nation, begin to achieve it? How can the impossible be made possible? The Japanese suffered during the war, but nothing happened. How can anything happen now only because they suffer? Shiina seems to be implying that the defeat at the hands of Western nations automatically confers on the Japanese a new ability to "return to one's own *shutaisei*." Is Shiina suggesting that the Japanese can discover self-identity and self-will by fiat? His sense of urgency is unquestionable, but his indifference to history and the current political situation causes the article to fall far short of being germane.

In "A Second Adolescence" ("Daini no Seishun," February 1946), Ara Masahito compares the Japanese people of 1945 to the Dostoyevsky of 1848, sentenced to execution and then reprieved at the very last moment. Now that Ara, like Dostoyevsky, has been saved from doom, he might as well think through the ideals of his first adolescence, which had proved nearly fatal. His earlier inspiration sprang from Christianity and altruism *(hyumanizumu),* both of which, when examined closely, revealed an underlying egoism. He was repulsed by this self-centeredness, but as he shed his youthful egoism, he also lost his adolescence to the war and with it his hope for humanity. The only way he could have kept his youth intact was by getting involved in subversive activities or by exiling himself abroad. Now given this second chance, he would rather confront the fundamental selfishness. Rigorously pursued to its limits, this philosophy of egoism might eventually prove to be a higher form of humanism. People who gave up their adolescence to the war must now embark on a journey to happiness, even if the pilgrimage should strike them as sordid and vulgar.

Ara's regret for having missed out on his first spring might win sympathy, and his resolve to be true to himself—which he insists on calling "egoism"—might be an honest enough strategy for life. Very much like Shiina's proposal, "A Second Adolescence" attributes the loss of his youth merely to a personal, psychological mischoice, as if the war that embroiled millions of people had little to do with it. Follow the right principle—"subjectivity" for Shiina and "egoism" for Ara—and history as well as your personal life will be amended.

In response to Ara, Kato Shuichi attacks egoism as too limiting to be a satisfactorily comprehensive vision. Humanism can never be founded on egoism, according to Kato, because it is "too bourgeois, too inert."[17] Kato, however, is not totally negative about Ara's idea of egoism. Insofar as egoism is defined as a purely formal proposal for the establishment of *shutaisei* in Japanese literature, Ara is on the right track; Japanese literature must be first rooted in a consciousness of self before it can aspire to transcendental and universal humanism. If Kato is distinct from Ara and Shiina in asserting the need for humanism, he is very much like them in setting up an undifferentiated notion of general humanity. History—which might be expected to particularize—is ultimately subordinate to this universal (i.e., Eurocentric) humanity. Japan lost the war, and it should rejoin the rest of the world, which would presumably embrace all nations including Japan without prejudice or discrimination.

Odagiri Hideo's "The Creation of New Literature: Toward a New Step" ("Shinbungaku Sozo no Shutai: Atarashii Dankai no tameni," June 1946) also celebrates the freedom he and others have enjoyed in recent months. To secure the pleasure of liberation, Odagiri argues, writers ought to be creating truly distinguished works, which, however, are nowhere to be seen. The essay, remarkable for its tortured zigzag argument, progresses in this fashion: How do they get around to writing great works? By having the right world view. But simply having the right view is not enough. Art needs real feelings. But feelings alone won't suffice either. Don't forget the world view, but heighten it with one's own felt experience. . . . When the essay finally comes around to close the circle, it leaves the reader with a recommendation of something like "reality as it relates to one's own raw experience" *(jibun to no kanren ni okeru genjitsu)*.[18] In concrete terms, the "reality" seems to mean the writer's own personal history of the last ten years, that is, the history of acquiescence and collaboration with war efforts. According to Odagiri, the writer's betrayal of his social responsibility is everybody's problem. In fact, unless all writers seriously examine their spiritual stigmata, there will be no new start in Japanese literature.

Odagiri does not explain what exactly constitutes wartime apostasy. Which failures are serious crimes, on the scale ranging from subversion of war aims by violence (which practically no single writer was willing to commit) to aggressive leadership in war planning (which likewise hardly anyone was guilty of)? Most writers, including the twenty-five whom Odagiri named as war criminals in another article, fell in the gray area between the two extremes. They were guilty because they acquiesced and cooperated; but they were also innocent because they were not informed and were under duress. Thus despite Odagiri's efforts to designate specific criminals, most discussion about war responsibility was likely to be deflected to collective guilt, although the "general penitence" that Prince Higashikuni had recommended was clearly inadequate.

Maruyama Masao's article called "The Logic and Psychology of Ultra-Nationalism" ("Cho-kokkashugi no ronri to shinri," May 1946) succinctly describes this situation of murky guilt and innocence as unique to Japan. He insists that the European state structure is neutral to cultural values, whereas in the Japanese state, constructed on the emperor system, emperor-worship fills private as well as public space. The lack of neutrality in the state structure makes possible the governmental control and subjugation of people's privacy and individuality. Maruyama believes that even the emperor himself lacks final authority, since unlike the European monarch he is held accountable to the authority of his ancestral succession.

Maruyama's analysis of the emperor system and its effects on Japan's intellectual and political history is astute, and his observation of the general absence of *shutaisei* in Japanese thought and action can be ignored only at a serious risk. His comparison of Japanese ultra-nationalism with German fascism, however, reveals an inexplicable predisposition toward Germany. According to Maruyama, German officials were fully conscious of their decisions and purpose and so were clearly responsible for their acts, while Japanese leaders such as General Tojo Hideki were merely following the dictates of their superiors in the hierarchy emanating from the authority of the emperor. Thus, at the war tribunals, Maruyama says, "A Tsuchiya turned pale, a Furushima cried, and a Goebbels roared in laughter," pointing to the intellectual superiority of the latter.[19] Does this mean that the Germans, who rationally and consciously committed the act of genocide, were somehow more intellectual, more enlightened, than the Japanese, who remained unselfconscious—that is, lacking in *shutaisei?* Exactly what is German "rationality"? Isn't Maruyama guilty here of a blind acceptance of the West, not uncommon among the elites of "less advanced" nations? Unlike the spokesmen of the newly liberated colonies such as Mao, Frantz Fanon, or Aimé Césaire, Maruyama is indifferent to the moral pitfalls of the West, having been bedazzled by its predominance in artistic, intellectual, and technical achievements. Isn't there a serious ideological failure in not recognizing an utter loss of sanity and humanity in what he calls German "rationality"? This purblindness is rather extraordinary for an agile and sophisticated mind like Maruyama's, especially because in the very same article he makes the pertinent suggestion that Japan's adventurism is "a modest attempt to follow the example of Western imperialism."[20] Yet he is all too satisfied to view Japan as uniquely irrational, as guilty of a special kind of ultra-nationalism that robs its subjects of clarity and choice.

The *shutaisei* controversy is cognate if not identical with the issue of war responsibility. And the writers' nervousness was widely visible in Japan. As Maruyama called it much later, a "community of penitence" *(kyodo kaikontai)* seems to have taken over the late-forties intellectual scene.[21] The one group that stood outside this embarrassed crowd was a small number of Communists who had firmly resisted the militarists, risking years of imprisonment or exile. Although even they did not go to the extent of bearing arms against the Japanese state, they were nonetheless heroic resistance fighters in the eyes of the liberal apostates as well as the general public. The prestige of Marxism in the postwar *shutaisei* discourse was at least in part due to the prominence enjoyed by Tokuda Kyuichi, Shiga Yoshio, Nosaka Sanzo, Miyamoto Yuriko, and her husband Miyamoto Kenji, for having remained uncontaminated. In addition to their personal presences as moral exemplars, the Marxists contributed to the *shutaisei* exchange by proposing a defense of free will and choice in the dialectic of historical inevitability. Umemoto

Katsumi, for example, argued that freedom was a historical product, and insofar as human freedom allowed choice, people must do all they can to remove the source of moral evil and social injustice. The acceptance of historical inevitability was perceived to constitute a ground for moral intervention. This essentially liberal humanist revisionism conducted on such a high level of abstraction eventually became undistinguishable from all others. The Marxists' euphoria with the American liberators and their ignorance of the Cold War[22] helped to sustain their argument as abstract, metaphysical, and, ironically, unpolitical.

A number of people who were worried about the blurred boundaries of war responsibility decided to join the morally pure Communist Party, thereby purging their guilty consciences. By the time they made up their minds to join the party, however, MacArthur had already begun to alter his earlier policy toward the revolutionary movement. As became painfully clear later on, not a few of them had to reverse themselves once again as the unpredicted prosperity of the sixties alongside the intensification of the East-West conflict made their party membership less than an association with glamorous heroism.

If the objective of this postwar soul-searching was to inquire into the conduct of the Japanese state in relation to its neighboring nations, it might as well have been directed to the larger context of international aggression and colonialism during the last century. Are not aggressive nations equally guilty? All individuals? Should there be distinctions among them in accordance with the severity of the crimes? What is the general war crime above and beyond specific acts of brutality and atrocity condemned by the Geneva Conventions? Is it a moral sin or legal crime? According to whose law? Are the Hiroshima and Nagasaki bombings justified? If the Allies, too, are guilty on specific counts, why are they not being tried? If they are guilty but not to be brought to trial, what is the status of the Tokyo Tribunal? Was the cause of the Allies wholly guiltless? Isn't it perfectly possible to argue, as did Takagi Yasaka earlier and Noam Chomsky later on, that Japan was following the precedent established by Great Britain and the United States, and was exercising its own Monroe Doctrine and realizing its own Manifest Destiny?[23] And if the Japanese version of Manifest Destiny is distinguishable from its acts of aggression and atrocity, how should the two be articulated? This type of fundamental inquiry was not attempted by most Japanese critics and historians either before or after the end of the Occupation in 1951. The writers seem simply to have presumed that war crimes had been committed by the Japanese, without asking about the precise charges.

There were several reasons for the Japanese reluctance to scrutinize the West's record. First was fear of Occupation censorship. In retrospect, one sees how arbitrary, ineffective, or even absurd the practice of censorship was in this—as in any other—case. But in the forties, when the Occupation forces were still hailed as Japan's liberators, the censor's moral authority and disciplinary power were very much revered and dreaded. The Japanese would do anything to avoid incurring SCAP's wrath, including keeping mum about the role of Western imperialism in the history of Japan's aggressive war. The silence was of course ironic in view of the self-examination that the Japanese were supposedly undergoing at the time. The abstruse philosophers who talked about the Kantian, Hegelian, and Marxian notions of *shutaisei* never took full cognizance of the moral and intellectual discrepancies that lay between the freedom they discovered in the abstract and the restrictions they accepted in actuality. In the course of investigating their past moral failure, they were once again failing to face up to the ongoing abuse of power. One cannot leave out, at the same time, the hypocrisy of those U.S. missionaries of democracy who as a matter of course banned the exercise of democratic principles once their own interests were involved.

Second was the discrediting of Pan-Asianism. Had fear of censorship been the sole reason for this silence, it would have ended with the conclusion of the peace treaty in 1951. Such was not the case. Even though the issue of war responsibility was kept alive after that date, Western hegemonism was not discussed except by a few sober critics such as Takeuchi Yoshimi and several right-wing revisionists such as Hayashi Fusao.[24] In order to understand this hesitation, one should recall that Pan-Asianism, which proposed the liberation of Asia from Western imperialists, had been thoroughly appropriated by the militarists during the war. Thus in those early postwar years few reputable writers would want to be associated with it. To be identified as revisionist was as serious a disgrace as being classified with war criminals. In 1955, for instance, Yoshimoto Takaaki wrote "The Poets of the Previous Generation" ("Zen sedai no shijintachi"), raising anew the question of war responsibility. In the essay Yoshimoto assails Odagiri and others for passing for resisters while they were actually collaborators. Yoshimoto is quick to point out contradictions between their wartime poems and their postwar statements. According to him, most of the writers who claim to have fought against the militarists are in fact hypocrites and opportunists, "quasi-fascist agitators earlier, and quasi-democratic sentimentalists now."[25] Yoshimoto is fierce and unrelenting in this essay, as always. But his disapproval seems limited to the domestic versions of hypocrisy, without considering them in the historical international context.

The third factor involved in this silence about Western responsibility was the International Military Tribunal for the Far East, which was, and was then perceived to be, totally arbitrary and farcical. The concept of the war crime tribunal, like the idea of the crime against peace or the crime of war conspiracy, was a World War II invention with no legal precedent. But the Japanese were forced to accept the verdict of the tribunal in accord with the terms of surrender. In the course of prosecution, moreover, the clearly innocent were punished while the manifestly guilty were left alone. The most obvious among the latter, the one who might best fit the description of war criminal, was Emperor Hirohito. If not directly responsible for the planning and execution of the war itself, he indisputably presided over the martial rites and ceremonies that moved and guided his loyal subjects. And yet, whether because of his supposed influence over his subjects or his prior understanding with the United States, he was safely placed under the Supreme Commander's protection. If he was innocent, no militarist leader could have been condemned. In this, as in other matters, the predictable verdict of the Tokyo Tribunal intensified the sense of moral futility. As the Japanese viewed it, justice was as usual one-sided. Radhabinod Pal, the only dissenting judge at the tribunal, mentioned the need to remember the general context of the alleged crime: "To appreciate what happened, it is only just to see the events by putting them in their proper perspective. We should not avoid examining the whole of the circumstances, political and economic, that led up to these events. This is why I had to refer to matters like the Britainocentric economic world order, the diplomatic maneuvers at Washington, the development of communism and the world opinion of the Soviet policy, the internal condition of China, the China policy and practice of other nations and the internal condition of Japan from time to time."[26] Hardly a full-scale inquiry into Western expansionism, Pal's argument was indeed a mild protest. Yet he and the Japanese defense lawyers were summarily dismissed, and others did not dare speak up against the blatant travesty of justice. In this act of silence, the Japanese reexperienced the history of compromise and acquiescence.

Fourth was the long-standing deference to the West. Ever since the Tokugawa isolation was shattered by the encroachment of the Western fleet, the Japanese had been fearful of the advanced technology and vast wealth of Western powers. As they learned about its civilization, they were similarly awed by its philosophy and literature, music and arts. The West was to be the center and the norm; and the non-West, peripheral and marginal. The early advocates of enlightenment urged their compatriots to abandon the ranks of Asia and join the West. Thereafter the Japanese, like most other colonized non-Westerners at that stage, had to cope with their own sense of insecurity. In its own people's eyes, Japan was a minor nation overwhelmed by the superior force and culture of the West. They were to "catch up" with the West, to model themselves after the more "advanced" culture on the monolinear scale of progress. Japan's xenophobic ultra-nationalism was merely the mirror image of this West-worship, which alone can explain the amazingly smooth transition in 1945 from the resolve to fight to the last soldier to the determination to build a peaceful nation.

At the same time, Japan was also one of the very few non-Western nations that had managed to keep itself unoccupied and unsubjugated until 1945. Hence, its pride and sensitivity about its supposed status as a "first-rate" world power, and its traditional exclusivism that often surfaced as outright contempt for the former colonies of the West. In fact, Japan's own colonialism had to be more brutal than the Western versions because they knew how much they had in common culturally and racially with their victims; in order to convince themselves, not to say their victims, of their superiority, they had to resort to naked force. Looking askance at the rest of the Third World, the Japanese considered themselves civilized and advanced. When they faced the West, they knew they did not quite belong. Racism is nothing but a form of self-illusion.

Postwar Fiction

With the resurgence of publications, fiction writers, too, were reactivated. Not that they were jubilant over the passage of a dark period. Attentive to the details of daily life by the nature of their work, they were even more bewildered than critics and commentators. But self-examination was urgent for them also. Their works offer further testimony to the postwar crisis of Japanese identity.

Old masters like Nagai Kafu, Tanizaki Junichiro, and Kawabata Yasunari resumed their disrupted work. The war seems to have left relatively few scars on them. Tanizaki completed *Silent Snow* in 1947 (*Sasameyuki;* translated as *The Makioka Sisters*). If the work's apparent lack of interest in the war is a mark of the author's resistance, its indifference to the postwar years may also point to a criticism of the Occupation-imposed reforms.[27] Nagai Kafu, too, published works that had been written earlier. The fact that he could print after the war what he had written under quite different circumstances says something about his perception of the war. As for Kawabata, he had made several contributions to the war effort, about which he remained rather taciturn. Does this suggest his unconcern with the matters of war and peace in particular, or with public affairs in general? What constitutes Kawabata's identity as a writer? How does he relate to the world surrounding him? These are no easy questions to answer. Kawabata completed *Snow Country* (*Yukiguni*) in 1948. The newly added parts do not betray any experience of the devastating war and defeat.[28]

The younger writers' involvement with the war was far more traumatic. During their formative years the war had expanded and intensified from Manchuria to China, then to the Pacific. Some had already started to write at the earlier stage of the war, while others began their careers after the surrender. They were impatient to speak up, although not always equipped with an interpretive will or

confidence. Many writers seemed to find consolation in merely recording their not readily decipherable experience. One group of
writers who were most conspicuous in 1946 were the Marxists, who
had engaged in some form of resistance activity in the preceding
years. Of these, Noma Hiroshi and Shiina Rinzo will have to be
noted.

Noma's "Dark Paintings" ("Kurai e") appeared in 1946. It describes a young student's search for his place among revolutionary
friends in the midwar years. The story is temporally unstable: at
several points the hero reflects on the narrated time from a postwar
vantage point. Nothing happens in the story itself, although it is told
that several revolutionists were arrested for subversive activities and
died in prison later. Various attitudes toward the revolutionary program are introduced, and the protagonist, characteristically, broods
over his possible choices: "There is no possible way of living for
him except finding a way to pursue self-perfection in Japan. For
Japan has not yet established individuality, and the establishment of
individuality is a serious question awaiting a solution. This idea
derives from a conviction about the need of achieving bourgeois
democracy, but [he] thought of it in terms of engraving on his flesh
the scars of continual efforts in pursuit of self-perfection."[29] How
this bourgeois self-reliance relates to his friendships with the revolutionists is not made clear, nor is Noma's postwar view of this
earlier adolescent self-search. His heavy-handed prose is literal and
unironic, demonstrating the postwar Noma to be still undistanced
from the midwar resolve of noncommitment. The protagonist, a
likely spokesman for the intellectual Noma Hiroshi, is quite smug
toward his father and other working-class adults, without whose
support and money young revolutionaries like himself are not likely
to survive even for a day. Noma's indifference to the economics of
daily life, coupled with the insistently arbitrary reading of Brueghel's
paintings of the title, make this initiation story depressingly self-centered and sophomoric.

Shiina Rinzo's "Midnight Feast" ("Shinya no utage," 1946) is a
story of unmitigated despair. The first-person narrator lives in a
shoddy apartment house in a burned-out Tokyo street. All the residents in the building are misfits from the lower depths, making do
from day to day on little nothings picked up from the city rubble.

Most characters including the hero are sick and dying. Among those dejected castaways, the only vigorous one is the hero's uncle who owns this prison-like apartment house. He is heartless, ugly, and lame. The hero and his next-door neighbor, who happens to be a young prostitute, are both about to be evicted by the ruthless uncle. As the two prepare for homelessness, they mumble to each other, "really, it's a miserable life. Besides, nothing can possibly happen."[30] As the girl pats him like a child, his hair falls out in strands.

Once again, nothing happens in the story. The hero lives by a creed of endurance: "Simply by endurance I become freed from all heavy burdens. To endure is, for me, to be alive." No one is in control, and those few who have any power over the others are vicious and ugly. Like the unceasing rainfall in the story, life never lets up. And yet the "I" refuses to give up hope. He must endure the unendurable. Shiina's *Ningen* article must be recalled in this light. One must not be nihilistic, one must endure. His idea of *shutaisei* proves to be a stoic determination to live on despite poverty and iniquity. In Shiina's view, then, there is finally no difference between war and peace, domination and surrender, justice and injustice, for evil is a condition of life. *Shutaisei* is, paradoxically, always attainable depending on one's fortitude. Shiina may be persuasive as a transcendental moralist, but as a Marxist historian of the intellectual and political conditions of Japan he is nearly useless.

Unlike Noma and Shiina, who both went through an activist stage, the members of the *Buraiha* (vagabond) group—Oda Sakunosuke, Tamura Taijiro, Sakaguchi Ango, and Dazai Osamu—are not closely associated with Marxist ideology. Tamura was arrested once, and so was Dazai, both in alleged violation of the Peace Maintenance Act. But the four are chiefly remembered for their so-called decadence manifestoes rather than their political creeds. The notion of decadence suggests sensuality and freedom, and hence independence and autonomy. Tamura's "The Gate of Flesh" ("Nikutai no mon") was a sensational success at the time of its publication in March 1947. The story describes a group of street girls who seek shelter in the basement of a burned-out building. In a world where the old order has crumbled and nothing has taken its place, the young prostitutes form a tribe for self-protection. They have one strict taboo: no sex except for money. The plot was even then a cliché: A young man shot by the police while committing an armed robbery joins the group. One of the girls falls in love with him and has an orgasm for the first time. As she is being punished by torture, she awakens to the pleasures of flesh. Her "body, encircled by a pale white halo, was resplendent like the prophet on the cross."[31]

The reference to Jesus, too, is quite a cliché (see Ishikawa Jun's "Jesus in the Tokyo Ruins" ["Yakeato no Iesu"], Dazai Osamu's *The Setting Sun* [*Shayo*], or Ooka Shohei's *Nobi* [*Fires on the Plain*] among others); there is no clear sense why Christianity suddenly becomes relevant—unless any *deus ex machina* will do.[32] At any rate, this sadomasochistic depiction of convulsive female limbs seems to offer a new expression of vigor and energy rarely seen in war-ravaged Tokyo. Flesh is honest, even mysterious. Against the wartime libidinal suppression, what was felt to be brute sexuality seems to have reaffirmed the actuality of existence. When re-read many years later, however, the story shows itself as full of fantasies and delusions. The warm camaraderie among the misfits, the clean-liness of underground communal living, the male power to endow women with purpose as well as pleasure—Tamura's idealizing of the illicit and fantasizing of male dominion are unrestrained. Rather than a witness to individual emancipation through sexual liberation, "The Gate of Flesh" is a paean to control and discipline, the only new departure being the sexist exploitation that has replaced military subordination. Sexuality may be a gate of flesh and may indeed serve as an opening to selfhood, but as it is depicted in this story, it is hopelessly bonded to the exercise of power.

Oda Sakunosuke is preoccupied in "Today's Scenes" ("Seso," April 1946) with the verbal surface that makes clear his affinity with Edo *gesaku* writers. And just as the works of the *gesaku* writers were heavily mediated by textuality rather than directly faced with raw experience, so Oda's writing is always distanced from carnal drives. The story is, typically, about a writer who is looking for subjects for his story. It takes the form of a string of episodes, some describing the narrator's encounters with people, and others re-peating the stories told him by these people. The story is set in actual places in Kyoto, and the time, too, is specific, consequently lowering the barrier between fiction and nonfiction. The representational level of storytelling is continually coalesced with that of the story told; an "Oda Sakunosuke" makes his appearance as a character, as is often the case with Oda's work.

Ostensibly, "Today's Scenes" depicts the changed—that is, degraded—scenes of contemporary Japan. Thus the protagonist wanders among the denizens of Kyoto, collecting sleazy episodes for the story that the author is in the process of writing under the title of "Today's Scenes." This complicated structure notwithstanding, there is a sort of core episode that concerns the notorious real-life murderess Osada, who killed her lover in the middle of lovemaking, severing his genitals as a token of their love. (This event forms the central plot of Oshima Nagisa's well-known film *In the Realm of the Senses.*) The narrator receives a copy of the court transcript of her trial that provides him with another episode. The owner of the Osada papers, his old friend who comes in and out of the story, is now intimate with the madame of the Cafe Dice, but as the story comes to its end, the man's past relationship with Osada herself is disclosed. The name "Dice" suggests Oda's philosophy of composition, namely that the narrative ought to remain without closure, with all its elements left to chance and accident. (In another story, "Soredemo watashi wa yuku," the plot unfolds as the protagonist throws a die at every decisive moment, thus turning the final work into a collection of characters and events barely connected in one integral unit.) Oda believes in the chance form, rejecting the authorial interpretive will that imposes its control on the work. Whether Oda's accidentalism is successful or not is not an issue here. His idea of "accidental fiction" *(guzen shosetsu)* is fascinating either way in view of the general emphasis placed on *shutaisei* at the time. In Oda's view and actually in his work, the author's authority, control, and responsibility are deliberately minimized. As though all such determination were finally trivial, Oda reverts to eighteenth-century conventions and locates Japan's contemporary scenes in that older context. It is indeed ironic that Oda—remembered for his willful decadence and demimonde licentiousness, qualities judged to be components of the *shutaisei* movement—should turn out to be a self-effaced occasionalist for whom randomness, not willed control, moves the world.

In his use of himself as a central persona, Dazai Osamu resembles

Oda. Of course, all "I-fictionists"—in fact, most Japanese fiction writers—are alike in this regard. But it is further in the concealment of their privacy under the masks of humor and irony that the two resembled each other. If other I-fiction writers exude the heated air of sincerity and honesty, Oda and Dazai are ostentatious in their studied insouciance. The two also depend on the accidentals of their real life for the plot of their work, not because these events are intrinsically important but because they are uncontrolled. They let accidents propel their story lines in random directions. Thus the verbal surface that deflects and refracts and the whimsical turn of events together work to effect open-endedness, ironically undermining the ostensible program for self-discovery.

One thing that keeps the two apart is Dazai's unashamed preoccupation with aristocracy. In *The Setting Sun* (1947) certainly, but also in many other works, Dazai keeps returning to recuperate and define the distinction of nobility.[33] He often insists that his is a moral and spiritual meritocracy, not a hereditary rank. But in Dazai's mind, aristocracy by birth and aristocracy by merit (a suspect category to begin with) keep merging. Especially after the legal institution of aristocracy *(kazoku)* was abolished and several sensational scandals involving ex-royals and ex-nobles were reported by the press in 1947, the decline of the once-glamorous group powerfully excited Dazai, who had always hankered after the rank of distinction. This sentimental attachment, very much like celebrity worship, was shared by other middle-class writers like Mishima Yukio. They all craved a mixture of exclusiveness, cosmopolitanism, affluence, and dandyism, using class terms to express their own claims to superiority.

Sakaguchi Ango, notorious in the immediate postwar years for his philosophy of "depravity," finally may not be radically different from Dazai or Mishima in snobbery, but he, at least, avoids class metaphors, as does Oda. In "On Depravity" ("Daraku ron," April 1946), Sakaguchi confronts Japan's changes since the previous summer. All that was prohibited is now permitted; those who were about to die for the emperor's glory are very much alive, earning their living on the black market. The intense beauty in the face of death and destruction is all gone. What is left now is the pain of survival, the routines of being alive day to day. "We fall not because we were defeated. We are degraded because we are human beings. . . . But we are too weak to keep falling forever. . . . Sooner or later we end degradation and find the way of the *samurai* or emperor worship. . . . By falling to the utter limits of degradation, we must find ourselves, our salvation."[34] Sakaguchi privileges degradation because his strategy for the recovery of *shutaisei* is the acceptance of decay as the necessary condition of life: letting go, instead of choice. Soon the ascent will begin. By accepting the vulgar and low, the individual will be relieved of the worries of the bourgeoisie.

A few months after "On Depravity," Sakaguchi wrote a story called "An Idiot" ("Hakuchi"). Set in the Tokyo of 1945, the story describes a seedy neighborhood where the protagonist lives. One day a schizophrenic neighbor's imbecile wife strays into the hero's house. He lets her stay and as the air raid becomes a regular event in Tokyo, they begin to sleep together. One night the whole neighborhood goes up in flame in an air raid. As the man takes the idiot woman along to escape from the fire, he wonders what it means to be with her. "Is the sun going to shine on me and on the pig who is standing by my side?"[35] The story was intended to exemplify the argument of "On Depravity." By reaching the bottom of degradation one can find the path of ascent. It is difficult, however, to apply Sakaguchi's decadence principle to this story. The protagonist is a thoughtful man throughout, and there is little in his act that can be called degraded. Is having sex with the idiot woman a depraved act, because a part of him can think of her only as a "pig"? Possibly. But as Sakaguchi tells the story, he sleeps with her out of kindness and responsibility rather than exploitation and brutalization. As a matter of fact, even the essay "On Depravity" itself does not fully explain what is meant by "depravity." Whatever is illustrated in the essay does not correspond to what is usually understood by the word. Sakaguchi describes a mild derring-do of bourgeois dimensions neither shocking nor even reprehensible by the most level-headed standards. Since his sin fails to reach the depth of degradation, his salvation, too, promises to be no more than a tiresome minor attainment. In Sakaguchi's world the self is not allowed to venture far in either its fall or rise. Sakaguchi closes another essay by saying "I just want to live for myself."[36] But even that perfectly reasonable wish, which he must express in a gesture of defiance, seems somewhat beyond Sakaguchi's reach.

Shiina, Noma, Tamura, Oda, Dazai, and Sakaguchi were all spokesmen for the darkest period of Japan in the late forties. But these writers who intended to mark the return of peace reveal no signs of individual freedom. Selfhood is inextricably woven into the fabric of Japanese society. The individual clamors for autonomy and independence are audible, but the voices seem drowned out by the tribal chorus of the fallen empire.

These writers are also all practitioners of "I-fiction" *(shishosetsu)*. Aren't I-fiction writers supposed to be autobiographical—that is, concentrated on the shaping of the self? Despite their self-preoccupation, none of the six writers is seriously critical about the core of selfhood. Shiina is too eager to flee from the self in transcendental affirmation; Noma's criticism is indulgent and incomplete; Tamura is bonded to the cliché; Oda surrenders the self to the accidental and uncontrollable; Dazai nervously performs to an audience; Sakaguchi, too, is bound by the dictates of his society. Thus despite their apparent defiance and independence, the I-fictionists are once again confirming society's unloosened control of their beings. Mishima's *Confessions of a Mask* (1949), too, is a timorous exhibition of a middle-class prig's breach of his society's normal expectations. The more they gaze at themselves, the more they see the shadows of their tribe instead.

The best way to approach this aspect of I-fiction, which might also throw light on *shutaisei,* is to read the work not as the author's moral and spiritual confession, but as a literal recording of the composition process. It has always been important for the Japanese writer to document the circumstances in which a poem was conceived, written, and read. Beginning with the oldest of the poetic collections, the *Manyoshu,* with its prefatory notes, the convention is alive throughout Japan's literary history, appearing in all the poetic anthologies, *zuihitsu* essays, and Basho's travelogue-diaries. Obviously the performative quality of Japanese literature requires discussion on its own. What is interesting here is that I-fiction can be looked at not as evidence of *shutaisei* (self-search, self-determination, self-identity) but as exactly the opposite, the public disclosure of the circumstance of the work's composition. Of the six works mentioned here, "Dark Paintings," "Today's Scenes," and *The Setting Sun* are clearly performative: they write themselves. As for Shiina, Tamura, and Sakaguchi, they wrote numerous works that have their texts themselves as their references. In the postwar years, when the individual's identity crisis was profound, fiction writers were not exploring the ground of the modern self so much as following the long-established habit of tracing the circumstances of their writing. The unprecedented circumstance of defeat and humiliation may have driven these writers into the abyss of self-doubt. But to see that is also to understand that the novelty of the circumstance made them retrogress even more compulsively to the process of writing. So viewed, postwar I-fiction is not new in any significant sense. Similarly, it is not *shutaisei* but its absence that is fascinating about Japan's orthodox fictional form.

Choices

Postwar actions and inactions, exchanges of ideas, and literary configurations form an intriguing picture of *shutaisei*. As the intellectuals eagerly assented to SCAP's dictates, they concealed their surrender by means of ungrounded abstractions or stylized sensationalisms. The program of *shutaisei* was from the beginning deliberately, and hopelessly, severed from the world they in fact inhabit.

A. Why Shutaisei?

Most intellectuals of Japan, either before, during, or after the war, seem to agree that *shutaisei* is not their conspicuous trait, and that its full development is desirable as a universal modern value. There seems to be little question that individuality in personality, autonomy in action, and freedom in thought and expression are not characteristic of modern Japanese society. The legal and political system of pre-1945 Japan testifies to it; the absence of resistance and the pattern of conformity throughout the war years provide further evidence; and the I-fiction as I have redefined it is also a witness. The postwar refusal to discuss seriously the history of Western hegemonism also adds credence to this proposition. Socially and psychologically, collectivism still prevails. *Shutaisei*, or subjectivity/subjecthood/independence/individuality, however, is of course not a universal value. Were it universal, Japan—like any other society—would have developed it on its own as a crucial cultural factor. It is of course no less historical and culture-specific than feudalism, Protestantism, or any other socio-psychological category. *Shutaisei* arose in the West in the modern period in response to specific events and developments, and if Japan has retained its collectivism despite its "modern" enlightenment and technology, it may well have its own reasons.

The world today certainly does not present a pretty picture. The Cold War between the so-called democratic West and Soviet East may indeed be over; yet hopelessly sundered between the rich North and poor South, the world is continually threatened with conflicts and miseries, if not with the eruption of the nuclear armageddon. Races and tribes battle—formerly in the context of the West-East confrontation and now more frequently in the name of economic expansionism or reactive fundamentalism—in the Middle East, the Americas, Asia, Europe, and Africa; factions and sects contend everywhere. Internal competition also fragments societies. Do nations, races, classes, sexes, and groups benefit from the unceasing assertion of individual interests and self-concerns? Doesn't brute power always lurk behind the rule of *shutaisei?*

Even history seems to require revision. As we reread Shakespeare's *Tempest,* Defoe's *Robinson Crusoe,* and Conrad's *Heart of Darkness,* we are gazing straight into the records of expansionism and colonialism. Once we fix our thought on the West, however, our speculation immediately turns to the nightmare of Japanese imperialism, which, too, hauled millions and millions to their graves. Japan's aggression may have been the one self-assertive act that Japan has "successfully" managed to learn from the Western model. If aggression is indeed inseparable from *shutaisei,* does Japan—or do we all—need *shutaisei?* Can we now afford *shutaisei?*

For Japanese intellectuals as well as for Westerners, the job may well be to see the absence of *shutaisei* in Japanese society for what it is, and to recognize how it operates in various areas. After all is said and done, the uncritical pursuit of *shutaisei* in Japan may be still one more example of Japan's gestures toward Westernization, and thus ironically proof of its lack of *shutaisei.* Conversely, the West may learn from Japan not just management techniques, but a model for truly civilized behavior as it studies Japan's longstanding avoidance of individualism. Isn't it possible after all to reject *shutaisei* without at once falling into the suffocating regimentation of conformism and collectivism?

B. The "Death" of the Subject

In the West, on the other hand, the death of the subject is very much talked about. According to Fredric Jameson, for instance,

> Such terms [the alienation and fragmentation of the self] inevitably recall one of the more fashionable themes in contemporary theory— that of the "death" of the subject itself = the end of the autonomous bourgeois monad or ego or individual—and the accompanying stress, whether as some new moral ideal or as empirical description, on the *decentring* of that formerly centred subject or psyche. (Of the two possible formulations of this notion—the historicist one, that a once-existing centred subject, in the period of classical capitalism and the nuclear family, has today in the world of organizational bureaucracy dissolved; and the more radical poststructuralist position for which such a subject never existed in the first place but constituted something like an ideological mirage—I obviously incline towards the former; the latter must in any case take into account something like a "reality of the appearance.")[37]

C. Lost

Japan's extraordinary economic success has been, up to now, largely unaccompanied by a spirit of self-criticism. Of course, there are occasional critiques by writers and scholars of the nuclear threat, cultural vulgarization, and environmental destruction, but they are sporadic and fragmentary. A general system of criticism is yet to be revealed.

Above all, Japan's immense economic power is exercised in conjunction with global corporate expansionism and the relentless consumerization of individuals. Systematically dehistoricized, the collective nonindividuals of Japan seem to be leading the whole pack of peoples and nations, in both the West and the Rest, to a fantastic dystopia of self-emptied, idea-vacated, and purpose-lost production, consumption, and daydreaming.

All-encompassing consumerism is, ironically, a version of *shutaisei,* since it is sensual, bodily, and systematic. If intellectuals of the immediate postwar period—such as Maruyama Masao, Otsuka Hisao, or Umemoto Katsumi—meant by *shutaisei* a kind of modern, Western, liberal individualism, Japan's present may have indeed fulfilled such a program, or at least realized what was implied by such an ideology: an ultra-intensified and super-accelerated form of "rational" (controlled) capitalism. By overleaping the modern age of Hegel and Marx, Kierkegaard and Nietzsche, Sartre and Chomsky, Japan may have already arrived at an empire of signifiers without a single signified—all advertising signs and trademarks, and no meaning. Isn't that the world of Tanaka Yasuo's *Nantonaku Kurisutaru,* the ultimate consumerist vacuity in which the act of buying alone serves as the confirmation and reassurance of individual beings?

The Lure of the "West":
Tanizaki Junichiro

Tanizaki Junichiro was an expansive writer. Unlike the *apure (après-guerre)* writers, he already enjoyed an established reputation long before the war and survived unbeaten both the war and its aftermath. In contrast with Kawabata Yasunari, who clearly suffered the impact of the destruction, as can be seen in *The Sound of the Mountain* and other works, Tanizaki continued to produce new and fresh works right up to his death in 1965 at the age of 79. Older than Kawabata by more than a decade, Tanizaki made his literary debut in 1910, while Japan's founders of colloquial prose fiction, Natsume Soseki and Mori Ogai, were still in ascendance. He was an avant-gardist then, playing with boldly sexual themes and images and experimenting with highly intellectual ideas in clumsily constructed stories. In addition he spent some time writing film scenarios—a lowly business in those days that very few elite writers would willingly undertake, but one that handsomely repaid its serious practitioners with solid training in dramatic timing as well as dialogic accuracy and visual precision. He also gained from it a better understanding than any other recent writer of his country about the relationship between popular and high culture. Tanizaki was one of the few who were unafraid of looking vulgar and commonplace among the snobs and mandarins crowding the scene.

Even if it does not encounter monumental historical events, a long writing career is likely to be checkered by changes in style and mood, if not in substance and commitment. Tanizaki's career, spanning the years before and after the war, could have easily produced a series of twists and turns amidst global incidents, as is the case with those "converts" discussed in the previous chapter. Although Tanizaki did not undergo conversions in public, he, too, made adjustments. But his changes were more obvious in the scene and landscape of his fiction than in his ideas and ideology. His attitude toward both the "traditional" and the "new" Japan was from the very beginning problematic—that is, equivocal, qualified, tentative, ironic—and he seems to have been quite at ease with this ambiguity. In this chapter I will examine the writer's approbation and rejection, his construction and decomposition of his culture and the concurrent process of his examination of the Other that has defined Japanese society.

To consider the "Japanese/traditional" and "Western/new" cultural components is to realize that this binarism is obviously an ideological invention, inasmuch as what is perceived as native is often alien, and what passes for Western is in fact indigenous. Perception and history do not always agree. Furthermore, a rigid binarism of this sort inevitably implies essentialism and exceptionalism, whether naive or perverse. The world is not divided into these particular antonyms. Besides, no national boundaries are ever watertight. With possibly a few obscure exceptions, world history is a record of exchange and traffic, if not entirely of invasion and conquest, and Japan is certainly not outside it. Further, a concern with the old and native is always a reaction to the perceived threat by the new and foreign; purism is always suspect, as either xenophilia or xenophobia. In a violently changing era such as ours, no category is stable, but all tend to mix and part, and traditions are constantly invented and reinvented in the face of ever new imports.[1] It is to Tanizaki's credit that although he did not hesitate to accept the East-West opposition as a framework for his analysis, he more often than not puzzled over the quality of the interface rather than made a clear-cut choice between polarized options.

Let us take his earliest and last works, for instance. "The Tattooer" ("Shisei"), published when Tanizaki was twenty-four, is set in the Tokugawa period, but the historical scenery is a mere back-drop before which the tale, immune to nostalgia, sets out to disclose the tattooer's sexual/aesthetic program. Imbued with exoticism, the story compares the Edo tattooer's ecstatic experience to a Middle Eastern motif ("just as the ancient Egyptians had embellished their magnificent land with pyramids and sphinxes"[2]) and presents the classic Chinese image of men being tortured by women as its cli-mactic figuration. For Tanizaki the tie between the erotic and the exotic comes naturally; and if he appears deliberately oblivious to the historical impossibility of such a worldly sensibility in isolated Tokugawa Japan, he seems to be lampooning history through such anachronism and rejecting cultural authenticity by exoticizing a do-mestic event. This confusional tactic runs through his entire career, providing a necessary counterforce to polarization.

One of his last works, *The Kitchen Chronicle of War and Peace* (*Daidokoro taiheiki*, 1962–63, untranslated), is a relaxed episodic tale of the lives of housemaids. Dismissed as sheer entertainment, it has never been subjected to a critical reading, and such a low estimate is perhaps well deserved. Yet *The Kitchen Chronicle,* which describes the romances and marriages of domestic servants, inevitably poses a counterpart to his major achievement, *Silent Snow* (*Sasameyuki*, 1947–48, translated as *The Makioka Sisters*). The earlier tale, written during the bleakest war years, unfolds a dazzling chronicle of upper-class sisters' elegant "traditional" activ-ities and arrangements; this later book keeps a humorous record of matter-of-fact couplings and uncouplings of country girls in the ser-vice of the well-to-do speaker's household. Against the background of the early sixties, when rising living standards began to eliminate the class of domestic workers, Tanizaki toys with the new idea of democracy as it was forcing a reinterpretation of the world of *Silent Snow.* If *Silent Snow* resisted—at least by implication—the asceti-cism of military Japan, *The Kitchen Chronicle* parodies *Silent Snow,* placing it in an unflattering light of privilege and stagnation. And the recognition of a kinship between the two works alerts the reader to the consistent ambiguity in Tanizaki's work: *Silent Snow* is not a nostalgic aspiration to the aristocratic life of *The Tale of Genji,* just as *The Kitchen Chronicle* is not a condescending pageant of lowly housemaids.[3] In Tanizaki's work the high and low, the foreign and native mix, as the traditional and emergent clash in ever more intriguing interplay.

This disposition does not, however, produce consistent permeation and plurality throughout Tanizaki's career; despite his zestful appetite, his work is not always syncretic or indiscriminate. It is possible to trace long-term changes in scenes and landscapes in response to shifting historical particulars. Although such periodization is more in the nature of modal accommodations than substantial transformations or new ideologies, still the changes cannot be ignored, if only for the purpose of accurately understanding Japan's wartime pressure on writers. Three stages present themselves. The first is from "The Tattooer" (1910) to *A Fool's Love* (*Chijin no ai,* 1924, translated as *Naomi*) and *Some Prefer Nettles* (*Tade kuu mushi,* 1929). Toward the end of this period—after the great Tokyo earthquake of 1923—Tanizaki left Tokyo and moved westward to the Osaka area. The second, from "The Blind Man's Tale" ("Momoku monogatari," 1931) to the completion of *Silent Snow* in 1948, more or less coincides with the Fifteen-Year War. The final period, the remainder of his life, produced *The Key* (*Kagi,* 1956) and *The Diary of a Mad Old Man* (*Futen rojin nikki,* 1962).

Westward Ho!

Tanizaki's early works—essays, plays, and stories—are consistent in perceiving life in Japan as dull and drab, and they all try to invent a space for escape in its midst.[4] Intellectual abstraction offers him only an inadequate refuge: despite his apparent familiarity with recondite European figures, he is clearly just name-dropping and is bored. The bizarre and grotesque, on the other hand, seem to enliven him. In these numerous early works (now safely tucked away in the first five volumes of the standard collected works), the motifs of masochism and death-wish recur time and time again. Humiliation, subservience, scatology, rejection, isolation, attachment to mother, suicide, jealousy, self-immolation—such is the stuff these early works are made of. Although these themes are to become Tanizaki's lifelong trademarks, with which he will frequently achieve brilliant effects in later works, in these earlier stories Tanizaki is too self-conscious or perhaps not self-conscious enough. Either way, most of these stories are pretty dismal reading and few deserve more than occasional excavations.

Alongside such freakish emotions is another quirk, persistent deference to the West and modernism, which is in fact very much a part of Tanizaki's general masochistic sensibility. As a utopian space, the West insists on intimidating and humiliating Tanizaki's own situation, which he identifies with Japan in general. In this view, the West stands for freedom, progress, and sophistication, and Japan represents restriction, stagnation, and crudity. As he enjoys sexual humiliation, so he savors cultural inferiority. As if to coalesce his personal and social perversity, the West he evokes is naturally the *fin-de-siècle* decadent version, and he sees a model spirit in Poe, Baudelaire, and Wilde among others. Whether his intercultural reading is right is not important here; that he found a territory that can be exciting and fertile for his writing certainly is. With a bold intelligence and single-mindedness quite rare among Japanese writers of the time, Tanizaki energetically pursued his pleasures, perverse though they may have been, as if he knew precisely where they would take him.[5]

A Fool's Love is a daring experiment with the hegemonic role of the West in marginalized Japanese culture. A sort of Pygmalion tale, it begins with the narrator's discovery of a ragtag café waitress named Naomi. The name sounds Western;[6] she also looks like Mary Pickford—two factors powerful enough to trip him headlong into love. He marries her soon thereafter. The narrator, Joji—a homophone of "George" in Japanese—tries to improve the slum girl by teaching her English, which of course fails disastrously. The rest of the story portrays his uninterrupted humiliation at her hands. This voracious and liberated Galatea openly sleeps around and entirely ignores her repressed Pygmalion. At the end he eagerly accepts all her terms for their continued marriage, which amount to her complete freedom and his complete surrender. In addition, they are to live in a Western-style house in Yokohama, an old treaty-port city, where they eat Western food, drink Western beverages, wear Western clothes—and in Naomi's case—sleep with Westerners. As Naomi and Joji see it, this is as close to transforming themselves into whites as can possibly be managed. (Plastic surgery was not available then.) A case of lunatic exoticism, or of colonial aspiration for the metropolitan center? How does *A Fool's Love* relate to this addiction to the West? Where is Tanizaki positioned in this work?

Two years before *A Fool's Love,* Tanizaki wrote a short story called "The Blue Flower" ("Aoi hana," translated as "Aguri"), in which a thirty-five-year-old man takes his teenage "woman" out to expensive boutiques to buy her stylish clothes and accessories. As the man pays for the purchases, he keeps having hallucinations of his having a heart attack while the girl, Aguri, stands by and shows no feeling but irritation and annoyance. At the end of the story, she is in a fitting room when the man has another attack and thinks he sees Aguri's face "light up with a radiant smile" (p. 134). Whether this last emergency is another bout of fantasy or a real illness is not made clear in the story. A precursor of *A Fool's Love,* "The Blue Flower" is obviously another Pygmalion tale. The title is borrowed from the German Romantic poet Novalis (who is widely known among Japanese readers). This suggests the solipsistic source of the protagonist's perceptions, including even the girl's "exotic type of beauty."[7] What confirms this suspicion is the girl's name: Aguri is not a Japanese name but the typical Japanese pronunciation of the English word "ugly." Viewed in this light, the girl's attractiveness—"exotic" or not—is in serious doubt. The story, and its author Tanizaki, in other words, are totally clearheaded about the main character's absurd solipsism and infatuation and, by extension, his aesthetics as a whole. Placement alongside "The Blue Flower" seems to encourage an ironic reading of *A Fool's Love.*[8]

That Tanizaki lived very much like Joji in Yokohama is well established. He and the sister of his first wife had a lasting affair that involved numerous stormy events like those described in the work. His household was a comic simulation of a Western life-style. There is no denying that Tanizaki was attracted to the dominant culture of the West. His masochistic orientation no doubt helped: he loved to be humbled, or rather, he loved to imagine he was humbled. But then—and this is important—he was absolutely clear that he was at least half willfully fabricating this illusion. Tanizaki's cultural criticism always has this ironic twist. He presents an absurd situation that is attractive enough in several aspects to fool its participants—and the reader—into believing him to be earnest and the event to be serious. But somehow or other, there is always provided an unmistakable hint that undercuts the authenticity of the situation. In fact, what makes Tanizaki's work so audacious is the confidence to appear—and, indeed, nearly *be*—so foolish while knowing all along that his intelligence will somehow show through.

The Japan of the 1920s was indeed ridden with strife. On the one hand, it was a time of the lost generation, the age of the *moga* and *mobo* ("modern girls" and "modern boys"), lost because the country was fast turning into an industrial and militarist power, and the rising middle class was not sure of what was in the future. The old structure was quickly crumbling, but the new one had not yet emerged. Was there to be an "enlightened" bourgeois capitalist Japan, or a recuperative nationalist imperial Japan, or both? On the other hand, after the First World War, capitalist Europe had lost its imperialist momentum and was faced with the aftermath of the Russian Revolution. The class struggle was intensifying in Japan also. In the year *A Fool's Love* was published, several proletarian literary journals were launched, and in the following year the notorious Peace Preservation Law (Chian Iji Ho) that would severely restrict freedom of speech was passed. The state's thought control was rapidly tightening. Even if Tanizaki was a closer kin to the lost souls than to the proletarians, he could not have been ignorant about the class problems. There were early signs of feminism, too. Aguri's and Naomi's triumphs over their bourgeois men can certainly take on an element of political meaning in terms of class and gender. And at the center of this critical turmoil were the ongoing questions of the East and the West, Japan and the Other.

Some Prefer Nettles (1929) is also remarkable in its resolution to keep ambiguous its position toward prevailing cultural options. Reflecting Tanizaki's personal life and set in the Kyoto-Osaka-Kobe area, the work describes a husband's inability to break out of his failed marriage. He cannot love his enlightened Tokyo-bred wife, nor can he get involved with a Kobe prostitute who pretends to be at least part European. He is happy about his wife's having a serious affair but cannot bring himself to let his young son know about the impending divorce. During this period of procrastination, he meets his father-in-law's mistress. A young doll-like Kyoto geisha, the woman is neither intelligent nor the type he is used to finding attractive. And yet he feels strangely moved by her acceptance of her master and her tranquility. In the last scene, the man is in bed and thinks he sees her image in an obscure corner, which turns out to be an old *joruri* puppet of an ideal female character. Then out of the dark the woman herself appears, carrying books for him to read while waiting for his wife's return.

The man is tempted by this convention-bound woman, but the chauvinist attachment is sharply undercut by the story. He knows that her allure is limited to the shadowy night or the puppet theater. In broad daylight he is repelled by the idea of a kept woman. What he really needs is not made clear. Split exactly down the middle, he is satisfied with neither the modern/Westernized/daylight/Tokyo model nor the traditional/Japanese/shadowy/Kyoto model. As if to ease him out of this dilemma, the closing scene converts the narrative strand into an arrested image, thereby flatly refusing to make any explicit comment. The reader is left with the visual beauty of the young woman, although the passage does not neglect to warn the reader against the coming rainstorm outside. Tanizaki quite frequently uses this form of visualizing a narrative closure, especially during the next period of historical tales, as if he trusted an image more than story and commentary. And if this technique aestheticizes the woman and thus turns her into an object, Tanizaki usually remembers to place the fade-out image in some ambivalence or ambiguity.

The work that exemplifies Tanizaki's ambivalence about Japan's cultural possibilities even better than *Some Prefer Nettles* is his 1926 tale "The Story of Tomoda and Matsunaga." It is a Jekyll-and-Hyde story in which the Tomoda side of the double personality is described as a fanatic West-worshiper, who works as the manager and pimp of white whores at his own establishment. The second half, the Matsunaga persona, is a traditionalist who quietly enjoys a provincial married life. The speaker of the story receives a letter from Matsunaga's wife, whose husband vanishes every four years (to assume the Tomoda aspect) and then reappears. The melodramatic details of the Tomoda portion reveal, as expected, a greater emotional commitment on the author's part; but what finally emerges from this story of alternating personalities is Tanizaki's admission of his utter inability to integrate the mutually exclusive urges that are directed to Japan and the outside world. I might also note that Tanizaki still defines the West as exciting and sexually uninhibited while characterizing Japan as staid and domesticated. He did not think through the meanings of such cultural simplifications but merely followed the vast majority of his countrymen since the nineteenth century, taking the clichés of the East-West opposition as self-evident. It took his second trip to China soon thereafter for him to begin to suspect a connection between the geopolitical conditions of the world outside and the cultural situation of Japan.

The "West" of Japan

Tanizaki moved in 1923 to the Kyoto-Osaka-Kobe area, known as Kansai, meaning "west of the checkpoints" (as against the Tokyo-Yokohama area, known as Kanto, "east of the checkpoints"). Before long he came to see in this "western" part of Japan what he had been long seeking and unable to find in Kanto, and he began at once to build an imaginary space. The factors that converged to lead Tanizaki to this construction are many and complex: exoticism, nostalgia, eroticism, historicism, the regional dialects, nationalism/chauvinism, and his encounter with Nezu Matsuko, his third and last wife.

The Kyoto-Osaka-Kobe area is geographically quite different from the Tokyo-Yokohama region. For one thing, because of its geological formation, the soil is dazzlingly light compared with the dark, loamy Tokyo ground surface. Everywhere one goes, there is the stunning contrast of the white sands and the dark green pine trees (or at least there used to be until the urban blight of a decade ago). The far longer history of the area has endowed the cities of Kyoto and Osaka with architectural legacies absent in Tokyo, which was established in the comparatively recent seventeenth century. For people from the drab, bureaucratic, efficiency-oriented Tokyo, the age and grace of the Kansai region are not just striking but nearly foreign. The often repeated regional comparison insists that people in Kansai are more relaxed and straightforward and yet softer; the past saturates the present with subtle ironies and qualifications, as it does not in Tokyo.

The Osaka and Kyoto dialects are different enough from the Tokyo speech—in accent, intonation, and vocabulary—to present to an outsider a difficulty in communication. When Tanizaki wrote a novel about lesbians called *Manji* in the Osaka dialect, he needed research assistants to help him master it. Tanizaki discusses the "feminine" sound of the dialect, comparing it with the Tokyo speech.[9] The latter was a Meiji production by the provincial new bureaucrats who had felled the shogunate and it was jarring to those brought up in the historical Edo dialect, like Tanizaki.[10] He hated this government-imposed Tokyo "standard" language; the western speech on the other hand charmed his ears and excited his writing.[11] He settled down in the area and wrote a large corpus of works that often used this heard music.[12]

Kansai had other attractions, among them a wide range of urban localities. Kyoto and Nara, the virtual museum cities of Japan, were capable of indulging anyone's nostalgia for old Japan. Kobe, on the other hand, was one of the two oldest treaty-port cities of Japan, full of "exotic" sailors and traders from all over the world offering the "international" flavor that Tanizaki in particular—but many intellectuals as well—thirsted for. The area offered not only the poles of old Kyoto and new Kobe, but the robust industrial and commercial city of Osaka (which also had a long history)—all in a milder climate and lovelier landscape than Tokyo's. To those who held themselves aloof from political bureaucracy, Kansai offered the possibility of a humane and sensitive life-style. Kansai was both Japan's cultural center and its political margin. Tanizaki the Tokyo man was an alien in it: he had to learn the foreign customs, and he loved the experience. To know the Other in Kansai and experience the difference indeed gave Tanizaki the pleasure he had been long missing.[13]

There are two other important factors: Tanizaki's marital situation and Japan's changing political conditions. Had he not met Nezu Matsuko, his residence there might have not been permanent, nor the effect of his residence there on his work so decisive. Soon after Tanizaki completed *Some Prefer Nettles,* he put into practice what he had fictionalized in it: he divorced his first wife and "gave" her to a writer friend.[14] Just about the time he married an Osaka woman who had helped him with the local feminine dialect in *Manji,* he met Matsuko, the one lasting inspiration for Tanizaki's writing. After a brief period, he divorced his second wife, and lived with the still-married Matsuko and her sisters—somewhat as in *Silent Snow*. The wife of one of the wealthiest Osaka merchants, who was now facing a decline, Matsuko fitted Tanizaki's idea of a haughty elegant beauty whom he could pine for without ever possessing. The object of his masochistic attachment, a distant and unattainable femme fatale, was embodied in Matsuko, who spoke the Osaka speech, a virtual foreign language, and behaved in an unfamiliar manner. Tanizaki needed to maintain distance from her while being close enough to allow sexual and creative indulgence. Tanizaki's published letters reveal the extraordinary efforts he made (with Matsuko's apparent cooperation) to behave as if he were a lowly and humble houseboy in the employ of this noble lady, even after the two were married.[15] In this Osaka woman, Tanizaki's attachment to his mother and fear of women—which are the likely roots of his exoticism, nostalgia, snobbery, self-humiliation, and aestheticism as well as masochism—converged to inflame a passion that was to sustain Tanizaki's productive energy until his death thirty years later. Matsuko appears and reappears in his works under different guises, always maintaining the pose of elevated distance.

Tanizaki's aspiration for Western culture and life-style did not cease immediately on his move to Kansai. As is shown in *Some Prefer Nettles* and other works, his fondness for Kobe (the surrogate West) continued. But as Matsuko loomed in his sexual and fictional imagination, there was a gradual shift in his exoticism from Kobe to Kyoto, from the future/West complex to the past/Japan nexus. Henceforth, exoticism was to take the form of nostalgia, although the two are finally cognate.

Aside from the effects of such personal events, however, there were public and political currents sweeping Tanizaki's restive search in a new direction. Japan's military adventurists were rapidly expanding their horizon of actions in China. In 1931, the Manchurian Incident was initiated by the (Japanese) Kwantung Army; in the following year, a puppet state of Manchukuo was established, and the Japanese troops assaulted Shanghai; the same year saw the May 15 military uprising toward a "Showa Restoration" at home; the February 26 Insurrection followed in 1936; then the Marco Polo Bridge Incident, executed by the Kwantung Army in 1937, plunged

Japan into an intense conflict with China that culminated in the Pearl Harbor attack in 1941 and the Hiroshima bombing in 1945. Throughout such a crescendo of hostilities, the internal control of speech became increasingly relentless. The publication of subversive and obscene ideas—which could mean just about anything under the sun—was ruthlessly suppressed. This pressure was felt by all writers including, of course, Tanizaki. His so-called return to Japan *(Nihon kaiki)* in his fiction around this time was at least partly a surrender to this policy of war efforts. And his relationship to Matsuko in the context of Osaka history did not discourage such a retroversion.

While Tanizaki's compromise is undeniable, there is another, generally unacknowledged aspect of this shift[16]—that is, Tanizaki's deepening understanding of the role of the West in Asia. Tanizaki never visited the West. His travel abroad was limited to two visits he made to China in 1918 and 1926. His first trip was pretty much as a tourist, limited to sightseeing and a few inevitable visits to the Chinese opera theaters and brothels. Tanizaki was unsurprisingly impressed by the colonial splendors of Beijing and Shanghai, whose high-rise buildings made them seem like Western cities. During his second visit, however, he met a number of Chinese intellectuals in Shanghai, including Tian Han, Guo Maruo, Ouyang Yuqian, and Zhou Zuoren, who were eager to build an alliance with Japanese writers. Their problem was China's slow pace in modernization and Japan's contrasting speed in facing the Western threat. Politically untutored, Tanizaki at first could not comprehend his Chinese friends' sense of urgency about Western encroachment. As he records this visit in "Shanghai kenbun roku" ("Impressions of Shanghai") and "Shanghai koyu ki" ("Friendships in Shanghai"), the Chinese writers and artists opened his eyes for the first time to the historical circumstances in which the Western presence in Asia was not just a neutral sign of progress but an imprint of domination. The prosperity of Shanghai and Beijing was deceptive, they said, since the real wealth and power were appropriated by Westerners, and the peasants of China were thoroughly exploited and impoverished. The Chinese were waking up to the economic invasion by Britain and the United States.

Parts of Tanizaki's essays appear to be word-by-word transcriptions of these conversations. He does not detail his response to the experience, but it is obvious that for once Tanizaki was enlightened about the connection between the "exotic" life-style of the urban Japanese and geopolitical conditions.[17] In this light, Tanizaki's "return to Japan" was not entirely a response to militarist pressure. There was a short spell when Chinese and Japanese intellectuals could seriously share their thoughts about the meaning of Western colonialism and cultural hegemony without the Japanese having to apologize for their country's own enormous misdeeds in China. The new traditional phase of his literary production was, just like his first Western period, to a measurable extent ambivalent, complex.

Tanizaki's evident accommodation to the war effort must be briefly noted here before discussing the major works of this period. First, there is no doubt that he was under pressure. Although there is no reason to believe he was enthusiastic about the imperial cause, he left several traces of willing cooperation. It has been pointed out that Tanizaki contributed a short piece for a propaganda collection called *Tsuji shosetsu shu (Streetcorner Stories),* which contained the work of more active collaborators.[18] But this inane eight-line "story" is nothing compared with the text of a speech he broadcast on radio, in March 1942, celebrating the fall of Singapore. Here Tanizaki is unembarrassed in loading the brief talk with imperial clichés. "Muteki kogun" (the invincible imperial army), "nisen roppyaku nen no nagaki o hokoru kokoku no rekishi" (the imperial history that is proud of the 2600 years of its unfolding), "zen Toa no kaiho" (the emancipation of all of East Asia)—those wooden words and phrases that were mechanically cited during the war are unashamedly deployed. The content of the speech is as empty as the style is worn, but he freely uses the idea of *seisen* (holy war): "wherever the imperial army goes, its achievement is fair and just, and unlike the history of European aggression, it lacks the record of injustice and brutality, truly deserving the name of a holy war."[19] There is neither irony nor reservation: Tanizaki's pride in his country's victory is total.

What is one to think of a statement of this sort? Was Tanizaki convinced of the justice of the Pacific War? Did he believe the propaganda? Was he so ignorant? Or did he feel under duress? There is no other answer but that Tanizaki was indeed carried away by the triumphant turn of events at the very beginning of the Pacific War. As for his ignorance, there is no way of knowing the nature and degree of Tanizaki's information regarding the atrocities committed by the Japanese army, or even the imperialist objectives of the war itself. Information was under strictest control then, and even a novelist of Tanizaki's fame probably had little access to the well-guarded news concerning the Japanese war machine. It might be necessary finally to be satisfied with Tanizaki's having written so few pieces in any way supportive of the war, rather than to be repelled by these few words of collaborative evidence.[20]

This was a period that produced Tanizaki's most accomplished works, from "Yoshino kuzu" (translated as "Arrowroot," 1931), "Momoku monogatari" ("A Blind Man's Tale," 1931), "Bushu ko hiwa" ("The Secret History of the Lord of Musashi," 1931), and *Asikari* (translated as *Ashikari,* 1933) to "Shunkin sho" ("A Portrait of Shunkin," 1933). He also wrote *In-ei raisan* (*In Praise of Shadows,* 1933), an essay in cultural apology, and *Sasameyuki* (*The Makioka Sisters,* 1946–48) which some readers consider Tanizaki's best work.

The stories are either set in the past or contain episodes set in the past. They are in the *monogatari* (oral tale) rather than novelistic form, with several noticeable features. As in the Heian tales, the characters are neither drawn in depth nor endowed with individualities. They are flat and external. Likewise, the plot traces a sequence of events without worrying much about causality. The events happen one after another, with every segment highlighting the sense of flow, the passing of time. The text is not heavily marked by punctuation. Cognate with this sense of flow is the inclusive unboundedness of the narrator's consciousness. These stories obfuscate point-of-view and temporality, as if the drama of the tale did not take place between characters but between humans and a-human powers. Thus often the initial narrator encounters a secondary narrator who in turn introduces a narrator at one more remove, bracketing the story's representational levels and blurring the narrators' distinct epistemologies. Quotations likewise abound, quotations within quotations within quotations. Some are from ancient texts, others are Tanizaki's inventions, and still others remain unattributed.

The text so fragmented is no longer composed by a unitary writing subject but is dispersed among many different voices. If one voice presents a story, another is ready to divert it. The plurality of voices is also temporal, thus calling into question the authority of the historical speaking voice. Out of these fragmentary yet coordinated parts, the text struggles to present often an image, at times a song, that seeks to transform the story to the image or the song itself, thereby nullifying the distinction between matter and form, the narration and the narrated, and creating a performative "itness." In fact, the materiality of a text is utilized to enhance this effect: the distribution of Chinese characters and *kana* syllabaries is meticulously calculated. A heavily *kana*-dependent text will slow down the pace of reading, increasing the need to sound out the text and making the story auditory. On the other hand, a text largely consisting of Chinese characters is hard to pronounce, thus making it visual. An auditory text intensifies the effects of "A Blind Man's Tale," for instance, while a highly visualized text produces the acute sense of sight irrecoverably lost to the couple in "A Portrait of Shunkin."

To take just one of these *monogatari* stories, *Ashikari* opens with an essay-like account of the "I" sauntering out to enjoy the full moon. At a historical site—which happens to be a densely allegorical sexual site as well[21]—he encounters the secondary speaker and they share drinks of sake; this inner speaker's story constitutes the major portion of the work. He tells the "I" that he visits this place every year on the night of the September full moon. The second speaker had a father who loved and worshiped a wealthy merchant's widow, Oyu, or Madame Play. The circumstances of the relationship are typically Tanizaki: the father married Oyu's sister to be near Oyu without consummating the marriage. Oyu was remarried to another wealthy merchant. At this point, a son (who is to become this second speaker) was born, and his father's fortune rapidly declined. As the son grew, his father brought him out every September full-moon night to spy on the beauty of Oyu as she amused herself in a most elegant banquet attended by her numerous servants. Even after his father's death, the speaker kept up the habit of spying on Oyu every September. Many details are left out: Were Oyu and the father sexually united? Who is the speaker's mother? *Ashikari* leaves such questions unanswered and ends with the doppelganger's enigmatic disappearance:

Thinking this strange, I said: "But surely, Oyu must be very old by now—almost eighty!"

But where he had been sitting, there was nothing to be seen save the tall grasses swaying and rustling in the wind. The reeds which grew down to the water's edge were fading from sight, and the man had vanished like a wraith in the light of the moon.[22]

The first speaker and the reader are left with the radiantly portrayed image of Oyu's exquisite beauty, the embodiment of play and poetry, into which the story is absorbed as it ends.

Ashikari is full of historical references and is continually interwoven with numerous poetic and historical texts, whose intricate interrelationships spark excitement. The plottable events of *Ashikari* are finally subordinate to this story of interweaving texts. It is a powerful story that appeals to anyone whose principal interest in literature is aesthetic, that is, formal, autonomous, and performative.[23] Displaying Tanizaki's aestheticism at its best, *Ashikari* is a modernist work that aims at universalism against a specific local commitment, that is, a political program. This work must be placed in the context of increasing wartime simplification: while most writers were preoccupied with the imminent war and its demands, Tanizaki took time out and tried to gaze into something less serious, something "human" and playful. Outside this context, his *monogatari* might seem to signify trivial escapism and collaborationism. In the specific historical context of the thirties and forties in Japan, the stories are remarkably bold attempts at resistance. Despite all the signs of *bon vivant* nonchalance, Tanizaki seems dead serious about the encroaching mindless allegiance to the imperialist Pan-Asian agenda.

In Praise of Shadows continues Tanizaki's old binary reductionism. The world is divided into Japan (or the East) and the West. The substance of the opposites remains identical: Japan is shadowy, inarticulate, repressed, and pleasureless, while the West is brilliant, wordy, uninhibited, and sensual. This opposition cuts through all phenomena, from language, literature, style, and fashion, to arts and architecture. In his earlier days—those days of *A Fool's Love* and "Jozetsuroku" ("A Garrulous Account")—the West received his adoration, and Japan his contempt. Whatever the reasons, his move to western Japan cured him of unbridled colonial aspiration for the

West. *In Praise of Shadows,* written between 1933 and 1934, reverses his approval and disapproval: now the shadows are in, the glitters are out.

Despite Tanizaki's apparent *volte-face,* however, there are stubborn constants: his obsession with the color of the skin, for instance. According to him, the dark undertone of Japanese skin, even when covered with a thick coat of white powder, is "plainly visible as dirt at the bottom of a pool of pure water. . . . Among a group of Westerners, it is like a grimy stain on a sheet of white paper." Thus, "We can appreciate the psychology that in the past caused the white race to reject the colored races."[24] All his cultural aesthetics derives from this stark binarism of white and colored skins, despite his conversion in favor of Japan/the East/shadows. An element of racism—though against his own race in this case—is undeniable, and to ignore it would be a mistake. One does need to recall, however, that this was written in the middle of gradually heightening nationalism and chauvinism. A few years later, *In Praise of Shadows* would have been at least frowned upon, if not outright censored. In that sense, perverse as it is, Tanizaki's aesthetic manifesto could be appreciated for refusing to surrender to the growing fanatic self-congratulation and for inserting a moment of self-mockery.[25]

Tanizaki made fun of his own Naomism earlier. As he worshiped the West, he ridiculed the worshiper in himself. Now, as he admires the aesthetics of shadows, he insists on its being an inevitable consequence of the need for the Japanese to hide their dark skin. All architecture and the arts as a result of a plan for concealment? This skin-color obsession and his brutally simplistic aesthetics are so absurd that one cannot help detecting a sense of subtle irony. He adores the exquisite details of the archetypal shadowy Japanese house, yet the structure of argument stands on the flimsiest foundation. In describing the actual architecture, Tanizaki's prose is taut; when he justifies it theoretically, he seems more sardonic than straight-faced. When his architect offered him a plan of his home in accord with the specifications of *In Praise of Shadows,* he is said to have flatly refused: "But no, I could never *live* in a house like that."[26]

A few words on a work that has been hailed by many as his best work, *Silent Snow* (as I insist on calling it). Very much like the traditional *monogatari* tales, it is episodic without heavy emplotment. Nor are the characters endowed with psychological depth. There is, of course, a central event: the marrying off of the woman referred to in the title, Yukiko ("Snow Girl"). Pages and pages are lovingly filled with every detail of family life, and there are a few identifiable subplots that comment on the main plot—such as the provocative rebellion of the liberated youngest sister, or the circumstances of a Russian neighbor family. It is quite possible to dismiss this novel as a nostalgic tale of an upper-middle-class family, bordering on pure soap opera (*rajio dorama,* as the Japanese counterpart used to be called). And yet this now-innocuous book was subject to suppression when it was first published in 1942.[27] The book's intention was to ignore the bleak war as much as possible and insist on recalling the more civilized prewar years in the middle of worsening living conditions. So considered, even this seeming bourgeois nostalgia could be thought of as a work of resistance and subversion.

It should be noted that the title Tanizaki gave the book translates not as *The Makioka Sisters* but as *Silent Snow* or *Fine Snow*. The reference to snow in the title of a book with no snowfall whatever in the story itself should send a signal to the reader. Of course, the heroine's name is Yukiko, and there is a scene in which the youngest sister performs a dance called "Snow Dance." But Tanizaki wrote that the title, which was decided early on, was an extension of the heroine's name, which had come first to his mind.[28] If snow was the key image of this work, he needed to find some snow-related theme or event in addition to the heroine's name. By the time he was at the stage of completing it, the war was over, and in the immediate postwar years the idea of *sasameyuki*—quiet, fine, silent, delicate snow—was not the most appropriate trope any longer. Nostalgia after the devastation of the war means something quite different from that in the war years. Tanizaki had to negotiate the changed relationship between the fragile title and a tough, ugly, and desperate age. In fact, he expresses his feeling that even earlier the work had to be more prettified than he had wanted because of the pressure of the war ("kirei goto de sumasaneba naranu yo na tokoro ga atta . . .")[29]: he really wanted to draw the degradation and decadence in Kansai upper-class lives. In this connection, there is an odd occurrence at the end of the book—in fact, the book's very last sentence enigmatically refers to it: "Yukiko's diarrhea persisted through the twenty-sixth, and was a problem on the train to Tokyo." The reader familiar with Tanizaki's scatological proclivity might find this quite characteristic of the droll writer. Diarrhea after hundreds of elegant pages? Why, it is the surrogate of the "silent snow"! For any other writer this might sound like a forced reading, but it was perhaps the only reasonable way for Tanizaki to write the final episode of this prettied-up story.

Tanizaki paid a toll during the war as did all other writers. His Westernism, which earlier appeared as Naomism, was replaced with Japanese scenes and landscapes. Throughout his changes in these years, however, he did not lose sight of the critical power of irony. Of all the Japanese writers in this century, Tanizaki is among the very few—possibly in the solitary company of Natsume Soseki— who confronted the problematics of modernity, with its full complexity of Eurocentric hegemonism as well as the marginal cultures' inevitable experience of discrepancies. As he was always self-mocking during the days of "Westernized" style, so his conversion was carefully qualified. In his so-called return to Japan *monogatari,* there is not one item that is nationalistic or chauvinistic. The tales are as preoccupied with aesthetic/epistemological queries as his works in the first period, though the subjects and settings in time and space are restricted to Japan. It is due perhaps to this relative absence of change in his frame of mind that he showed far less exhaustion in his postwar works.[30]

Postwar Years

As most *apure-geru* writers were struggling with postwar disorientation—some in search of subjectivity and autonomy, others seeking pleasure and decadence—Tanizaki seems to have been relatively unperturbed. If we are to believe his published diaries, he spent 1946 writing and revising the last of the three parts of *Silent Snow* and soon began to arrange the reissue of practically all his earlier works. Having not gone through a marked wartime "conversion," Tanizaki was also not on the SCAP censorship list.[31] And his post–Peace

Treaty writing does not reveal any marked change. Like everybody else in these immediate postsurrender years, he worked hard at surviving, although according to his diaries he may have been a little better provided for than the literally starved majority of the people.[32] *Silent Snow* was brought to completion in May 1948 after eight long years, and the second translation of *The Tale of Genji* that began in 1950 was finished in 1954.

The publication in 1956 of *The Key (Kagi)* startled Japan's reading public, which took it to be an *apure-geru* specimen of America-induced sexual libertinism—although it was by a seventy-year-old recipient of Japan's most prestigious imperial Order of Culture. Certainly the story that describes in graphic detail a middle-aged English professor's nightly pastime—getting his wife drunk and taking Polaroid pictures of her inert naked body while she is unconscious, with the help of his daughter's fiancé—cannot help being read as such. A film based on the work, released in 1960, encouraged such a treatment of *The Key* both inside and outside Japan.[33] Tanizaki's novel, however, is unlikely to be just soft porn.

The finally indeterminate story suggests a vague outline: the husband's excitement as he watches his wife's body becomes intensified as he manages to involve the young man in the escapade. He wants his wife to participate in his pleasure, too, but not through bodily intercourse. The pleasure must be mediated by his "diary," which he expects her to read regularly, without admitting that she does so. The wife knows his plan and cooperates to an extent, although she has her own game plans and keeps her own "diary." Meanwhile, the young man's role gradually changes from a passive assistant voyeur to the wife's full-fledged lover. But even this transition is left deliberately unclear. The two tightly woven strands of conjecture, knowledge, and manipulation grow more and more entangled as *The Key* unlocks events. Points of uncertainty increase. Does the wife initiate her adultery or is she following her husband's subtle requests? Does her pleasure grow with her husband's knowledge? Does the husband enjoy the knowledge of her delight in his awareness of her infidelity? The role of their daughter in relation to this ménage à trois is also obscure. Is she aware of the affair between her mother and her fiancé? Does she participate in it? Is she a passive observer or an active intervener? All the answers provided in the two diaries are no more than invitations to the reader to further questions. At the moment of aroused curiosity the husband has a stroke while making love to his wife. With her husband paralyzed, the wife becomes the sole writer. But the change from the dialogic to monologic narrative form merely heightens the sense of uncertainty, especially since the wife's credibility has by now been thoroughly diminished. Furthermore, her knowledge of her own situation is also limited, after the husband's death changes the relationship between her and the young man. It is suggested at the end that she will not be the only writer of the plot for long: her daughter and the young man are about to enter the story as new clandestine readers.

The Key probes the pleasure of sex in its many dimensions—voyeurism, exhibitionism, necrophilia, foot-fetishism, masochism, and sadism, as well as simple carnality. *The Key* is also a funny book. It exaggerates the details in bold strokes and breaks up prurient concentration with grins and laughter. To take one example, the husband's last entry just before his stroke ends with a reference to his wife's ankles, a genuine Tanizaki trademark. No one could read the book for long without an occasional giggle. Of course, feminist readers may well object to this reading: after all, the husband's treatment of his wife is essentially necrophilia. Although this objection to *The Key* as sexist is finally sustainable, Tanizaki cannot be Tanizaki if he is that simple-minded. After the husband's stroke, there is a hilariously bizarre passage where the wife turns the tables by describing her husband's paralyzed nude body—as the doctor examines his scrotum. The wife is at least allowed to retaliate in this grotesque game of visual rape.

The book is also a study of writing and reading. The reader is urged on to grasp the unfolding events, but the attempt is always frustrated. There is a subtle query into the nature of inscription, for instance. As the husband lies inert, the wife must pretend to him that she is no longer keeping her diary now that he is not there to pry into it. But since she is in fact still continuing the habit, she must show him a blank notebook together with the old diary as if she had not written after he became ill. Here the two books, one inscribed and the other blank, are placed side by side, ironically suggesting the identity of their contents. Inscription is no different from blankness; they both tell lies.

The Key also opens up to a world in which communication has virtually ceased. The husband and wife never talk with each other, and if they write, the purpose of writing is to mislead, dissemble, and manipulate. The only available pleasure, sexual or otherwise, is finally the kind that cannot be shared and confirmed by the other; everyone is bound to his or her self-generated text, even when it is meant to be read by the other. And yet Tanizaki does not give up. Although the wife admits that she lured her husband "into the shadow of death," the wife also claims that she gave him "the kind of happiness he wanted."[34] Murder and love, too, seem to coincide, just as earlier the images of the husband and the young man became double images of the same person for both the wife and the husband in their moments of climax. In Tanizaki's world, faith and adultery merge, just as killing can be an act of love.

The same theme continues in *The Diary of a Mad Old Man*, serialized between 1961 and 1962. The work consists of the old man's diary entries, Tanizaki's favorite dramatic monologue form, this time with no dialogic responses. It is another tour de force, a brilliant examination of an old man and his decaying body. The story is quite simple: The aged "I" admires his son's young wife and, with the son's tacit understanding, tries to buy her favors with expensive gifts and other inducements. He is especially infatuated with her feet and is willing to go to any length to see, feel, and kiss them. The young daughter-in-law is totally undaunted and coolly takes advantage of the crazed old man's mendacity and her husband's unconcern. An unembarrassed comedy of foot fetishism, the work deliberately makes the old man out to be grotesquely ugly and, in contrast, his free and modern daughter-in-law to be stunningly attractive. Of course, the testimonies are all his own, and there is no way of verifying them.

With his characteristic control, Tanizaki allows the old man to make the most shocking admissions as if he were writing about matter-of-fact daily events: his earlier pederasty, his begging of a kiss in exchange for a cat's-eye ring, or his contemptuous disregard of his wife. He is always cool, even when he confronts his own incredibly ugly face in the mirror, because the uglier he is, "the more ravishingly beautiful" she looks.[35] He maintains distance from his body as if it were a trivial inconvenience. And as he senses the coming of death, he devotes all his energy to designing his grave.

His beatitude is the dream of lying dead under a tombstone carved with the young woman's footprints, passing for the Buddha's. Such ecstatic images are continually placed alongside the statistics of his pulse, blood pressure, and temperature, or the names of his drugs and the medical terms for his condition, as if the more diseased his body is, the more ecstatic his vision of the woman he worships. Tanizaki's comedy reaches a climax in the appended professional reports from the old man's nurse and doctor, declaring him to be not yet quite mentally ill. Tanizaki at seventy-six seems to gaze at his decaying body and remain amused by the follies he has perpetrated and is still ready to commit.

In his last works Tanizaki is no longer positioned between Japan and the West. In *The Diary of a Mad Old Man,* the old and the new mingle just as crazed fantasies and medical examinations mix and juxtapose. Tanizaki's lifelong exoticism, directed either toward the Other in the West or toward the Other in the past, has finally left him. Nothing is pristine, in fiction as in life. Despite the outrageous admission of follies and foibles, Tanizaki never gave up the habit of seeing, the exercise in criticism. Although he is not free from the charge of sexism, he was far more aware of his own foibles than nearly any other Japanese male contemporary. He has almost learned to live with the Other, and thus with himself.

Stepping beyond History:
Mishima Yukio

Much of Mishima Yukio's dazzling performance now looks merely flamboyant, or even kitschy. The list of his works is long, but the list of those that might as well remain unread is nearly as long. The few books I personally might reread are *Confessions of a Mask* (*Kamen no kokuhaku,* 1949), *The Sailor Who Fell from Grace with the Sea* (*Gogo no eiko,* 1963), the tetralogy, and a handful of short stories. But even these works have lost their luster. His prose, once hailed by Japanese critics as "classic," is stiff and snobbish rather than elegant or eloquent, targeted to a social imaginary that is embarrassingly adolescent or commodified. His plot and characters look staged—out of date and out of place—in today's Japan, where literature itself might be facing extinction. The books are also remarkably shapeless and incoherent, taxing the reader's patience, which might be better expended on other writers. And yet Mishima Yukio the man is still very much remembered, whether with respect or revulsion. The bloody image of his suicide at the end of the turbulent 1960s stands as a monument that violently and enigmatically sums up that crucial decade. What compels our attention and demands our understanding, therefore, is not Mishima the writer or the thinker but Mishima as a presence or an event.

Nowadays, any artist seems to receive less and less critical attention *qua* artist. Increasingly it is realized that an artist is deeply mired in his or her time and place; furthermore, art is felt to be dispersed, or "worldly,"[1] and the textuality of a work is seen to emerge only as the reader or critic recognizes or even forms it. Put another way, the notion of art as autonomous and ontological is itself a product of social and economic conditions whose time has long passed. In this sense, a historicized rereading of Mishima is as unexceptional as any reading of any writer. Yet the memory of Mishima seems to compel more emphatically this historicization, this contextualization within the 1960s, his last decade, during which *The Sea of Fertility (Hojo no umi)* was conceived and produced.

Such a reaction, however, is more pronounced within Japan, while Mishima is still being read abroad with a kind of seriousness that is not easily understandable to the Japanese reader. There was a Mishima revival in West Germany, France, and other European countries in recent years. In the spring of 1989, for instance, Ingmar Bergman staged Mishima's *Madame de Sade* (*Sado Koshaku Fujin*, 1965) in the Royal Theater of Stockholm; a few years earlier, Marguerite Yourcenar wrote *Mishima: A Vision of the Void* (trans. Alberto Manguel; New York: Farrar, Straus, and Giroux, 1986). More translations of his work have recently appeared in the United States, too. Several points must be noted here. First, obviously, Mishima is not owned by the Japanese, and anyone can read him in any way he or she pleases.[2] Second, Japanese intellectuals, having little confidence in their own judgment, often accept with docility evaluations made in the West about their own artists and writers. What is interesting here is that, for once, they are not buying the foreign assessment of Mishima's work. Yourcenar's praise—which is distinctly, and uncharacteristically, unintelligent and uninformed—has not affected the more or less unanimous rejection of Mishima in Japan. Does this mean that the Japanese are now gaining some confidence in their own cultural appreciation? Third, some critics have been speculating about the reasons for Mishima's popularity—or rather his status as the only Japanese writer read and remembered in the First World. The issues raised in my first Chapter might explain that to some degree; his construction of an exaggerated masculine body housing a psychologically feminine makeup might also provide some clues.[3]

The best comments on the matter come from a conversation between Oe Kenzaburo and Kazuo Ishiguro:

> *Ishiguro:* Mishima is very well known in England, or generally the West, largely because of the way he died. But also my suspicion is that the image of Mishima in the West confirms certain stereotypical images of Japanese people for the West. . . . in the West he is being used to confirm some rather negative stereotypes. I wonder what you think about Mishima and the way he died, what that means for Japanese people, and what that means for a distinguished author such as yourself.

> *Oe:* The observations you just made about the reception of Mishima in Europe are accurate. . . . It was the superficial image of a Japanese as seen from a European point of view, a fantasy. . . . [Mishima] said that [the European] image of the Japanese is me. I think he wanted to show something by living and dying in exact accordance with the image. That was the kind of man he was and why he gained literary glory in Europe and the world.[4]

I am curious to know if European and American readers are going to listen at least this once to Japanese views of these foreign views of Japan. It does seem about time.

Mishima was born in 1925, a year before Emperor Showa's reign began—not that this emperor's rule played a decisive role in the details of Mishima's everyday life, or even in the conduct of the state, at every moment. But the era of Showa was marked by violent turns deeply engulfing every citizen of the country: after the short span of the so-called Taisho democracy, it saw the rapid rise of nationalism and militarism around the time of the Depression, the bloody Fifteen-Year War, and the destruction and impoverishment that accompanied the inevitable defeat, along with the humiliation of the unprecedented foreign occupation. Within a few years, however, the U.S. Cold War policy enabled Japan to regain productivity at a rapid pace, and before the end of Mishima's life Japan had already been set on its way to monumental economic prosperity. How vulnerable and battered Mishima was in this swirl of history is obviously indeterminable, and yet his pose of dandyism and nonchalance, his studied loud laughter and exuberant wit, seem to have concealed a great deal. So does his fiction. For instance, his early

Confessions of a Mask, which masks the story of a life in the sense that its self-conscious tone, style, and mood carefully seek to transform a report into fiction, is thoroughly autobiographical. In Mishima's work concealment and revelation are always engaged; while an impulse to conceal resorts to transcendence, confessionalism binds his words to experience. Despite his vaunted cosmopolitan freedom, Mishima's work is finally saturated with the atmosphere of his time and place. Mishima was a writer of Showa Japan par excellence.

Younger than Tanizaki by a generation, Mishima had no recollection of Meiji Japan. Tanizaki had loved the downtown *(shitamachi)* Tokyo that had tenaciously preserved old Tokugawa merchant life. In his time an area of working-class people and their little shops and factories, it was still lively, unpretentious, and neighborly. As Tanizaki saw it being destroyed, first by the officious bureaucrats who lived in uptown *(yamanote)* Tokyo—largely uprooted provincial elites who had moved to Tokyo to construct a centralized state—and second by the great earthquake of 1923, he fled to Japan's "West."

Mishima was too young to know that part of Tokyo's history. Besides, he was born on the wrong side of the tracks. The Tokyo he knew was the city of bureaucrats, the uptown Tokyo, colorless, elitist, pretentious, formal, timid, humorless, unimaginative, conformist, repressed, methodical, obsequious, and arrogant—in short, horridly bourgeois. Not only did Mishima grow up in the upwardly mobile uptight Tokyo, he was reared by his grandmother, who lived in her memory of the old grandeur. Furthermore, he was educated at the power center of statism, an exclusive school managed by the Imperial Household Bureau. Since his father was no more than a second-rank civil servant who pulled himself up from a nondescript background largely by dint of a diploma from the Imperial Tokyo University, and since his claim to distinction rested solely on a remote connection to the shogunate through his grandmother, Mishima, a commoner student, must not have enjoyed the prewar snobbery of Gakushuin Schools. As an institution they were built on the principles of discrimination and difference. At the top were the emperor's children and relatives, then aristocrats, then the power elites of the empire. Belonging to none of these groups, Mishima was lonely and isolated despite his brilliance and precocity.

He was fatally ambivalent about being there. On the one hand, he was a snob enough to be proud of being among the snobs; on the other hand, he knew at every moment that he was not one of them—close enough to the center, but unreachably distanced from it. The seeds of his hunger for power and glitter were sown while he was still a young student there. No matter how hard he feigned to despise orthodoxy and hierarchy, he craved them so that he might reassure his fragile self and distance the threatening Other.

Tanizaki required difference, too. His strategy, however, was to place himself in a "foreign" space, thereby feeling humiliation and estrangement, which would then stir his fantasy and drive him to write. The world was condensed into the Kansai region, and his identification was more often than not with the marginal and decentered. His strategy was similar to that of Oe Kenzaburo, who was born in Shikoku, farther west than Kansai, and came to Tokyo for school in his late teens. The shock of dislocation from a mountain village to the metropolis was lived and relived throughout his writing career. With his remarkable scholarship in French, English, American, Italian, Russian, Asian, and other literatures (and many languages), Oe constructed an imaginary village with its own history and geography that at times overlap with those of Japan—seen, however, from a distinctly off-center perspective. In contrast to Tanizaki and Oe, Mishima audaciously insisted on his centralist position.

As I discussed in Chapter 4, the first task that most leftover intellectuals undertook in 1945 was to resurrect themselves as closet liberals, pacifists, humanists, democrats, westernists, or Marxists at last freed from police and militarist control. They were eager to claim legitimacy as the leaders of a new Japan by learning or re-learning "democracy." The transformation was not so much a voluntary act as a response to the orders of the Supreme Commander of the Allied Powers. Thus, not surprisingly, there were a few who remained faithful to the myth and ideology of emperorism. This small minority despised the new-fangled democratic humanists as unsightly hypocrites. They were silent, biding their time just as the liberals and leftists supposedly did during the war years.

Mishima was too young to have had to confront the choice, but he was old enough to remember the barbaric and attractive simplicity of nativist indoctrination. As long as he subscribed to the faith during the war, he had no need to question and rationalize. Reason always followed faith, and besides, the impending death in the course of the war only heightened the erotic thrill of commitment to it. Such an abandonment of the self paradoxically provided a self-enclosed space that was under no threat of outside interference. As Mishima witnessed the unseemly sight of the postwar converts now dancing to a different tune in the ever-looming presence of the Occupation authorities, he reacted by devising an imaginary nativist style of elegance and force, which he recovered from the wartime fabrication of courtly grace and martial discipline. Violence was to supplement beauty. Such a concern with style was always vital to Mishima, because style was capable, when properly utilized, of sidestepping history. By inventing the idea of "traditional form" that presumably escapes time by enduring, Mishima, and others like him, clung to his remembered faith and managed to sail over the wildly shifting tide of events. Nostalgia for old Japan enabled these Romantics *(Roman-ha)* to ignore the American interlopers in their land; it also allowed them to remain aloof from the opportunistic liberal converts. Mercifully for them, the sway of Western liberal democracy lasted only briefly in Japan.

The Supreme Commander actively supported the continuation of the emperor system, although the emperor's leadership in the war and the complicity of the imperial system with militarism were nearly unanimously recognized by both Japanese and American intellectuals in the immediate postwar years. Wartime leaders were quietly brought back, and the ideology of centralized state power was reinstated. The institution of parliamentary democracy of course received endorsement from the United States, as did the postwar Constitution. But the political pluralism was in name only; and the Constitution, too, was continually subjected to reinterpretation. Thus the rule of the conservative Liberal Democratic Party has been practically uninterrupted since 1955, and the resurrection of the military in the so-called Self-Defense Force was—at least at its inception—a product of the changed U.S.-East Asian defense policy. The emperor and the imperial system were modified under the new Constitution, but their position and role in the state structure were removed from further query and challenge. Japan's democracy was thus more a consensual style than a political ideology.

The decade of the sixties was as crucial to the future of Japan as it was to that of the United States. It began with a violent year. In 1960 the ratification of the revised Japan-U.S. Mutual Security Agreement was before the Diet, and the issue rocked the entire nation. The conservative party in power favored a capitalist alliance with the United States, while the opposition, consisting of labor unions, students, and city voters, feared that remilitarized Japan would be swallowed up by U.S. hegemony, and so they advocated independence and nonalliance. Unprecedented demonstrations raged in the streets of Tokyo. The progressives were well organized, and yet they failed to penetrate beyond the educated middle class. In fact, at no time during the period of protest in 1960 did the agitation spread outside the limited bourgeois opposition to the program of remilitarization under U.S. patronage. The minority problems, the working conditions of the poor, and Japan's war atrocities in Asia—in Korea, for instance, or even in Okinawa—were all excluded from the focus of the struggle. Thus once the revised Security Pact was ratified, the opposition crumbled fast, although the prime minister was forced to resign under the pressure from the opposition. And with the continuing high economic growth in the following years, aided by U.S. demand for goods and services, the succeeding prime minister's promise of doubling the per capita income no longer sounded like just a campaign pledge.[5]

Throughout the sixties, especially after the intensification of the war in Vietnam, Japan served as the logistic depot of the U.S. forces in the Far East, which meant a rapid and great expansion of economic and industrial capacities. Japan was increasingly obsessed with economic success. What began as a dream increasingly became a realizable program, as the Japanese began to think about economic self-sufficiency, security, prosperity, and finally leadership and even domination of the world scene. High-growth economy, based on centralized planning, concentrated investment in production plants and equipment, and governmental aid to the basic industries and giant corporations, in addition to the hard-working, frugal, and disciplined populace, swiftly transformed Japan from a war-ravaged importing country into a comfortable exporting country by 1965. National unity was seen as the key to success, and the ideology of agreement and homogeneity was carefully tailored to fit the program for prosperity. Few were tempted to resist it.

It ought to be recalled here that the same sixties were a time of dissent and conflict in the United States. The civil rights, anti-war, and university reform movements—soon to be followed by women's liberation—formed the foci of the protest during that decade that divided the nation in private homes, in the inner cities, on the campuses, and at the seats of power. Conflict often exploded into violence. John F. Kennedy, Malcolm X, Martin Luther King, and Robert Kennedy were assassinated, and behind these bloody events loomed a far bloodier drama, the war in "postcolonial" Vietnam. The global hegemony of the United States was for the first time visibly shaken, and Japan began an imperceptible move toward the challenger's position.

The decade of the sixties, marked by such bloody violence, was also a period in which the American people took it upon themselves to reexamine the course of their nation's conduct and their responsibility for it. Dissatisfied with their leaders' decisions and counsel, a large number of people sought to participate in the conduct of the state. If their idealism was often undisciplined and disorderly, it led to what was at least in the earlier stages a genuine popular uprising. Thus every social assumption and practice was exposed to scrutiny. The issues of U.S. hegemony were at once linked to those of domestic injustice, and the questions of academic freedom, intellectual responsibility, racial equity, and equal rights for both sexes were argued in public places with the same vehemence. And although its immediate impact was largely limited to clamorous protests and demonstrations against the state without much tangible effect, the spirit of criticism and inquiry was not completely quenched at the end of the Vietnam war. The passion for protest, however, waned before long, and in the mid-1970s and 1980s apathy, cynicism, and egoism seemed to replace idealism. And yet under the surface the spirit of critical inquiry has continued to survive into the 1990s, even if it has not risen to inspire a new collective movement. In different areas of concern—in minorities discourse, in feminist criticism, in the earlier stages of deconstruction, and in environmental studies—criticism and opposition are by no means extinct even now.

The Japanese uprising in 1960 had a different outcome. As the opposition was defeated, progressive intellectuals, who were no longer in tune with students or labor forces, withdrew into their bourgeois daily lives, as if their real concern had been simply Japan's national independence from the United States rather than a more general criticism of modern history and Japan's place in it. The Marxists' demoralization resulting from the revelations of the Stalinist horrors no doubt played a role in this, but the subsequent apathy of the intellectuals is better explained in terms of the phenomenal rise in the standard of living. As long as their criticism was targeted mainly to limited domestic issues, they found less and less to criticize. There were sporadic protests around environmental issues (including the still ongoing opposition to the construction of the Narita Airport outside Tokyo) in the 1970s, and this environmentalist movement preceded those in Europe and the United States. But the ruling conservatives no longer found it necessary to engage ideologically with the left. Serious oppositions dissolved as consumerism grew. When the Mutual Security Agreement came up again for ratification in 1970, it was the more isolated and radicalized students who took the main brunt of the establishment's suppression. Their professors were no longer with them. Very much like their pre-1945 counterparts, the intellectuals were once again allied with the ruling managers of the state. The Liberal Democratic Party felt quite secure about itself and its future.

Mishima Yukio was very much a man of his age. His fiction—which was never completely comfortable with the personal[6]—began to take on public issues toward 1960. His postwar strategy of transcendence was brought down by peace and prosperity to confront his own time. How was he to distinguish his aestheticism from the aesthetics of consumerism? All around him he saw the preoccupation with commodities, which, though always seductive and available, could never be other than temporarily satisfying, if not outright demeaning. And yet he saw himself very much immersed in the culture of consumption: more than just a bon vivant, Mishima knew he was an unashamed commodity fetishist. He liked to talk about Tiffany and Jaeger. He bought and displayed brand-name goods. His bizarre "Western" house was his own design, in which he took unrestrained pride, although he tried to conceal his vulgar satisfaction behind nonchalant laughter. Still, he was restless. The fulfillment he sought was becoming increasingly elusive as the comforts and satisfactions of daily life diluted intellectual and spiritual exercise. Mishima needed an absolute that was both spiritual and erotic, which would allow him to escape from the lifeless politics of homogeneity and agreement. His snobbery and arrogance were to serve as a gateway to ecstasy. After the critical failure of *Kyoko's Home* (*Kyoko no ie,* 1960), which allegorized contemporary Japan, Mishima's work became more and more explicitly engaged with the problems of the day. But where was the way out and beyond?

For Mishima the answer had to be found in the memory of his earlier years. His adolescent fixation on early death (which preserves unaging youth, that is, changeless beauty), his attraction to young men (which is cleansed of the muck of procreation and domesticity), and above all his enchantment with the threat and thrill of extinction (which lets one forget the boredom of bourgeois life) suggested a powerful aesthetics that would take him out of history once again. Paradoxically, however, this strategy against history required a gesture of politics. For Mishima must be different, must be among the select. And in order to attain to the distinction, he needed a bridge to the transcendent, a means to overcome the mundanity of democracy, and a legitimation of his snobbery. Psychology must thus be justified by politics, just as aesthetics must be transformed into politics. Insofar as Mishima's last work needed to be dignified, it had to borrow the form of an epic, a myth, a public spectacle—unhistorical politics, aesthetic politics, or rather politicized aesthetics, but aesthetics nonetheless. It was the space Mishima needed in order to cope with the society of reproduction and cloning in which he was forced to live.

At the 1960 protest against the U.S.-Japan security pact, Mishima remained an observer. As his sense of personal and national crisis intensified in the sixties, however, he began to think of a scheme for his final work, which would coincide with his final action. No one knows, of course, when he began to think of self-termination, but it is fairly clear that by 1962 he had conceived *The Sea of Fertility,* his last work, which would involve imperial absolutism, self-destruction, and reincarnation.[7] The thematic determination was nearly inevitable. His earlier works all tended toward that choice. *The Sailor Who Fell from Grace with the Sea* (1963), for instance, is about a hero who ought to have lived dangerously and kept his glory instead of playing it safe and turning domestic. The sailor must be murdered as the punishment for his betrayal of fate. As Mishima approached his fortieth birthday, he felt his time was running out, and by extension he thought Japan, too, was facing at least the end of an era. He must write his final story that would show the world how to experience an end. He must also act out that end.

Mishima's will was not to interpret but to present. His fiction, which always tries to conceal and at the same time reveal, is thus inhabited with melodramatic, not dramatic, characters. The melodrama's hero was easily supplied by his autoerotic imagination, but its quasi-epic side needed another hero, the public god who would send the characters to their commedia of joys and return them to their tragic ends. The causus primus of the tale was to be found in the person of the emperor *ex cathedra,* whose denial of divinity after the defeat, as Mishima saw it, had turned Japan into a cultural and spiritual desert, the lunar *Mare Foecunditatus.* Although no emperor makes his personal appearance in any of the four volumes, the tetralogy is meant to be full of the imperial deity, either in presence or in absence.

The events narrated in the tetralogy cover sixty years, beginning at the second decade of the twentieth century. *Spring Snow* (*Haru no yuki,* 1965–67), the first volume, is set in 1912 and ends in 1913, the first year of Emperor Taisho's reign; the next volume, *Runaway Horses* (*Honba,* 1967–68), moves on to around 1932 during Hirohito's rule, when Japan's invasion of Manchuria had already commenced. The second half of the tetralogy, *The Temple of Dawn* (*Akatsuki no tera,* 1968–70) and *The Decay of the Angel* (*Tennin gosui,* 1970–71) are set in the postwar years after the emperor renounced his divinity in 1946.[8] The first two volumes are related at least thematically to the monarch's presence, one with its simulation of the Meiji/Taisho production of "graceful" Heian court life and the other with its invention of martial loyalty to the sovereign. The two are Mishima's pastoral quasi-Hollywood hymns to beauty and force in Japan's past as he reconstructs it. The last two volumes, on the other hand, describe the world from which the emperor has absconded. The emperor having now declared himself a democratic "symbol," a sort of rational political institution, his mystery is, according to Mishima, gone and Japan has lost its center. The war dead have all died in vain.

Through these works, one character, Honda, is always present, watching everything that goes on around him. The hero of the first volume is Honda's friend; each succeeding volume is provided with a new main character who is his reincarnation. The theme of metempsychosis, complete with the sign of three moles in the armpit, is at times hilarious, although laughter can hardly be the intended effect. The four tales placed at twenty-year intervals are meant to coincide with the transmigrating soul's incarnation at crucial moments in twentieth-century Japan's history; each lives for twenty years and after death is reborn in the next character's body. For many readers, the identifying nevoid signs serve merely as a plea for them to read the tetralogy as if it were a coherent story. *The Sea of Fertility* was obviously meant to be a serious statement.

The first half of the tetralogy presents Japan positively, under the heavenly guidance of the emperor. In *Spring Snow,* supposedly modeled after the twelfth-century *Hamamatsu chunagon monogatari (The Tale of Middle Counselor Hamamatsu),* fabrication of the past is at full pitch.[9] The elegant aristocratic life of pre–World War I Japan that this volume depicts is a romantic simulation, oblivious to the dire poverty of the majority of people as well as to the bottom-line shabbiness of Japan's upper classes at the time. Had he been serious about history, Mishima might have filled the book with the complex relations of power, violence, and order—the ruthless uses of force and machination that greatly contributed to the making of Meiji Japan. For Mishima, however, these were the halcyon days from which every sequence has been only a decline: the characters are young, rich, and beautiful, and they even choose to die young. The hero's love for the heroine is passionless until the heroine becomes affianced to a royal prince with the imperial blessing. The young lovers are now inflamed, and defiance of the imperial taboo, a challenge to the will of the absolute, elevates physical sexuality to a spiritual ecstasy. Somewhat like Tanizaki Junichiro, who invented a sumptuous world of elegance and wealth during the bleakest war years in *Silent Snow,* Mishima demonstrates what might be possible with the return of the *deus abscondus.*

The second tale continues on a positive note. This tale of a youthful right-wing assassin indeed comes even closer to Mishima's agenda at the time. The increasingly militaristic climate of Japan in the thirties was still not radical enough for nationalistic activists. In their eyes, the ruling circle of the imperial advisors was liberal, pro-Western, and degenerate, and must be liquidated. The young patriots involved in several coup attempts in the thirties had reached no consensus about the political form of the so-called Showa restoration. Some believed in direct rule and guidance by the imperial authority; others, like Kita Ikki, wanted the restoration as a means for a revolution that resembled in some ways that of National Socialism.[10] Mishima read the history and forged his version. The instrument of change must be heroic violence, as he saw it, purified by fierce loyalty. His young activist schemes for an armed insurrection. Totally idealistic and completely ineffectual, he gets caught before putting his plan into practice. Although this part ends with the young man's successful killing of a prime target, the tale's drama is not so much in the eventful plot as in the idea of the sanctity of the emperor, the fierce loyalty of the youthful samurai, and their "pure" male bonding. The ideology tends at every point to assert itself in separation from the narrative drive.

Mishima's idea of the samurai was a fantastic revision of the historical Tokugawa bureaucrats, who needed a warrior's mask to hide their parasitic existence. He could have detected the bureaucracy and commercialism of the samurai employment contract that passed for "selfless loyalty,"[11] but Mishima was in love with violence without knowing violence firsthand. He was too much in need of a theology and aesthetics of emperorism to be bothered by history. Here one might compare Mishima's hero of this volume with Oe's activist in *The Silent Cry* (*Manen gannen no futtoboru,* 1967) where violence and activism are ruthlessly scrutinized side-by-side with contemplation and stagnation. Mishima is less concerned, at any rate, with the overall argument of *The Sea of Fertility* than with drawing separate images, such as the rising sun before which the young hero commits harakiri, or with composing an unintegrated tract on a nineteenth-century samurai revolt against the new government.

The first two volumes at least have continuity, and they struggle to hang together. Despite the distracting insertion of the Shimpuren insurrectionist tract, the second volume manages to propose an alterity, a divergence, a disagreement, albeit unreasonable, violent,

and ineffectual. In the second half of the tetralogy, however, such
interest in telling a story and urging a course of action seems largely
dissipated.[12] Of course, the events, now set in the postwar days and
thus after the disappearance of god, are of necessity depraved, and
the scenery is bound to be barren. And yet the sense of futility one
experiences in reading the second half comes not from the book's
depiction of an arid land but from the design of the book itself, which
is now torn by disparate impulses in several directions. The frag-
mentation already evident in the second tale is more substantial in
the third volume, which is divided into two nearly unrelated parts.
The story moves to Thailand for no particular reason, except for a
vague suggestion of *Hamamatsu chunagon monogatari.* The author
mechanically lectures on Buddhism as if he had nothing else to think
of doing. All the details involving Thai aristocracy, lesbian liaisons,
and senile voyeurism seem dreary, not so much to the reader as to
the author. In the last tale, *The Decay of the Angel,* the distraction
is not an encyclopedic entry as in volume three but rather the young
hero's diary. And if the diary's entry reads very much like Mishima's
earlier works such as *Confessions of a Mask* or *The Temple of the
Golden Pavilion,* the reader finally finds the fact unimportant. The
author does not seem to care, and at this point the reader cares even
less.

What is by now clear is Mishima's own boredom with the work.
He had lived through the war, when everything was reduced to the
bare essentials of survival. The intensity of the experience enabled
life to swing wildly between ecstasy and despair. As long as day-to-
day living was an uphill struggle, there remained a clear objective
that organized details of life into meaning. In the sixties era of high
economic growth, however, such amplitude of passion was reduced
to the monotone of reasonableness. Bourgeois happiness leveled
everything. Every citizen aspired to the same tepid goal, reasoned
in the same routine fashion, and was more or less content. Collective
consumerism resulted in a peace that, as Mishima saw it, was
nothing but a living death. His rage against the barrenness of living
and the repetitiousness of pain and pleasure had to explode in the
stillness of the void that postwar Japan had now become.

The parts of a tetralogy are usually related: the four poets in the
renga practice, Beethoven's last four quartets, or the four seasons

in a Chinese screen painting. Mishima's tetralogy, however, is not held together by any promise, hope, change, or contrast. No telos drives the four parts; there is only deadly repetition. Mishima cannot have believed that the birthmarks alone could unify the four incarnations (the original, plus two real and one inauthentic). Nothing less trivial, however, connects the four parts. The books fall apart, as do the idea, the statement, and the ideology. After imperial grace vanishes, all that is left is futility, ugliness, and boredom—not in the life narrated, but in the narrative itself. The sameness of daily life alone, in interminable ennui and indifference, replicates itself. The simulated political violence—assassination, terrorism, and insurrection—is also delusive. It is in this all-pervasive sterility and boredom that *The Sea of Fertility* is inscribed.[13]

To the extent that it intends to reassert Japan's cultural and national identity as separable from all-encompassing Western "universalism," *The Sea of Fertility* fails to define its distinguishing features. Postwar Japan may be a history of failed attempts to simulate the West. Japan in the sixties may have required a fundamental reexamination of its place in the world. Furthermore, Japan's liberal-conservative orthodoxy may indeed have stifled intellectual pluralism and diversity. But Mishima's version of the alterity to modernization and Westernization is merely self-indulgence. The ill effects of Japan's economic expansion cannot be undone by stylized emulations of courtly elitism and samurai violence. There must be a thorough study of Japan's past as well as the West's; the economics of production and consumption and its impact on the critical intellect must also be understood. Mishima was right in detecting the dismal futility of culture in the 1960s, which has continued to hover over Japan through the 1980s and into the 1990s. In attempting to flee from history, however, Mishima seems to have failed utterly.

It is important to recall that Mishima's emperor, according to *The Defence of Culture* (*Bunka boei ron,* 1968) and other essays, is not a political institution. Unlike ultra-nationalists—who range from Kita Ikki, the militarist revolutionary of the thirties, to Eto Jun, a current leading revivalist, and who advocate the emperor's meta-constitutional political position—Mishima defines the emperor as the spiritual and cultural center that would sustain the essence and purity of the Japanese. Because the divine emperor would constitute the Other to the people, also providing an alterity to the modernized, Westernized, and depraved Japan, the nation could again be creative, generative, and erotic. Also because he would be divine, and thus transtemporal and metahistorical, Japan would be seen as pure style, evading all historical restrictions. Mishima's version of emperorism is thus a proposal against the growing ideology of homogeneity as an instrument for high economic growth. In this view, democracy, either capitalist or socialist, is an imported uniformalist idea that deprives Japan of its unique spirituality.

Crazed though this cultural/political discourse might seem as a whole, it contains at least a shrewd reading of Japan's official cancellation of heterogeneity. Mishima's emperorism could be seen as a prescription for the restoration of heteroglossia. As Tanizaki required the "west" to be his Other and found it in the western parts of Japan, Mishima had to find his Other overtly in anti-democracy and covertly in homosexuality. He was maddeningly wrong at the same time in failing to see that the homogenization of the people was inseparable from the very emperorism he was trumpeting.[14] The emperor as the sanctified and eroticized Other is bound to be a device for elimination of Otherness altogether. And yet Mishima refused to choose; he wanted both.

Mishima was contemptuous of the fragility of the postwar Constitution, which could be amended only regressively. The 1947 Constitution that defines the emperor as the national "symbol of the State and of the unity of the people" (as if the word "symbol" had nothing to do with "representation") is hopelessly ambiguous and vague. The emperor is not allowed to take any political action of his own, since he is merely a symbol; at the same time, as long as he is the symbol of the unity of the people, people are expected to be unified and conform. The emperor can be an instrument, or even a coercer, of unity among his people, suppressing dissent and heterogeneity. Thus the Constitution guarantees or restricts little or nothing as to the emperor's interventionary power. Likewise, the renunciation of the armed forces is subject to compromise, as it in fact has been compromised from nearly the beginning of its proclamation. The emperor is securely written into the fabric of Japanese society, and the likelihood of republicanism is nil for the foreseeable future. And yet Mishima wanted the apolitical return of the old absolutism—without ever spelling out the costs.

The chronology of *The Sea of Fertility* progresses steadily. The last volume, which began serial publication in July 1970, opens with the description of an event supposedly taking place in May 1970. A fussy reader will note that its Section 17 depicts the month of October 1970, and Section 18 refers to 1971, skipping over a few months. As we recall, Mishima's suicide took place on November 25, 1970, a date that is conspicuously printed on the last page of the tetralogy as the date of its completion. Although there is no doubt that Mishima took great care in giving the impression of the simultaneity of the two events (the completion and the suicide), nothing happens on the fictional day of November 25 in the narrative of *The Sea of Fertility*. What is interesting, however, is that the novel, which continued to appear in a periodical until January 1971, continues to narrate events that are set in the future. In the famous last scene, set in a temple garden, Honda, the book's consistent narrative voice, meets again the heroine of the first volume after three books and some thousand pages and is told that she had never once met the hero of *Spring Snow*. And this climactic scene is set in July 1975, nearly five years after the author's death! If *The Sea of Fertility* was to be a tale of incarnation, and the myth of the immortal imperial deity, Mishima could not have been mindless of this transmigration of his life into his fictional characters. Mishima died and lived in his fiction. Is this meant to be his last prank? A challenge to history's inevitable force? No doubt a thin joke, it still prophesies the possibility of reincarnation, if not of Mishima or his characters, then of the myth of the emperor who as he dies seems to live once again. An omen of an untoward future? It is a chilling thought as one tries to laugh off the bored sterility of *The Sea of Fertility*.

Problems

Out of Agreement:
The Emperor and Christmas

If the critical rage of 1988 in the United States was postmodernism, that of 1989 was the Other—colonialism, feminism, minorities, multi-cultures, alterity. And 1990 might be remembered as the moment of retrogression, the "triumph" of capitalism and power. What is interesting about these developments is that many works in cultural criticism seem to keep reverting to a concern with the circumference of the self, either in self-adoration or in self-loathing, as if solipsism were the inevitable destination of all speculation.[1] The situation was not markedly different in Japan. This chapter focuses on a few uses of the idea of the Other and their cultural and political significance: first, Emperor Hirohito's death and the use of the event as a means to suppress the Other; then, several war films that treat inter-national encounters. The objective is to examine the circuit of gaze from the point of origination (the observing self) to the object of scrutiny (the observed Other), then to further terminals of seeing (onlookers, bystanders, reflections, mirrors) to determine the nature of inequality and imbalance among the powers of those involved and their effects on the definitions of both self and Other.

Hirohito the Symbol

The Japanese emperor has been positioned at the site of generating power since the mid-nineteenth century, when the formation of a modern nation-state was felt to be an urgent need in the face of Western colonialist threats. The Tokugawa shogunate was no longer able to keep Japan unified enough to respond to such threats, and the reinvention of the myth of imperial Japan was found to be both necessary and effective. A young emperor was thus recovered out of the shadows of the shogunate. How much power the emperor's office or person has in fact wielded since then is a matter yet to be settled.[2] The old constitution "granted" from above by Emperor Meiji one hundred years ago specifically defines the emperor as Japan's sovereign and the head of its imperial armed forces, calling him "sacred" and "inviolable." By assigning the emperor a meta-legal position, the Meiji framers made the whole legal structure a-legal, that is, overtly political. In pre-1945 Japan, the state could initiate whatever policy it found expedient domestically or abroad, in the name of the emperor within the framework of the ever malleable constitution.

Constitutions are not the same everywhere, of course: some are more constitutional than others, and the Meiji version is an example of lesser legalism. At any rate, *de facto* emperorism does not seem to have amounted to a full dictatorship; nor does it seem to have been a mere ornament at any point in the last hundred years. The truth lies somewhere in between, although far closer to the absolutist end. Hirohito's war responsibility—in the sense that he knowingly approved of the commencement of war and participated in its conduct—is indisputable. Whether he could have had the power to alter radically the course of war against the will of his "advisors," and to what extent, are perhaps slightly more arguable. Regardless, Hirohito's war responsibility, if not criminality, was nearly universally recognized at the end of the war until the United States changed its policy regarding Japan in the context of the Cold War.[3] Under the new Constitution, literally dictated by the U.S. Occupation Forces, the emperor is defined as "the symbol of the State and of the unity of the people,"[4] and this vague phrasing contains the genie who might create quite a bit of mischief, given an opportunity.

What has intervened between the Japan of 1945 and the Japan of 1990 is of course its subsequent recovery and prosperity, hardly planned or predicted by the United States or Japan at the initial stage. With the phenomenal advance in its economic power, its political influence, too, is on the rise, although in a far quieter fashion. Despite such changes in the politico-economic conditions, however, what is often called the "cultural" realm has shown little alteration. Japanese society is still seen by outsiders as closed, provincial, exotic, traditional—with all its characteristics and mythological qualities such as aestheticism, unintellectualism, and collectivism still intact. Japan's social imaginary remains outside the mainstream of world civilization. It still is the alien Other to most people outside Japan. Whether motivated by a self-sufficient narcissism, a reactive defensiveness, or an economic strategy, most Japanese, too, regard themselves as unique and therefore unchangeable—albeit with variants.

To the extent that Japan finds and wants itself to be separate from the rest, the emperor myth and system function quite well. According to this myth, all Japanese nationals are genealogically, if not genetically, connected to the emperor at some fantastically remote point in the past, at the beginning, so to speak. (I have in mind here Kenneth Burke's idea of "the temporizing of the essence."[5]) The nation is strategically compared to a family. As the emperor's "children" (sekishi) offered their lives to defend their "father" in wartime, so in peacetime all its citizens are said to share a common objective, interest, and taste ("the unity of the people").[6] One might recall here Matthew Arnold's culturalist strategy in nineteenth-century England. Arnold would invoke Edmund Burke to conjure up the mythical "state" that presided over strife-ridden nineteenth-century British society, divided among the three classes of the Barbarians, Philistines, and Populace. For Arnold, the idea of culture is the solvent for conflicts not only between the past and the present, but also among religious sects and class interests. The function of his culture was to depoliticize social criticism and to promote "disinterestedness," so that a secular, liberal, capitalist political ideology might be quietly reinserted into the English nation.[7] For Japan's cultural planners, Arnold's mythical state is already inscribed in the office and person of the emperor. Even under the new Constitution, he can demonstrate that his state consists in a homogeneous and classless people, whom he "symbolizes," though not "represents," as the changeless essence of their culture. Far more easily than Matthew Arnold did, the Japanese cultural planners have discovered a formula for the elimination of difference inside Japan.

How effectively this formula works even in peacetime—at the height of prosperity without any external threat—was shown during the recent death of Emperor Showa, the state funeral, and the new emperor's succession soon thereafter. During Hirohito's final illness which lasted for three months and a half, the Japanese were placed under so-called self-restraint (*jishuku*). The extent of the restraint was startling: loud music, drinking parties, neon advertisements, foreign travel, festivities, or any other highly visible events were restricted or canceled. Most entertainment performances were allowed to continue, presumably as long as they were contained within a definite and inconspicuous site. There were no explicit rules of conduct because—and this is a little unsettling—people tacitly understood what to do and what not to do. Does this mean, then, that the restraint was truly self-imposed? That there was widespread agreement about the need for some sort of ritual expression—restraint—is beyond doubt. At the same time, it is also unquestionable that a sizable number of people were deeply disturbed by this conformist and repressive gesture. It is more than probable that most people were not very interested in the event one way or the other: for them, like most bourgeois in any other society, state occasions were a matter of mild curiosity, no more. And yet the country, reputed to be wholly obsessed with money, lost a considerable portion of its national production in this program of self-control. When the emperor finally proved himself to be mercifully mortal, the country went into mourning, and "self-restraint" was once again unofficially proclaimed.

There are aspects of the event that are truly fascinating as well as disturbing: people's responses and media representation. First, what was the nature of this "universal" self-restraint? Did it accurately reflect the feelings of the general public? After the emperor's death, there was a show of grief over the end of the Showa era (1926–1989), a long and eventful reign by any standard, and, according to the media, the whole nation was redolent with reminiscences of the experiences during this period. The wartime images of the emperor on a white horse, the devastation of Japanese cities and the destruction in China and elsewhere, as well as scenes from the recently prosperous Japan, inundated the channels of communication. According to one report, however, video rentals soared during the funeral week, when the media broadcast only emperor-related news and documentaries. In order to retain its audience, the National Broadcasting Corporation (NHK) was forced to cancel the last day of what had been planned as a three-day program.[8] Further, there were numerous letters to the newspapers protesting the excess in restraint and challenging the legitimacy of the emperor system.[9] Although a poll taken in February 1989—soon after the new emperor was enthroned—overwhelmingly supported the institution of the emperor as the national symbol (retain, 83 percent; abolish, 10 percent; strengthen, 4 percent), it also showed the people as divided regarding the question of Emperor Hirohito's war responsibility (can't decide, 38 percent; no responsibility, 31 percent; responsible, 25 percent).[10] In short, there was a strong undercurrent beneath the public exhibition that does not seem to have received fair representation.

Second, no one knows, or seems to care, precisely where this "restraint" was generated. Were there identifiable instigators in this interminable "spontaneous" expression of concern and grief? The national government no doubt set the tone, taking the cue from the nexus of the Prime Minister's office, the ruling party, and the Imperial Household Agency. The municipal governments transmitted it throughout the country, establishing a network of message services to convey people's concern *(kicho)*. And business organizations—chambers of commerce, trade associations, and the like—of course cooperated. But is Japan so well knit as to enable a single chain of command to be so effective? Why was the opposition so enervated and unorganized?

The typical newspaper pages seem to have been carefully planned and formatted to provide the reader with all sorts of unsorted and fragmented responses, both pro and con, on the emperor issues. They seemed also to have aimed at leaving the reader with an overall impression that these were unimportant differences. They seemed persuaded, and ready to persuade others, that people were more or less in agreement—despite their differences—on the larger question of emperorism as a needed institution. The brief items offered consisted of simplified arguments, supplemented with similarly abbreviated episodes (such as an old woman tearfully reminiscing about her only son, killed in Okinawa, or a young man kneeling in the dusk on the Palace ground). Scholars and commentators were of course mobilized, but they were either given small space or placed in a roundtable discussion *(zadankai)*[11] where coherent views, if there were any, were deliberately or inevitably pulverized. Magazines and periodicals devoted whole issues to the topic, but most were produced in similar formats—clichéd views, fragmented impressions, declamatory assertions, and the ubiquitous *zadankai*. The enormous journalistic output more than satiated the public, but left little space for sustained criticism.[12]

Third, does this mean that Japan had succeeded in eliminating all elements of alterity? Were all Japanese editors of one opinion, and was there no possibility whatever of serious dissent, strife, protest, or even disagreement? The mayor of Nagasaki's statement on Hirohito's war responsibility in December 1988 apparently provoked 7,600 people to write to him. Out of these, a mere 600 were critical or condemnatory of the mayor.[13] And yet this minority seems to have pressured the majority into nearly complete agreement with them. Even after the mayor was the target of an assassination attempt on January 18, 1990, the protest demonstration in his support in Tokyo organized by two noted writers gathered only a hundred people, swelling later to two hundred.[14] Many of the writers of letters to the newspapers who were unusually animated about the nature of "self-restraint" also requested anonymity for fear of a possible right-wing retaliation.[15] Indeed, when *Sekai,* one of the very few surviving serious journals of opinion, published a critical roundtable discussion about the conduct of the media after the emperor's death, the periodical had to print it without disclosing the identities of the concerned journalists who participated.[16] Fear was palpable all around, and it was indisputably accountable for the unanimity in press reports, or nonreports.

Perhaps even more disturbing—for us in the United States—was the deafening silence of most American Japan experts. Unlike the

Japanese, they were under no threat of violence. On the contrary, they were now in a favored position, since many of their Japanese colleagues needed their counsel and support. And yet these Japanologists either remained silent or, worse, made fatuous, unsupported remarks such as the statement that the emperor had been a consistent peace leader opposed to the militarists.[17] One can only speculate as to what motivated the silence in the United States and Britain. Was it fear of possible retaliation from Japanese government agencies? Or more simply, the loss of research aid and grants? The fearful suppression of difference, self-generated or otherwise, seemed to spread across the Pacific.

What is curious is the media coverage of a certain period after the funeral. A few weeks after the torrent of imperial trifles spilled over every form of publication, the coverage abruptly stopped: no remark whatever on the emperor, the dead one or his living son, was to be seen anywhere. As far as I can determine, all memory of the death, funeral, not to say life, of the last emperor was completely erased from the papers for several weeks. Aside from some gossip about the current empress and other royal relatives, not even the new emperor was mentioned in any publication.[18] Did people at last reach the point of saturation with imperial matters? Were the prime minister's scandals, which followed Hirohito's death, so absorbing that all that had preceded was forgotten?

There was another imperial event in the spring of 1990. The new emperor's son fell in love with a commoner's daughter and demanded that he be allowed to marry her—with a threat that in the case of denial, he would resign his royal status. Although the crown prince, his elder brother, had not yet married, his parents—and the usually adamant Imperial Household Agency—gave in, and people seem to have responded warmly. The media, and a reported majority of people, apparently became enchanted with the romance. The memory of Hirohito's death seemed to lapse swiftly. Perhaps Japan's consumerism is radically reducing the attention span of its population—quick to get excited, and even quicker to cool down. Or is someone controlling the mood and temper of the entire nation? But then who has the magic wand? If the substance of history is conflict and struggle, is history over in Japan? Has Alexander

Kojeve's post-history finally arrived?[19] Once again, there seems to be no one in Japan—nor in the world outside—who is curious about such questions.

I had a visitor from Japan recently, an intelligent and sophisticated scholar who had just finished a two-year period of study and teaching in France. He had kept in touch with what went on in Japanese intellectual life. According to this professor of modern French and Japanese literature, the Japanese have managed to erase the Other entirely. Although the country now has a dramatic shortage of labor, and the importation of cheap Asian workers is both a necessity and an actuality, no one is willing to face up to the issue. Exploitation and abuse are rampant, yet they are ignored by both the media and intellectuals.[20] He finds an analogy to this situation in France, where, however, the Algerians and other minorities do have intellectual friends—such as Kristeva and Todorov in their new works, for example.[21] Remembering *On Chinese Women* and *The Conquest of America,* I am not sure that I can embrace their ideas of the Other wholeheartedly, but that is not important. The point is that this Japanese colleague was visibly excited about his discovery of the idea of the Other in France through the writing of these two intellectual refugees. I am of course radically simplifying his complicated ideas, but one of the points he stressed while he was here was that he would not have been able to come up with the idea of the Other had he stayed in Japan, despite the presence of hundreds of thousands of aliens now employed there. The idea of recognizing and encountering the Other for this scholar—as for others—is European. In order to discover the Other, with all its ramifications of "critical humanism," "heteroglossia," and "living with the Other in the self," Japanese intellectuals need to travel to the cosmopolitan center in Europe and there, for the first time, discover the Other.

It is ironic that most Japanese intellectuals still regard as the real center Europe and not America, and certainly not Japan. (Thus even the study of the discourse of racism—one of the genuine contributions the United States has made in the intellectual sphere thanks to its own bloody racial history—must be authenticated, not here, but in Europe.) And even more ironic is the fact that all the while their own Asian, nonmetropolitan, non-Western Otherness has not been seriously noted. The Japanese visitor to San Diego concluded his lecture with a moving plea to outsiders to intervene so that Japan can gain an external perspective, restore sanity to the production and consumption of goods, and find a way out of the ideology of self and homogeneity.[22] That at this critical moment American experts on Japan choose to be silent about the emperor and the Other—the most crucial issues facing Japan today—is the final irony.

Japanese Prisoner of War Wardens

The consideration of three films, British, American, and Japanese— David Lean's *The Bridge on the River Kwai* (1957), Steven Spielberg's *Empire of the Sun* (1987), and Oshima Nagisa's *Merry Christmas, Mr. Lawrence* (1983)—and their similarities and dissimilarities in the representation of the Other, may throw light on the Japanese consciousness of alterity. These three movies are thematically identical: they are all stories of Westerners in Japanese prisoner of war camps, in which the authoritarian and inhuman Japanese captors brutalize the powerless but resourceful white prisoners. They are set in closed-off spaces controlled by the Japanese army; the camps are located in the Western colonies of Burma, Shanghai, and Java, respectively. They depict interracial, intercultural contacts—or even understandings and alliances—though in varying modes and degrees. The majority of the characters are military figures, although the principal roles in *Empire of the Sun* are given to civilians, one English boy in particular. I will go over the British and American films quickly, since they will mainly provide a context for Oshima's film.

The Bridge on the River Kwai, the oldest of the three, depicts a company of British soldiers under the command of a British colonel in a POW camp directed by a Japanese colonel. On both sides, the commanders tower in significance over their subordinates. There are a few other officers, but they merely serve as commentators. The plot is, briefly, as follows: The Japanese try to use the British officers to build a strategic railroad bridge, which however is impossible because the Japanese lack engineering skills and the British refuse to submit to the enemy's will. The struggle is soon embodied in the persons of the two colonels—one proud, Japanese, and therefore aesthetic and unskilled; the other proud, British, and therefore practical and competent. A peculiar understanding is established between the two eventually: the bridge will be built, because the Japanese need it for a logistic purpose, and because the British need it in order to demonstrate their superior engineering skills and reaffirm their imperial prerogatives as a colonizing power. Power is at the heart of the two colonels' conflict, but even this struggle is soon so internalized as to render the British-Japanese rivalry forgotten. Colonel Nicolson's strife-ridden interior (as acted by Alec Guinness) gradually replaces the external battlefield: he must assert his, Britain's, and the West's supremacy, and to accomplish that mission all other concerns and persons must be overpowered. In other words, *The Bridge on the River Kwai* has only one side to present. The Japanese colonel and the Allied officers prove to be no more than stage props, just as the whole encounter between two armies and two cultures is in fact a shadow-boxing in which no Japanese ever participates. In this self-filled and Other-absent world, a bridge is built, but before a train can cross it, the bridge is blown up by the master builder himself. As it shatters to smithereens, nearly everyone is killed, friend and foe alike. In a much later film, David Lean reexamines E. M. Forster's *A Passage to India* (1984) and concludes somewhat more wistfully than did the novelist that the bridge to the Orient is still unbuildable. I wonder if for over twenty years Lean hasn't been simply rebuilding the same bridge that merely connects one side with itself. (I might add that the Burmese population in *The Bridge on the River Kwai* is represented mainly by lovely women whose sole mission in the film is to turn Jack Hawkins/William Holden's dangerous commando assignment into an idyllic sex picnic.)

One of the most striking features of *Empire of the Sun* is the way it, too, erases the local people—in this case, Chinese—from its drama. The masses and masses of people constitute merely the background against which something really important is presumably taking place. What is this event that obviously involves but categorically ignores the existence of the Shanghai people? It is an English boy's survival in alien city streets and then in a Japanese prison camp, having been separated from his wealthy colonial parents in the confusion of the Japanese invasion. During his struggle, he encounters a Japanese boy of the same age who—like himself—loves aviation and airplanes. A quiet friendship grows between the sons of the two colonial functionaries. Just as the Japanese army is facing defeat, the Japanese boy is shot to death by an American who misunderstands his movement beside the English boy. Their friendship, which had developed by ignoring the incomprehensible grown-ups' war, is destroyed by the same uncomprehending grown-ups. At the end the only way the English boy can greet any stranger is to repeat, "I surrender."

The film romanticizes the friendship of children from warring imperialist countries. In so doing, it sets aside the possibility of mature cultural encounter, as if it were too remote to be considered seriously. In two memorable scenes, the English boy bicycles around and around in a frenzy—the first time inside the deserted mansion of his parents, and the second time in the camp, also completely deserted—as if he were trapped inside the escapeless prison by his absent parents and absent grown-ups. The Japanese boy, too, seems always abandoned to play by himself. In *Empire of the Sun,* the colonized natives just do not enter the picture. As they press themselves against the windows of a Rolls-Royce, these colonized poor seem to see only a privileged group of whites who inhabit a totally different dimension. And as the English family inside the Rolls-Royce cannot be concerned with the staring eyes of the unknowable outsiders, so Spielberg's camera is oblivious to the interiors of the Chinese people. The empires of the sun are built, one realizes, in a discriminatory political space that unflinchingly excludes the alien Other.[23]

Merry Christmas, Mr. Lawrence, a Japanese film, is sharply different from those by Lean and Spielberg in several significant aspects, and such variances might indeed offer us a clue to the current, nearly unanimous silence in Japan. Although all three films are based on English-language novels, *The Bridge* and *Empire* were both written and directed by Westerners who belong to the same side of the schism from which the films presumably gaze across at the non-West. *Merry Christmas,* on the other hand, based on a novel (actually two works that were later published under one title), *The Seed and the Sower,* by South African–British writer Laurens van der Post, was directed by Oshima Nagisa, a Japanese. Van der Post, who was born in South Africa, had lived in Japan before he joined the British army and was held captive in a Japanese prisoner of war camp in Indonesia until 1945.[24] Thus the fiction writer's perspective and the film director's would seem to conflict; but Oshima loves to confront conflicts. He cast in the two principal roles rock idols of England and Japan, David Bowie and Sakamoto Ryuichi, who were both extremely good-looking, not a little androgynous, and inexperienced in film acting, as if the introduction of the similarly different and the similarly unfamiliar were a meaning in itself. The film's crew, too, came from several nations, including New Zealand, the United States, Japan, and Britain.[25] This assortment of backgrounds is unusual in any film, but particularly for the normally homogeneous Japanese picture.

According to Oshima, he read *The Seed and the Sower* in 1978 and completed the film in 1983.[26] He seems to believe that the film represents the novel accurately. Although there is no reason that he should be any more inhibited in his interpretation of the source materials than any other filmmaker, the film and the novel are, of course, different. In what way does this Japanese film depart from the South African novel—aside from the obviously different features between a written novel and an audio-visual motion picture as media of representation? How do the two works intersect within the context of intercultural encounter?

The Seed and the Sower (1963) consists of three more or less discrete tales loosely connected around the main narrator (the unidentified and authorial "I") and a Colonel John Lawrence, his comrade during the Pacific War. The three parts were not written and published together originally, and in spite of the evident efforts to cement them together, they clearly remain disparate. Part I, called "Christmas Eve," is followed by "Christmas Morning" and "Christmas Night." Van der Post's emphasis on Christmas is perhaps an afterthought, since the holiday is intrinsic only to the first story, published years earlier than the subsequent parts. It is likely that the author tried to give the impression of coherence to the three separate tales by placing them all in one Christmas setting where the storytelling takes place. The emphatic Christian theme in Parts II and III may also be attributable to the same circumstance.[27]

The first part was originally published under the title "A Bar of Shadow" (published in *The Cornhill*).[28] The story is told by the "I," whom Colonel Lawrence visits for Christmas. The two men reminisce about their Japanese POW experience, and Lawrence tells a timely Christmas story that is more or less identical with the Colonel Lawrence and Sergeant Hara episode in the film. Lawrence is released one Christmas by the brutal noncommissioned officer Hara from an isolation cell while waiting for execution. For some reason Hara seems to believe that Christmas is an important occasion for everyone, even non-Christians. The Hara of the story matches the movie representation in general with his supposedly samurai code of behavior—that is, cruel and inhuman, but in his own way decent. At the end of the war, Hara is arrested to be tried before the War Crimes Tribunals. Lawrence pleads for him, but without success. As in the film version, Hara sends for Lawrence on the eve of his execution, and their last conversation ends with Hara shouting to Lawrence, "Merry Kurisumasu, Rorensu-san."

This part is told entirely from Lawrence's point of view, and the "I" merely listens. The narrative situation is often awkward, revealing at various points that Colonel John Lawrence, the "I," and Colonel Laurens Van der Post are barely distinguishable. The story of Hara and John Lawrence is complete in itself, not involving Major Jacques Celliers and Captain Yonoi, who are the principal characters of *Merry Christmas* as a whole. Very much like Van der Post in his nonfictional work on Japan,[29] Colonel Lawrence is full of theories about his enemy country and its people. Hara as he sees him is "faithful and responsive to all the imperceptible murmurings of Japan's archaic and submerged racial soul" (p. 16). Hara can't help himself, according to Lawrence, because "it is not he but an act of Japanese gods in him" (pp. 17–18). The "moon-swung" Hara and his countrymen are "still deeply submerged like animals, insects and plants. . . . They [are] subject to cosmic rhythm and movement and ruled by cosmic forces beyond their control to an extent undreamt of in the European mind and philosophy" (pp. 21–22). So goes the Lawrentian anthropology, which quite obviously receives Laurens Van der Post's fullest endorsement.

The next part of Van der Post's book, "Christmas Morning," contains nearly all the major components of *Merry Christmas, Mr.*

Lawrence, except for the Hara story. The nameless "I," who was the listener in Part I, is now the storyteller, filling in the earlier life of Jacques Celliers. Actually, the story, told via a bundle of notes left by Celliers to the narrator, is a confession of his betrayals of his younger brother in South Africa. It recalls the similar device used in Conrad's *Lord Jim,* which *Merry Christmas* in many ways resembles. While in the film Celliers' acts of betrayal, described in a series of flashbacks, seem irrelevant to the main story, in the novel it is quite clear that Celliers' bravery and heroism in a remote colony would redeem the earlier betrayals, again very much as in *Lord Jim.*[30] The memoir lasts for four chapters, more than a third of the whole book; its is radically shortened in Oshima's film.

The second part of the novel returns to Celliers' pre-incarceration career. There is a good deal of religiosity in this part, which Oshima more or less erases from his rendition.[31] Also, of Van der Post's South African background—he has been a liberal anti-apartheid activist—no trace is left in the movie. On the other hand, several episodes—such as a Korean guard's rape of a Dutch soldier; Hara's decapitation of the guard;[32] Yonoi's sword practice; Celliers' numerous defiant acts such as smuggling in a shortwave radio, distributing food among his fellow prisoners, and attempting escape; and many details that powerfully suggest homoerotic tension among the two male couples—are new additions in the film. Celliers' reckless act of kissing the Japanese captain before the entire Japanese and British companies, his subsequent punishment by being buried alive, and Captain Yonoi's clipping of Celliers' hair, the film's climactic events, survive from the novel. In both versions, the officers from the upper classes are depicted—without any self-consciousness or criticism—as more poised, sensitive, and intelligent than those from the lower classes. There is no explicit scene of mutual attraction between Celliers and Yonoi either in Van der Post's version or in Oshima's, but there is a discernible difference in the modes of representation. In the film, the Japanese officer is hopelessly infatuated with Celliers, who remains almost completely indifferent. In the novel, however, Celliers is very much aware of the effects of his good looks on the Japanese officer—in fact, this self-awareness is presented as deeply enmeshed with his sense of guilt over the betrayal of his physically unattractive but spiritually gifted younger brother.[33] Oshima seems intent to present the Japanese-English relationship as more one-sided than in the novel.

The third part of *The Seed and the Sower* describes Colonel Lawrence's encounter with a young Englishwoman. The romantic story in which the two fall in love under the threat of Japanese invasion is compressed in Oshima's hand into a verbal (unimaged) reference lasting only a few minutes—an element that is quite superfluous even at its brief length. *Merry Christmas,* it seems, tries hard to retain much of the novel, with the result that several of its episodes are not only irrelevant but unintelligible.

In addition to the confusing narrative situation, Van der Post's various themes refuse to intersect. Encounter with the alien Other is the most pronounced concern in the Lawrence-Hara episode; the conventional moral motif of betrayal and redemption dominates in the Jacques Celliers portion; the Celliers-Yonoi affair is an intensification of the male bonding that is always implicit in any war story; the heterosexual and ethnically homogenous romance in the last part offers an apology, so to speak, for the exclusion of the female from the rest of the book. In fact, gender politics is carried into the narrative framework itself in the quarrel between the narrator's wife and Colonel Lawrence about the propriety of a sword and a doll as Christmas gifts for a boy and a girl. (The book ends—rather inexplicably—with the critically aware wife accepting Lawrence's and her husband's sexist views.) These components are placed in discrete sections and parts that neither suggest an integral meaning nor interact as fragments.

Oshima's job was to devise a film out of these materials. First, he eliminates the narrative frame, together with its placement on Christmas years after the event. There is no equivalent of the "I" or his wife, thus also removing the concern with feminism or, simply, women. *Merry Christmas* is self-consciously male and homosexual both in intention and execution. For this purpose the removal of the "I" (who is absorbed into the character of Colonel Lawrence) is both necessary and successful. Instead of the two pairs (Hara and Lawrence, Yonoi and Celliers) being observed by the "I" or described to him, the film audience is directly introduced to them, in their pairings and in occasional criss-crossings between Hara and Celliers, Yonoi and Lawrence. This male concentration is complicated further by Oshima's invention of the rape of a Dutch prisoner by a Korean soldier, an episode expanding the context of the central pairs. The most physical relationship between the Korean and the Dutch soldier lines up with the largely unconscious intimacy between Hara and Lawrence, and finally with the self-conscious Yonoi-Celliers affair. Oshima seems intent to provide a complement to his two immediately preceding films, *Empire of Passion* and *In the Realm of the Senses,* in which he tried to make sexuality overwhelm pornography. To present eroticism in homosexuality before a presumably heterosexual audience, and to have homosexuality represent friendship and love in general, and finally to prove that love and friendship are possible between enemies are among the objectives of this film, according to Oshima.[34]

Merry Christmas in this sense is another experiment by Oshima in perception and representation of the strange Other. He offered in an interview that Van der Post's novel had intrigued him because he thought its representation of the Japanese was "remarkably good" and wondered what it might be like to reexamine the foreign representation of the Japanese.[35] When asked for his opinion of Van der Post's ambivalent representation of the Japanese, he said that perhaps the present generation of Japanese would take the vantage point of Colonel Lawrence, although he himself would be a Yonoi or a Celliers, a soldier committed to his own side. He also said that "although he might take an objective viewpoint like Colonel Lawrence's, he himself could empathize ["kanjo inyu dekimasu"— as a Japanese?] with Yonoi and Hara" (p. 417). What is interesting about this confusing exchange is that Oshima seems to believe that Lawrence—and by extension Van der Post—is not a partisan but a disinterested observer who can see the Japanese in the true light.

Oshima published a book titled *I Answer!* (*Kotaeru!,* 1983) that collects in self-celebration all the positive and enthusiastic reviews and comments the movie received while he went on a promotion tour to England and the United States. This book includes quotations from interviews in which he makes self-promoting remarks about the movie; it also approvingly quotes numerous brief mentions of the film that appeared in British and American publications. Throughout he insists that the film's representation of the Japanese is accurate. In support, the European and American views of the film are accepted as the final word on the film by its maker, just as Van der Post's novel is accepted as the accurate representation of the Japanese. And therein lies the clue to Oshima's interpretation of the Japanese, which many intellectuals of Japan seem to share with him.

Let me reflect on Oshima's career for a moment. During the sixties he made a number of political films. One of his preoccupations in them was the racial conditions of Japan. *The Catch (Shūku),* based on Oe Kenzaburo's wartime story, depicts a black American flier who parachutes from a bomber only to be captured by country villagers. The villagers keep him alive but blame him for all the trouble that befalls them; they finally slaughter him just as Japan is about to surrender. The film presents people's greed and stupidity, which their children clearly see through. Oshima also made *The Forgotten Army* for television, which treats disabled Korean veterans of the Japanese imperial army who are abandoned by both the Japanese and the Korean governments and are now reduced to panhandling on the streets. Perhaps the best known in this category is *Death by Hanging,* based on a true story of a Korean boy who passed for a Japanese until the life of deprived identity and welfare led him to murder two Japanese women in an act of rage and revenge. The boy ruthlessly analyzes the relations between race, sex, crime, law, and death. Throughout, Oshima is determined to locate himself in the place of the Other and to look back at himself, the Japanese, and their complicity in the boy's murder of the women as well as in the legal execution of the boy.[36]

Merry Christmas is a continuation of this program of recognizing and representing the Other. In contrast to *The Bridge on the River Kwai* and *Empire of the Sun,* it stares at the enemies without absorbing them into their self-reflection. Whereas Oshima's earlier films look at Japan and the Japanese from the viewpoint of the victims of racism, *Merry Christmas* observes them from the vantage point of the white prisoners of war. Oshima seems to regard racial minorities and prisoners alike simply as victims of Japanese control and brutality. Furthermore, Oshima's acceptance of Colonel Lawrence, a.k.a. Sir Laurens Van der Post, as an authority on Japanese people and culture is so uncritical and unexamined that one cannot but conclude that he is unconcerned with the fundamental difference between the victimization of Asians and the brutalization of British prisoners of war.

Quite obviously I am not excusing the latter atrocity, which is as damnable as any other. Japan's imperialism in Asia, however, plays a more structurally constitutive part in world history and requires a different dimension of argument. Let me simply refer back to Japan's experience of the Western imperialist threat in the nineteenth century. As has been discussed earlier, the country's answer to this threat was to utilize maximally the ideology of emperorism to centralize and "homogenize" its people domestically, to assert their uniqueness at home and abroad, and at the same time to represent them as an equal to the "advanced" peoples. Japanese nationalism sought to coerce internal agreement and loyalty. To the extent that Japanese nationalism was a response to Western aggression and domination, and strictly to that extent, Japan's aspiration was understandable—if not laudable—like many other decolonization attempts. The fundamental problematic of Japanese liberationism, however, was that unlike Pan-Arab nationalism, Pan-African nationalism, or any other independence movement, it immediately inverted, or perverted, the program into its own colonialism and imperialism, and initiated its own agenda of aggression and suppression in the Pacific islands and continental Asia as well as at home. It was a semicolonized country attempting to colonize others without a dominant metropolitan culture. During the process, Japan desperately needed legitimation of its claims by the "advanced" nations. Its cultural exceptionalism, for instance, is a logical extension of a strategy to place itself outside the categories of both "advanced" nations and "underdeveloped" nations. And despite its economic leap into a high-growth phase twenty years ago, this cultural self-consciousness has remained unchanged to this very day.

As far as the Indonesians are concerned, Oshima, too, evacuates them from *Merry Christmas:* there is not a single Javanese character in it. The film's background music, which apparently is meant to suggest the native presence, was entirely composed by Sakamoto Ryuichi (who plays Captain Yonoi). The supposed Javanese music is a synthesized gamelan whose New Age simulation placed against a rock rhythm is an insult to the highly sophisticated Javanese music—insofar as the film attempts to represent the encounter of cultures.

Oshima has known all along the absurdity of Japan's exceptionalism. Thus he has been consistent in objecting to the discrimination against Koreans and other minorities on the basis of
difference. At the same time, his concern with the minorities in
Japan was humanitarian, that they be regarded and treated equally
and identically with the Japanese. His idea of social structure did
not suggest the reality and desirability of heterogeneity, but the equal
absorption of all into an assimilated and homogenized Japanese
nation, which is after all no more than an imaginary. Exactly in the
same fashion, humanity means for Oshima that of the modern West,
Europe in particular, which supposedly embodies "common humanity" ("jinrui kyotsu," *Kotaeru!*, p. 177). Oshima may have intended to pursue in *Merry Christmas* the fundamental ambivalence
the Japanese feel toward the West—love and envy pitched against
hatred and contempt—and its disastrous outcome in the last war
(Sato, *Oshima Nagisa*, p. 415), but his own resolution seems to
accept the hegemonic and hierarchic view that would rank nations
and races on a scale of progress and development. He displays an
unconcealed aspiration and admiration for Europe and the Europeans. This is the only way to explain Oshima's unembarrassed
infatuation with David Bowie's white skin, blond hair, and blue eyes
(called "God's gifts," "to be born so beautiful"—"kami no medeshi
hito," "annani utsukushiku umarete kite"; Sato, *Oshima Nagisa*,
p. 427) which Oshima ecstatically exclaims as he reminisces about
his collaboration during the film's production in New Zealand.

The one puzzle that remains unsolved is the question of the film's
intended audience. Does the film require particular familiarity with
both societies? Does Oshima as a grand container of cultural differences understand the effects of particular scenes and images on
different viewers? Is a Canadian, not to say an Egyptian or a
Hungarian, audience supposed to know what Yonoi means when he
refers to the February 26, 1936, army insurrection in Tokyo? For
another instance, when the same captain mumbles in the courtroom
scene "To be or not to be, that is the question," the audience in the
theater where I sat in Berkeley, California, responded with a ripple
of embarrassed giggles.[37] (Cultural literacy!) Was the laughter calculated? To what effect? Oshima says in a recent article that his
films are no longer for the Japanese (who have ceased to invest
money in such risky ventures) but for an "international audience."

What does this internationality mean precisely? In 1986 Oshima made *Max, mon amour* with a French producer, in which a French actress sleeps with a chimpanzee, and the film's effects seem to hinge on her English husband's response to the ménage à trois. It is a completely French film without a trace of Japanese life. Is this the final destination of Oshima's search for Otherness?[38]

Unlike the visitor to San Diego, who needed to travel to Paris to discover alterity, Oshima earlier saw Koreans and other Asians for what they are. And yet when he became engaged in the program to represent the Japanese, he had to fall back on a European observer for an interpretation. Thus while his earlier films powerfully indicted all Japanese for the act of exclusion and discrimination, *Merry Christmas,* his first big-budget, big-name production, almost eagerly participates in European hegemonism.[39] Oshima the lifelong rebel has finally rebelled his way into intercultural agreement.

This is a parody of James Clifford's by-now-famous episode in which an ethnographer visiting Gabon asks for information about the meaning of a ritual term. In the story, the native chief runs back into his home and consults a sacred book, which turns out to be a work by an earlier visitor-ethnologist.[40] Oshima is the tribal chief here reading from Raponda-Walker/Laurens Van der Post, offering their representation as authentic. By accepting the international consensus concerning the world's center and its margins, he tries to join that center itself. Very much like Oshima's own reminder in *Death by Hanging,* the charge of "anata mo, anata mo, anata mo" (and you too, and you too, and you too) must now be directed to Oshima himself.[41] He must be indicted for his complicity in agreeing to the dominant. He may not have openly endorsed emperorism yet, but he certainly has embraced the universality of Christmas and the hegemony of the West. As the emperor sits at the center of Japan, so does the West preeminently preside over the affairs of the world—in the consciousness of the Japanese. Centrality demands agreement. Thus our own way out seems simply to insist on challenging that agreement. In today's Japan at least, disagreement is the only way toward the recovery of dialogue and argument, without which no serious and meaningful agreement can possibly be found.

Gathering Voices: Japanese Women and Women Writers

There was no one like Mary Wollstonecraft in the late eighteenth century, nor a counterpart to John Stuart Mill in the mid-nineteenth century, in Japan. Should there have been? The answer will have to be no—and yes. No, simply because it would be absurd to ignore history. Mill did not emerge out of nowhere; bourgeois capitalist Victorian England was not Meiji Japan, where imperial statism was about to reinforce a version of absolutism and capitalism better adapted to modern geopolitical conditions than Tokugawa feudalism. Yes, on the other hand, because the suppression of women was a historical fact in Tokugawa and Meiji Japan, and suppression of any kind cannot be left uncontested anywhere, anytime, even in the context of the unalterable past. An ahistorical and transcendental truism of this sort, however, has little meaning unless it is to serve as a corrective and standard for a society in a given time and place. More reasonable questions might be whether Japan has had a Simone de Beauvoir, and whether there are women's rights and women's study programs *now* in Japan. Should there be? How do the conditions of women figure in today's Japanese literature, and how is feminist discourse positioned in Japan now?

Gender, Class, and Ethnicity

We might begin by considering the three cardinals of injustice—
ethnicity, class, and gender—as they relate to each other. Any historical condition or instance of oppression, at least since the process
of global integration commenced in the Renaissance, cannot be
viewed from any one or two of these perspectives without taking all
three into account, inasmuch as they are finally cognate. Take concerns with class. Crucial shortcomings of earlier Western socialism,
in retrospect, are found in its Orientalist and patriarchic indifference
to race and gender resulting from an all-absorbing preoccupation
with class struggle and an incomplete understanding of power. The
Marxist notion of the "Asiatic mode of production" is an obvious
instance; so is its acceptance of colonialism as a necessary evil for
the sake of the general progress of humanity. The idea of progress,
itself a product of Enlightenment, has unavoidably implicated Marx
and Engels.[1] Socialism's neglect of gender issues, too, must be kept
in mind. Even today some social planners are convinced that class
is the fundamental and central problem while dismissing gender
concerns as peculiar to bourgeois women and accepting Eurocentricity as a universal given. Working-class men, victims of
economic exploitation, often scoff at the gender issue as an irrelevant and trivial pastime of the well-to-do, ignoring the plight of
women of their class, who doubly suffer from abuse by the rich and
by men. Working-class women all too often concur with these sentiments. In addition, the economic frustration of the working class
is often channeled into race hatred. Of course, sexism and racism
are present everywhere across class and gender lines. They are
simply more successfully concealed among the upper classes,
whereas the bigotry of the lower class, with its lesser resources, is
shown with less guile and exploited by the media. In fact, racism
and sexism are at times encouraged as a useful instrument of containment by those in power, matching the poor white against the
poor black, men against women, in the labor market. Most white
male intellectuals, supposedly disinterested arbiters of all matters,
are simply unwilling to take seriously race, gender, and class perspectives, on the simple ground that the truth as they see it has been
revealed only to the select group of Western male intellectuals

whose views and values are naturally neutral and universal, thus uncontaminated by class, race, and gender ideologies—even on the questions of class, race, and gender themselves.

Those concerned with race issues, too, are much too often exclusive in their preoccupation. A notable number of activists for racial liberation are uninterested in the issues of gender and class. The history of the civil rights movement is tarnished by the experiences of women whose aspiration for racial equality was overwhelmed by despair and outrage at the inequality in gender rights. Indifference to class problems obviously works against the establishment of a racially just society. Yet the white middle-class voter-registration workers of the early 1960s, for instance, failed to gain a full understanding of the conditions of poor whites in the South.[2] Colonized natives are usually divided between a few haves and a vast number of have-nots, the former likely to be compromised by the colonizers as their surrogates over the latter. The use of tokenism and elitism is both policy and practice in the management of the oppressed, nearly always employed in colonial situations. Colonialism, conversely, is itself a part of the strategy to contain surplus labor at home at the expense of the poor, especially the female poor. The discourse against colonialism, however, is at times oblivious to class problems even as it is engaged in the examination of day-to-day political struggle. The characterization of a revolutionary in public and an imperialist at home too often applies to the Third World patriarch as well as the First World progressive.

Historically, the struggle for feminism and against sexism was the last in the triad to emerge as a political force. Although all kinds of victims of domination have voiced their rage and suffering ever since the beginning of history, such *cris de coeur* against racial and sexual bigotry were not gathered into a discursive context until recently. Of the two, anti-racism became a social issue earlier: even at the height of imperialism, J. A. Hobson's *Imperialism: A Study* (1902), for instance, powerfully protested against the idea and practice of racial inequality.[3] His protest was seconded by Lenin and Rosa Luxemburg, among others. And yet their analyses were not incorporated into general academic discourse, and the views and voices of the oppressed were rarely considered in history, sociology, or political science courses. It is indeed remarkable that Edward Said's

Orientalism, published as recently as 1978, should have had such a great impact on a wide range of disciplines from anthropology, history, and sociology, to literary criticism. Unprepared for the thrust of his argument, which had been unmistakably implied—or even articulated—in anti-colonial liberation ideologies since 1945 and in the civil rights movement at least since the 1960s, the social sciences and the humanities reacted as if caught by surprise, as can be seen in rapid developments in critical anthropology and cultural criticism that ensued.[4]

On the feminist front, the works of Wollstonecraft, Taylor and Mill, and Margaret Fuller were not accepted by academic and intellectual leaders until a much later date: Wollstonecraft was largely ignored throughout the nineteenth century, and *The Subjection of Women* went all but unnoticed by Victorian liberals such as Arnold, Bagehot, and George Eliot as well as reactionaries like Ruskin and Carlyle—and, more important, by twentieth-century experts in the history and literature of that era. Virginia Woolf was considered a minor novelist in the shadows of Joyce and Lawrence, or even H. G. Wells and Galsworthy. Nearly two decades after the appearance of Simone de Beauvoir's *The Second Sex* (1949; trans. 1953), and only after the anti-Vietnam movement and minority protests of the late 1960s revealed profound gender injustice even among the ranks of progressive activists, did feminism become an articulate force in the United States. Even then, women's liberation was at first a largely social event and not an academic program; it was only at a painfully slow pace that tradition-bound academic establishments and authorities began to show interest in and respect for feminist criticism. Although in recent years the humanities disciplines, and increasingly the social sciences, have been avidly embracing feminist criticism—many academic departments could not perhaps survive without a serious commitment to gender studies now—this alteration in the academic scene did not begin until the mid-1970s.

Once the new direction was established, under pressure, the old male canon was challenged with more and more alacrity. The core curriculum of the college English department, arguably the most intellectually conservative institutional unit (defined by the boundaries of two hegemonic nations), has been conspicuously in need of a massive transfusion from outside. The continuity of "great books" has been questioned everywhere and challenged by the growing interest in more marginal work. No longer do Chaucer, Spenser, Shakespeare, Milton, Pope, and Wordsworth constitute an unrivaled all-male apostolic succession; rather, off-center texts such as works by Chinese-American writers, Caribbean novels, and African oral tales are offered to students. The orthodoxy of English and other national literature departments has been clearly altered from formalism, traditionalism, and authoritarianism to historicism, marginalism, and oppositionism, and from masculinism to feminism. Evidence of this unmistakable transformation can be seen by comparing the programs of the annual conventions of the Modern Language Association of 1970—or even 1980—with that of 1990.

As American and other Western students begin to look into non-Western cultures, they might once again be caught in the act of universalizing their newly formed convictions. This is not meant to imply that the First World students of Third World cultures are less sophisticated or alert than those engrossed in their own culture. On the contrary, possibly the reverse is the case, especially among younger, less socialized scholars. And yet the memories of the United Nations Conferences on Women in Mexico City and Copenhagen in 1975 and 1980 are still fresh in our minds. The delegates from the First World were eager to instruct and emancipate the unenlightened from the Third World. Like their forefathers who traveled to remote regions for missionary work, the women of the West were there to evangelize, not to listen and learn about the plight of the rest. Some of them were even unwilling to recognize that different societies might face different problems and act on different agendas, and that the charts of progress are not identical everywhere.[5] The gulf that gaped wide at the earlier conferences was considerably narrowed at the Nairobi meeting at the end of the U.N. Decade for Women in 1985.[6] And yet as I turn to consider the position of women in Japan, it is crucial to remember that a different configuration of race, class, and gender operates in Japan as well. As has been repeatedly asserted in this book, Japan's technical and industrial advance is hardly accompanied by the social and cultural change that one expects to see alongside it in the First World.

Modern Japanese Women

There is no room here to go deeply into the history of modern Japanese women, but a few points ought to be recalled. According to the German-inspired New Civil Code of 1898—adopted after the 1889 Old Civil Code had been found to be too French, radical, and anti-traditional—men and women were to be sharply distinguished and differentiated as to their rights and privileges. Not only was it stipulated by the Imperial House Act (Koshitsu Tempan) that the emperor was always to be male, the head of the family was also to be male, and his rights and privileges were carefully protected by the Civil Code from the challenges of the female in nearly every possible way. The patriarchic system was made so completely pervasive in the structure and function of Japanese society that women's status in marriage, family, education, occupation, and law was indelibly defined as inferior: the man as head of the household held all rights as regards lineage, property, divorce, and child custody; the woman's rights were subordinated to those of her husband, parents, and sons; higher education in any state university was denied to women (with a very few exceptions later on);[7] most professional jobs were closed to women; and women had no voting rights. Most of these were legal restrictions, and social practice was inextricably enmeshed with such *de jure* stipulations.

The Meiji Constitution and the 1898 Civil Code not only institutionalized and even extended the oppressive Edo gender practice but further intensified the domestication of women to help men meet the imperialist demands placed on them. Law was largely an articulation of state policy. And the relationship of women to men was devised by the rulers and planners of the state to be subordinate, reproductive, and nurturing. Regardless of their class, women were brought up to assume the role of the "good wife, wise mother" *(ryosai kenbo),* which was not Confucian in its ideological source but a shrewd borrowing from the bourgeois capitalist West.[8] Women's highest responsibility was to bear children, especially sons, who would grow in turn to be heads of households and perpetuate their family names and serve their country. Articles 4 and 25 of the Assembly and Political Association Law (Shukai Oyobi Seisha Ho) of 1890 forbade women to join any political organization or even to attend a political meeting, virtually nullifying their chance to improve their condition. The Association of New Women (Shin Fujin Kyokai) was formed in 1920 to challenge these restrictions, and the Peace Preservation Police Law (Chian Keisatsu Ho) was amended in 1922 to allow women at least to be present in a political assembly. Yet the Association rapidly declined thereafter, as its middle-class orientation was attacked by an emerging radical group of socialist feminists.[9] Women were not permitted membership in political organizations until the end of World War II.

Women were also prohibited by social pressure from mingling with men, who were, however, free to patronize the legally sanctioned prostitutes. Women in the "water trade"[10] were daughters of poor peasants who sold them to the proprietors of entertainment houses. Respectable women stayed home. The law concerning adultery was also quite one-sided. For a wife, adultery was both a civil and criminal offense. A husband, on the other hand, was free to commit adultery as long as he was not involved with a married woman; if the husband of the married adulteress brought suit against him, he could be divorced by his wife, though he was not vulnerable to criminal prosecution himself.

There were exceptional female artists and writers, some of them bohemian enough to determine their own life-styles, or defiant enough to form their own political programs; but such brave souls were extremely rare.[11] Most women generally cooperated with the state ideologues by associating only with other women, inculcating, rather than resisting, the program of submission. With the rise of militarism, male domination became even more uncompromised. The few feminist writers from well-to-do families had to pay an exorbitant price for their acts of opposition, as we will see in Miyamoto Yuriko's life. There were feminists from the working class, too, but in a society where the idea of civil rights was carefully kept suppressed, a full awareness of equality in race, class, and gender was beyond comprehension for most of its members.

After the surrender, most discriminatory laws were abruptly abolished; the American-dictated 1947 Constitution and various subsequently established laws and codes provided women with equal rights on a sweeping scale. The legal change so realized, however, was not achieved by a people's determination and sacrifice in the struggle against oppression but, rather, a command imposed on them from outside. The democratic rights conferred without a struggle were neither appreciated nor even understood by most people, who had a long history of their own—whether it was a product of mystification or not—to which they were accustomed and responsive. Most people, especially men, believed that the unwanted and newfangled democratic way of living was a penalty exacted for losing the war, and that they were obliged to humor their youthful, naive, crude, rich, and mighty conquerors. The social and political practice of Japan was thus alienated from the new law of the land and has remained surprisingly unchanged to this day. In the name of Japan's old and indigenous tradition, the pre-1945 habits and manners were preserved out of either nostalgic or nationalistic sentiments, even when they worked against Japan's own interest. The myths of strong manliness and soft femininity and the doctrine of male supremacy *(danson johi),* invented during the samurai-militarist periods, are still firmly held by many men and women as if they were permanent features of the mythological "Japanese race." (In this view, Western nations are seen to operate by the doctrine of female supremacy [*joson dampi*], which is considered a significant cause of their general decline and degradation.) These sexist—as well as racist—opinions are still voiced with impunity by high government officials and cultural leaders.[12] The whole world knows the sex scandals surrounding the prime minister and high cabinet officers of the conservative party in 1989. But these incidents are by no means exceptional, nor are they taken very seriously. The Japanese media took them up only because of the loud clamor made about them in the United States. To take just one more example, a writer called Miura Shumon reportedly asserted in 1985 that "a man not strong enough to rape a woman ought to be put to shame."[13] For anyone to make a violently ignorant statement of the sort is itself an outrage, but it is even more disquieting to find out that the man who made the barbaric pronouncement occupied at the time the official position of Director-General of the Cultural Affairs Bureau (Bunka-cho Chokan). Sex scandals may indeed be ubiquitous around the world, but the relative indifference—even among women—to the inexcusable behavior and remarks by national leaders is quite rare in most industrialized nations.

Miyamoto Yuriko

The long history of female writers in Japan had, as everyone knows, an illustrious beginning centuries ago. During the Heian period (ninth to twelfth centuries), it was not male courtiers but women in aristocratic service who produced prominent literary documents. Forced to write in the "easier" *kana* syllabaries rather than the masculine, official, and "difficult" Chinese characters, they resorted to native forms of poetry and fiction. Their writing is still read; the men's, hardly remembered. In fact, Murasaki Shikibu's *The Tale of Genji* has served as the sacred text and received annotations and commentaries as if it were the Bible or the Koran. Although Lady Murasaki's tale was in some ways replaced in importance during the late Tokugawa and later militarist years by the *Great Chronicles* (*Kojiki* and *Nihon shoki*) and some of the *Imperial Anthologies* (*Manyo shu, Kokin shu,* and *Shin kokin shu*) that better served to legitimate the imperial powers, its authority was never seriously called into doubt. *Genji* also infiltrated the layers of popular culture through parodies and updates.[14] The female practice of writing itself, however, drastically declined once the bloody civil wars tore apart Heian court life and a series of shogunates contended for mastery—when male domination was assumed as a matter of fact. Yet modern women writers certainly did not lack precedents or role models in Japan. Their calamitous oppression notwithstanding, Japanese women of the late nineteenth and early twentieth centuries also responded to the increasing challenges of modern Western feminist writers. In spite of the male hegemony, a good number documented their sufferings, registered their protests, and even struggled against their society. Earlier in the Meiji period, middle-class female writers like Higuchi Ichiyo (1872–1896), Yosano Akiko (1878–1942), Nogami Yaeko (1885–1985), and Hiratsuka Raicho (1886–1971), among others, put their advantages to good use and helped younger women turn to serious writing with fewer difficulties and impediments.

One of the most outstanding resistance writers is no doubt Miyamoto Yuriko, née Chujo Yuri (1899–1951). Miyamoto's writing is almost always autobiographical, very much in line with the orthodox *shishosetsu*. That is, Miyamoto locates the subject matter of her tales in the life she chose to live and experience. This means that the fictionality of her works consists in the selection of episodes, organization of materials, structuring of commentaries, and above all interpretation of the life she narrated. Miyamoto says in various places that in the earlier stage of her career she admired Shiga Naoya's *A Dark Night's Passing* (*Anya Koro,* 1921–37),[15] but her discrimination and evaluation in life as well as in the narratives that define her life are far more rigorous than Shiga's in his self-indulgent style. What she learned from the aristocratic male author is thus largely his disciplined decorum in choosing words and sentences, certainly not his ideology of aestheticism.

Miyamoto's father was one of the earliest modern architects of Japan, who built several large office buildings in Tokyo. Her mother's father was a well known "moral educator" who participated in the early "enlightenment" movement called Meirokusha and later headed the Peers' Girls' School (Kazoku Jogakko); Miyamoto's mother was a graduate of this exclusive institution.[16] Miyamoto thus began her career as an elite member of society and rejected her privilege as she grew up, not so much out of material necessity as from moral and intellectual compunction. Hers was an act of *noblesse oblige,* not of *ressentiment,* at least at the initial stage. She began to write early in high school. After spending a term at Japan Women's College (Nihon Joshi Daigaku, one of the few private institutions for women beyond high school), she withdrew from it and devoted her time to writing. One of her earliest stories, "A Crowd of the Poor" ("Mazushiki hitobito no mure"), published when she was eighteen, shows signs of her lifelong dedication to the cause of the wretched as well as her typically reportorial and analytic tone.

In 1918 she accompanied her father to the United States and did some informal studies around Columbia University. As she continued to write in New York, she met a graduate student from Japan. In defiance of the objections of her family and friends, she married him soon afterward. The marriage was a disaster from the beginning; her husband, fifteen years her senior, had neither the intelligence nor the vigor that an energetic and bright young woman might naturally look for in a companion. He was also desperately poor. Still, she accomplished an important task in severing the ties to her parents, who had tried hard to tame their free-thinking daughter into a proper bourgeois lady. The marriage lasted nearly five years despite the serious discontent the young idealist felt with her husband, who had never managed to form a serious interest in moral, intellectual, or even material life. The divorce was inevitable. It was her second lesson in rebellion against traditional family obligations, according to which she was expected to play the role of "good wife, wise mother" in addition to "obedient daughter." During these miserable years, she was squarely faced with the problematics of modern Japanese marriage.

She began to live in 1925 with Yuasa Yoshiko, a female scholar of Russian literature, with whom she studied Marxism. In 1927 she and Yuasa arrived in Moscow and stayed in the Soviet Union until 1930. The next year she met Miyamoto Kenji, her junior by ten years and a member of the Japan Communist Party, and married him soon thereafter. Her relationship with Yuasa was undoubtedly intense during their seven-year cohabitation. When Miyamoto Yuriko disclosed her intention of marriage, Yuasa is said to have exploded in rage, even resorting to physical violence. The exact nature of their liaison is not clear; Yuasa was a self-identified lesbian,[17] while Miyamoto seems at this stage to have been bisexual. Yuasa, at any rate, not only gave Miyamoto an introduction to Marxism but also taught her uncompromisingly to reject bourgeois conventions, especially gender restrictions. Miyamoto and Yuasa no longer saw each other after this breakup.

In 1933 Miyamoto Yuriko was arrested and detained briefly for violation of the Peace Preservation Law, while her husband went underground as the Communist Party was outlawed about the same time. Miyamoto Kenji was arrested shortly afterward, not to be released for twelve years. In fact, he was sentenced to life imprisonment in January 1945, and his appeal was rejected in June of the same year. Miyamoto Kenji's freedom was regained only after Japan's surrender a few months later, which meant that the Miyamotos lived together only for a few months in all their married years during the Fifteen-Year War. One cannot speculate on what might have happened had they lived together throughout that time. But it does seem clear that Miyamoto's isolation from her husband at least allowed her to be free of the domestic routines of married life and to devote her time and energy to political struggle. Actually, Miyamoto Yuriko was herself never far from the prison during this time. In addition to her frequent visits to her incarcerated husband, she, too, was arrested and kept in prison from time to time. One might call this her third act of rebellion, this time against the power of the state itself. In these years she wrote whenever she could, despite the strictest control over expression, but the opportunities were indeed few: she was often ill from overwork and malnutrition. In January 1941 the publication of her work was banned altogether.

Thus the end of the war came as a happy tiding to the couple. The husband was released from a Hokkaido penitentiary and joined his wife in Tokyo, where they resumed activities together as members of the Communist Party. She lived long enough to witness the "reverse course"[18] begin once again to purge those with leftist convictions from the arena of national politics, this time under the aegis of the Allied Occupation Forces. The two persisted in writing and lecturing. Yuriko, however, died early in 1951 at the age of fifty-two without completing her autobiographical account of the years she lived apart from her long-imprisoned husband. Miyamoto Kenji survived his wife and is in fact still a powerful leader, currently the chairman of the Japan Communist Party. Although the global storm against the communist party bureaucracy finally seems to have caught up with him in Japan, he remains firmly in power as of the autumn of 1990.[19]

Miyamoto's early story, "A Crowd of the Poor," is characteristically self-analytic as it portrays a deprived village of tenant farmers. The speaker watches her relationship to the people as she visits her wealthy grandmother every summer. The young Tokyo girl intends to help the poverty-stricken villagers she meets. But how can she help? She soon discovers that the poor do not react as they are supposed to do. They will do anything—cheat, steal, fight—to get what they want. The stark reality of the poor, with their intelligent egotism and cunning greed, disgusts the outsider speaker until their desperate situation begins to sink in. She is disabused of her sentimental generosity: the romanticization of the poor is an outcome of the romanticization of herself. Philanthropy is often an act of charity for nobody but the donor. Worse still, gifts and donations, even when well meant, have a way of turning toxic and harmful to their beneficiaries. The poor are not grateful, nor do they have a reason to be. Although the story—written when Miyamoto was a protected schoolgirl of seventeen—does not articulate a social analysis, it nonetheless betrays an acute perception of structural injustice: the fundamental inadequacy of private generosity and yet the paradoxical need for intervention.

Miyamoto's program for liberation was designed for both the personal and the public. *Nobuko* (1924–26), a long account of her life in New York, her first marriage, and its deterioration, is a study of a woman's place in Japan's restrictive family life. As Miyamoto tells the story, her past experience is organized and reorganized into the heroine's life not only to yield a story but also to serve as a blueprint for what Miyamoto is and will become. Every past event in the lives of the heroine, her father, and her husband is scrutinized from the vantage point of the speaker as she writes it. Discrepancies between the beliefs and emotions of Nobuko's past and the judgment and evaluation of the present writer generate irony, while consistencies between them contribute to the reaffirmation of a moral position. *Nobuko* in this sense is one of the few documents in early twentieth-century Japan that questions a woman's position in the family, as a daughter and a wife, and proposes an unambiguously alternative independent life.

Nobuko's criticism of her husband is directed not so much at his lethargy and hypocrisy as at his will to tolerate whatever she chooses to do, in a determination to keep her in control. He can endure any problem so long as the family shell remains intact. Such stoicism hides his plan to dominate her beneath the mask of magnanimity and open-mindedness. Utterly stubborn and unimaginative, he neither understands her aspiration nor is interested in knowing it. Doggedly following his own deadly routine, he is in fact contemptuous toward Nobuko's frustration and misery. His use of sex as a tool for the preservation of marriage begins to irk her. Increasingly bored and dissatisfied with the role of a bourgeois wife, she is repelled by his passivity and possessiveness. As she feels the weight of depression, she finds herself continually reacting to him with hostility. In this dead-end situation, Nobuko meets a woman who has no fear of living alone. No explicit sexual attraction is mentioned here, but a friendship grows quickly between the two women, as in Miyamoto's real life.

The last section of *Nobuko* (VII, 10) is a remarkably poised presentation of the last moments of Nobuko's married life. It begins with the man's desperate plea for reconciliation and Nobuko's awareness of her own apathy; then it records her unexpected sexual arousal at his seductive advance. After sex, with his confidence restored and with his feeling of control and domination in place, the old imprisonment resumes. She gathers her courage and insists on parting. The final episode may be a trifle too pat even in the Japan of 1926: the husband breaks the wires of their birdcage, freeing the birds. They fly away at once, but one of them returns to the cage. As he cries, "Even the bird comes back. Why don't you . . . ?" Nobuko averts her eyes and says to herself, "How could I be compared to a bird in a cage?" Nobuko has read Ibsen, as did Miyamoto and many other Japanese women.

In I-fiction writing such as Miyamoto's, a text does not claim autonomy as a Western novel is likely to do, although this does not mean that the text is a factual record like a ship's log or a police record. Miyamoto ponders her future as she writes off her past. The future that quickly turns into the present has continuity from the past text as well as past life. Miyamoto Yuriko of the 1930s continues the struggle that had formed "The Crowd of the Poor" and *Nobuko*. In turn, when Miyamoto writes the sequel to *Nobuko* in 1947 under the title of *Two Gardens (Futatsu no niwa),* the writer remembers from the distance of twenty years extricating and liberating herself from the two "gardens"—presumably her husband's and her parents'. (Alternatively, *Two Gardens,* which describes Nobuko's life with her female friend, Yuasa Yoshiko, might be suggesting a different pair. The cohabitation and her first marriage, both rejected later, could be the two gardens of the ironic title.)

History guides the direction and shape of an I-fiction text. In the case of Miyamoto in the 1930s, it played a great role—through the state apparatus of "thought control"—by restricting, obstructing, and finally outright prohibiting publication. During the twenty years following the publication of *Nobuko,* until 1945, Miyamoto's fiction writing mainly consisted of brief stories that sketch the underground life or prison experience of the outlawed activists. The tales are moving accounts of oppression and resistance. Her writing of the time is, however, not often chiseled with care—such was neither her intention nor her ability at the time. "Hour by Hour" ("Koku-Koku") and "A Breast" ("Chibusa") are notable for their exceptional moral courage and provide evidence for Japan's resistance and conscience during these bleak and depressing decades.

Banshu Plain (Banshu Heiya), published in 1946, begins with the daily routine of Hiroko, Miyamoto's surrogate, on August 15, 1945. As she listens to the emperor's announcement of surrender, she wonders about the safety of her husband, who has been jailed over a decade, and hopes for his safe return. She must visit his family near Hiroshima, where his brother has been missing since the atomic bomb explosion. As she returns from Hiroshima on broken-down trains, she witnesses endless miseries in war-ravaged cities and villages. The devastation of the entire nation and the exhaustion of the whole population are drawn with clarity and vision, albeit in profound sadness. Unlike so many postwar writers—the disillusioned *"apure"* generation—Miyamoto had no war guilt to cloud her conscience. One of the extremely few who did not go through the process of conversion, she welcomed the day of liberation and democracy with genuine joy and ease. In addition, *Banshu Plain* describes the sufferings of women who stayed home and supported their men, who were herded to the battle fronts. For many of them the war was not over yet, faced as they were with a long hard struggle for survival without their husbands, sons, or fathers.[20]

Miyamoto presents a wider canvas in *Banshu Plain,* while in *Weathervane Grass (Fuchiso,* 1946) she once again concentrates her gaze on her personal life with her husband. The story takes place soon after Japan's surrender, which resulted in the freeing of all political prisoners under SCAP orders. Her husband returns to fill his long-vacant place in daily family life. As the wife (Hiroko) tries to help him adjust to his unaccustomed domestic role, friction and misunderstanding inevitably arise between them. The more lovingly considerate they are with each other, the more intricate are their subtle reactions and interactions. Defensive about her overconcern with his prison-acquired illness, the husband strikes back by remarking on her toughened "widow-like" independence and control. The wife reflects on the vicissitudes of the past decade that have unavoidably hardened her demeanor. The two quietly talk about a moment of uncontrolled irritability. Such strain and stress cannot be removed at once. The husband who was forced to work as a tailor in prison life corrects his wife's sewing; she playfully complains about his need for her help in his effort to put on civilian clothes. Such petty incidents hurt them unexpectedly. They remember those many years—till the autumn of 1945—when they were together only in thought. Now there are their physical presences to cope with. The wife also yearns to begin writing again, and so does her husband.

Miyamoto includes in *Weathervane Grass* another episode from her life. Before the commencement of the Pacific War, a literary association of which she was a member renamed and transformed itself into the Literary Patriotic Association (Bungaku Hokoku Kai), and she was automatically given membership in it. This was before she was banned from all publication in January 1941 and was still in a state of uncertainty. She thought then that her outright withdrawal from the Association might attract more attention to her subversive politics. Thus in answer to the new Association's request, she submitted a story for possible inclusion in its publication. One day after the war, the wife finds by chance an official Association envelope that contains her rejected manuscript and shows it to her husband. He at once reminds her of his advice from prison to cancel her membership. The wife of course agrees on the soundness of the advice, but she realizes how little he knows the economic and psychological hardships she faced in her lonely life at the time. True, she was not in jail, but wasn't her trouble at least as serious as his? And yet even now she restrains herself from telling him about the past difficulties. The story ends with the wife's visit to the newly opened editorial office of the *Red Flag (Akahata),* the organ of the Japan Communist Party, where she meets various actual party leaders, now freed after many years of imprisonment. The last section describes a film being shown in memory of the party martyrs (including the assassinated proletarian writer Kobayashi Takiji) and in celebration of the political freedom regained, or rather granted for the first time in Japan's history. Her husband appears in the film as a hero of the moment while she quietly watches it from the audience.

The domestic relationship of the husband and wife may not be adequately resolved in the story; nor perhaps is the final film description free from propaganda hype. And yet Miyamoto's rendition of the daily life of a politically exceptional couple is remarkably astute and powerful. In this story at least, the husband's suffering

in prison is not allowed to overshadow his wife's misery and fortitude during those long years of isolation and loneliness. His egotism
is matched by hers, with rare insight and self-understanding. And
the strain and stress in the couple's regained family life are drawn
with uncompromising honesty and intelligence. *Weathervane Grass*
is one more exercise in Miyamoto's politicization of personal life
and personalization of politics, that is, in seeing everyday life in
history.

Miyamoto Yuriko is a prolific writer who filled thirty volumes of
collected works in a relatively short and severely disrupted life. The
topics in her essays range extensively. The works dealing specifically
with issues about women alone fill two volumes, 1100 pages. Since
she introduces ideas and reports from the woman's perspective on
nearly all subjects she touches, her work remains—together with
Takamure Itsue's—one of the most fertile resources of feminist
discourse in Japan. Although she addresses problems such as suf-
frage, political responsibility, prostitution, family, birth control, occupation, higher education, arranged marriage, adolescence, dowry,
femininity, labor, the opposite sex, friendship, and many others, one
topic remains conspicuously unmentioned—at least from the point
of view of the reader in the 1990s in the United States: the issue of
sexuality. A few passages in her fiction suggest sexual acts, albeit
in high abstraction. As far as I can determine, however, she never
discusses sexuality of any kind in her essays. The only passage
where Miyamoto does touch on it is in a long letter she wrote to
Yuasa Yoshiko on June 15, 1924, that reveals her to be acutely
conscious of the interplay between sexual desire and intellectual
communication, between sexuality and power, and between the
sheer pleasure of carnality and the inadequacy of tamed love. She
both admits the attraction of raw sensuality and confesses a sense
of shame about it.[21] Startlingly intelligent, the letter nevertheless
remains opaque and vague.

One wonders in this connection about the restraint placed on
Japan's intellectual circles even well after 1945—when so-called
sexual emancipation was loudly proclaimed in the media. Whether
Confucian or bourgeois in genesis, taciturnity such as Miyamoto's
about sexuality—male, female, heterosexual, homosexual, or autoerotic—in intellectual discourse is still prevalent. Its existence is as

disturbing as it is puzzling. Is there a concealed relationship between this and other taboos, such as that on imperial matters? Is sexual repression—in respectable quarters, even in 1990 approaching the Victorian ideal—a function of economic and industrial expansionism? Especially in view of the print market glutted with violent sexual comics, sleazy pornographic pictures, and popular media trash, which are indeed tolerated, this taboo on serious discussion of sex and gender matters might prove even to share the same ideology that operates to encourage and promote the sex industry.[22] In her sexual attitudes, at any rate, Miyamoto Yuriko was no exception.

Mid-Century Women Writers

Among Miyamoto's contemporaries, Hayashi Fumiko (1903–1951), Sata Ineko (b.1904), Hirabayashi Taiko (1905–1972), and Enchi Fumiko (1905–1986) must be mentioned at least briefly. These four women, with several others, constitute a second wave in the history of Japan's modern female writers. What is immediately striking about them is how little they have been translated into English or any other Western language, compared with their male contemporaries and antecedents. Perhaps the reason for this neglect is the general male-centeredness of both Western scholars and their Japanese colleagues. There may indeed be some specific factor involved in what Japan as a society has presented to the West in the past century and a half.[23] Whatever the reason, very little is known about these writers—or about Japanese women—outside of Japan, except in very clichéd terms. Inasmuch as their work is at least as interesting as that of their male counterparts—or even more fascinating, depending on the reader's point of view—it is of critical necessity that these writers be translated for a more balanced view of Japan's everyday life.[24]

Hayashi, Sata, and Hirabayashi began as proletarian writers, surviving on temporary hand-to-mouth jobs as café waitresses or factory workers while in and out of wedlock. They were all more or less active on the leftist front in their youth, but Hayashi and Sata abandoned the cause, and Hirabayashi became too ill to be active as the Fifteen-Year War intensified. In fact, the three writers' transition to bourgeois and wartime ideology was rather seamless. In the case of Hayashi Fumiko, her early success enabled her to travel to the Soviet Union and Western Europe in the early 1930s, and soon after her return home she seems to have been thoroughly acclimated to the comforts of middle-class life. Her dispatches after her assignment in 1937 as a war correspondent for the *Mainichi* newspaper in Nanjing, for instance, betray no sign of criticism of the aggression and violence of the Japanese armed forces. She also worked for the Cabinet Information Bureau, regularly publishing stories on the invasion troops in China and later in Southeast Asia. A prolific writer, she is best known for her early work *A Vagabond's Record* (*Horo Ki,* 1930) and a number of short stories such as "The Late Chrysanthemum" ("Bangiku," 1948).

While hopelessly poor, Hirabayashi managed to produce several stories in her youth such as "Self-Mockery" ("Azakeru," 1927) and "At a Clinic" ("Shiryoshitsu nite," 1927). As she began to attract attention from left-wing critics, however, she was arrested on account of her membership in the Japan Proletarian Writers Alliance and soon thereafter became desperately ill with tuberculosis. Because of her poor health and leftist convictions, she published no work at all between 1938 and 1945. After the war, she wrote a number of autobiographical stories such as "This Kind of Woman" ("Koyu onna," 1946) and *A Desert Flower* (*Sabaku no hana,* 1955–57), which provide detailed records of a woman's life in these difficult years. Hirabayashi's popular fiction became eminently successful, and she soon abandoned critical distance from the dominant social views.

As for Sata, her formal education ended in elementary school, although she continued to read and began to write early. To escape from poverty she married a young man from a well-to-do family, and the marriage unsurprisingly proved a disaster; she eventually tried to commit suicide. She later met and married a Marxist writer in 1929, and became recognized as a writer herself, only to be incarcerated soon thereafter. She, too, suffered from isolation and poverty and before long compromised with the repressive authorities. Thus during the war she accepted assignments by the armed forces to entertain Japan's invasion troops. During the immediate postwar years, she like most others had to face her own past of "conversion" but gradually eased into the peaceful and prosperous mode of recent Japanese life. Sata's latest works are characterized by a quiet and delicate sense of irony. In a way, Hayashi, Hirabayashi, and Sata paid a great price in their struggle against material poverty and patriarchal domination. Bare personal survival rather than public or social problems loomed largest in their lives. Compared with Miyamoto Yuriko, whom all three knew well, they were less ideologically committed to the issues of war and race, although they persisted in several ways in their opposition to male domination.[25]

Of these four women, the most personal and "literary" writer is Enchi Fumiko. A daughter of an eminent professor of Japanese literature, she was well tutored in classics from her early days. She wrote mainly plays until the war, when she too was mobilized to join the corps of writers to report on the imperial army activities in China. After 1945, her work was largely prose fiction, in which the theme of women's disillusionment and resentment against their men occupies a prominent place. Accomplished in narrative skills, Enchi examines the man-woman relationship from many angles. Thus *The Waiting Years* (*Onna zaka,* 1955) opens with a scene in which the wife of a provincial Meiji bureaucrat visits Tokyo in search of a suitable mistress for her husband. Set in expansionist imperial Japan, the story portrays the husband's steady climb in the hierarchy of officialdom just as he absolutely dominates an ever-expanding household. The heroine manages to survive her egotistical husband's neglect and affronts by hoping for an early widowhood. Her waiting, however, proves futile; it is she, the abused and trampled wife, who must die first while her husband remains alive and vigorous. The tale ends with her bitter refusal of a normal burial; instead, she cries out from her deathbed, "Tell him to dump my body in the sea."[26]

The Waiting Years abounds with melodramatic movements, theatrical gestures, and stagey proclamations. Nevertheless, Enchi's focus on women's miseries that cut across class boundaries is impressive. Not just the heroine, who is forced to become the manager of a vast household of relatives and servants—all more or less her insatiable husband's mistresses—but practically every woman in this virtual harem suffers from isolation and humiliation. Yet there is a sort of camaraderie among the women. Instead of jealousy and suspicion, there is an unmistakable celebration of solidarity among the co-victims, which nearly compensates for their general bitterness toward men.[27]

In Enchi's fiction, the familial relationships between a woman and her son-in-law, or between a man and his daughter-in-law, for instance, tend to blur into sensual connections, either to avenge women for their lifelong deprivations or to magnify men's unlimited lust and avarice. Enchi, however, seems uninterested in providing social or historical commentary, an enterprise that she apparently feels belongs essentially to a masculine domain. One does register, however, her lifelong gaze at men who seduce women in order to dominate them, and at women who are never able to free themselves from hovering between desire and despair. In a number of stories such as "Fox Fire" ("Kitsunebi") and "Epipsyche" ("Yukon"), Enchi faces up to the limits of a woman's discipline and endurance, and repeatedly dwells on the situations of adultery and incest. As she imagines such counter-strategies, however, her character is likely to remain within the framework of erotic daydreams and fantasies rather than move boldly in action and event, thus depriving her narrative of emplotment.

Enchi also utilizes her familiarity with classic resources to blunt the sharp edges of contemporary life issues. Thus she often places layers of narrative within narratives, diffusing subjects and identities, obscuring the temporality of events, and merging points of view. Her tale characteristically rejects linear arguments and sequential developments, allowing the drama to take place on the borders of rage and desire, frustration and eroticism. Her prose is studded with aesthetic objects that, being glitteringly attractive, resist surrender to the narrative. Underlying Enchi's attachment to discrete things—very much like Kawabata Yasunari's—is a commodity fetishism that has not been sufficiently taken note of. Her narrative is also at times veiled by a wistful longing for mysticism. Unexplained events and transnatural perceptions suggest themselves in her work. The sharp outlines of alluring objects against such a misty background are among the stunning effects created by her power of narration.

Enchi is not an articulate strategist for feminism, nor is she an intellectual speculator on social history. She is thus finally incomplete, inasmuch as she refuses to confront the material historicity of contemporary Japan, taking refuge instead in erotic daydreaming and unresolved discomfiture located in a transcendental personalism and aesthetic culturalism.

The Prospects for Women

The 1960s were a crucial decade for Japan as for so many other industrial nations. Since around 1970, social agitations have steadily subsided to a virtual whisper, or even less. Economic expansion has been uppermost on the agenda of the Japanese state. What this suggests is that the managers of Japanese society—the whole machinery of industry, the media, academia, and the state apparatus (such as the Ministry of Education or MITI)—have been determined to maintain the status quo, with the cooperation of the all-too-willing majority. The myth of Japan as homogeneous has to be continually reinvented and maintained; the Japanese tradition must be constantly reinforced. The imperial household is skillfully deployed as the centerpiece of the undertaking. The imperial family adroitly manipulates its presence among people with a crowded schedule of tactical state events. Royal travels, both domestic and abroad, receptions of foreign dignitaries, and imperial home events such as births, betrothals, and weddings, all project powerful images of the family, serving to attract and distract people's attention from politics as well as demonstrating the stabilizing power of the unchallenged national and familial father figure. Ceremony is never innocent. And the mass media—with NHK, the National Broadcasting Corporation, as their flagship—are fully prepared to orchestrate the imperial performance as "the symbol of the State and of the unity of the people." The goal is the removal of dissent and disunity of any kind. Agreement must prevail.

Under the circumstances, the disclosure of gender asymmetry and inequality would endanger the ongoing social structure, firmly built on the ideology of an unflagging patriarchic hierarchy. Male domination of the family base is felt to be indispensable to the welfare and integrity of an economic and industrial Japan; women must be incorporated subtly but decisively into its productive and consumptive process. The equal rights of men and women guaranteed in the Constitution must be implemented with utmost caution.[28] Feminism is not likely to prosper in the immediate future in Japan. The scandals surrounding the Prime Minister's involvement with geishas and his Agricultural Minister's edicts about a woman's place may have brought down the cabinet in the summer of 1989, but the ruling party's hastily assumed "feminist" gesture (the appointment of a woman to the position of the cabinet secretary) lasted only a few months. Once the crisis was over and the Liberal Democratic Party won the subsequent election, the party swiftly returned to an all-male cabinet, and the voters hardly uttered a murmur. The attention span of the Japanese is as abbreviated as that of people elsewhere.

Although the dominant gender ideology is hardly contested, feminism cannot be wholly contained indefinitely. The steady rise in the economy is unavoidably accompanied by certain developments.[29] First is an increase in free time. By now Japanese women have the longest life expectancy among all the women of the world. Together with the declining rates of childbirth, the establishment of the nuclear family, and the improvement of household efficiency, this demographic shift has released an enormous amount of time in the lives of Japanese women. The time saved has not as yet been translated into activities outside of the production and consumption cycle of commodified life. There are signs, however, that Japanese women are becoming more sensitized to the predicaments of industrial wealth that simultaneously doom its supposed beneficiaries to a routinized, dehydrated, or even de-eroticized life, with few dreams, little grace, and no criticism. Once fully activated, this sensitivity is bound to lead Japanese women to a room of their own in which to reflect on their relationships with men, parents, children, and family, both personal and national. As of now, this possibility—not yet an actuality—of autonomy and freedom has not been fully explored, nor has it been fully assessed in a deliberation of social objectives.[30] In view of the nearly total male absorption in the production and consumption cycle, however, it seems a fair enough expectation that Japan's egress from the cycle is incumbent upon its women. Finally, Japan's official program for "internationalization" may be as of now no more than a ploy in the overall trade strategy, and yet Japan does not belong outside global integration. The period of autonomy and insularity is forever over for Japan. Patriarchy cannot remain unchallenged much longer, even in Japan, in the name of exceptional national tradition and culture. So-called cultural aspects of social life need to be scrutinized in the context of the history of Japan *in the world,* not in its transcendental essence. Here, too, women as marginalized members are likely to intercede and wrench men from their "utopian" unintelligence.

Writers represent, reflect, and intervene in such changing situations. Younger women writers, like their older sisters and brothers, are largely foregrounded in the bourgeois problematics of Japan, as if there were no social differences, no underclass, no minorities, no gender inequality. They are also nationally and regionally determined despite their frequent travels abroad and the country's official cultural policy of internationalization. Oba Minako (b. 1930) and Yamasaki Michiko (b. 1936), for instance, write about their lives abroad, but their perspective is unquestioningly "Japanese," a clichéd vantage-point assumed monolithically and monologically. These writers are self-defensive and self-enclosed in tone and observation, making no special insights available to the readers of their host countries. Among the practitioners who are critically alert and historically intelligent are Kono Taeko (b. 1926), Ariyoshi Sawako (1931–1984), Tomioka Taeko (b. 1935), and Tsushima Yuko (b. 1947). The last mentioned, and the best of her generation, will be the last topic in this chapter.

Tsushima's fiction is nearly always deployed around the persona of an indomitable though solitary woman. She can be a young mother (as in *Child of Fortune* [*Choji*], 1978; *The Territory of Light* [*Hikari no ryobun*], untranslated, 1979; and *Woman Running in the Mountains* [*Yama o hashiru onna*], 1980),[31] an adolescent (as in *Burning Wind* [*Moeru kaze*], untranslated, 1980), or a grown woman paired with an adolescent (as in *By the River of Fire* [*Hi no kawa no hotori de*], untranslated, 1983). She can be from the middle class or the working class, but either way she is utterly uncompromising in guarding her idiosyncrasy. The fierceness with which she keeps herself free and independent is what runs through each of Tsushima's works, be it a short or a long *shosetsu.*

It is almost as if to keep this fierceness untamed that the author keeps her prose relentlessly short and trimmed. There are no convoluted qualifications, nor are there many *gitaigo*[32]—words that function to loosen up a tight syntax and to colloquialize prose. Tsushima modulates the tautness of her prose with dexterity, although her phrases never run lax and loose.

Woman Running in the Mountains describes a young girl who becomes pregnant after sex with a man she hardly knows. Her life with her poor, tired, and morose parents, who were set against her having the baby and feel no love at all for the infant, is presented in the grimmest and drabbest terms. No one who means anything ever enters her life, nor does anything break up this dullest monotony. Nearly total bleakness fills her diary entries, which record the baby's bodily intake and output and little else. In this life reduced to that of a barely maternal animal, the girl yet refuses to succumb. Never yielding to her parents' demand to give up the child, she struggles on to survive. About midway in the book, she finally lands a job as a manual laborer at a plant nursery. Hope returns to her life and to the narrative.

On a truck being driven through the city streets, she feels the movements of trees and plants and the outdoor air. Once out of her parents' claustrophobic home, she learns the freedom of movement. She comes to know a male co-worker who quietly talks about his love for his retarded son. She has never met a man before who is at ease with being a father. And through knowing this man's presence, "her acts of giving birth to Akira and nurturing him have been given an expression."[33] To love a linguistically handicapped child is to learn a wholly new language—or to learn what language truly is. What has been hitherto unnamed is now named, and with it a new realm of language and meaning is initiated. She is no longer just working at a plant nursery. Her workplace turns into mountains where animals leap, dreams run free, and people care for each other. One of the most pastoral of Tsushima's tales, *Yama o hashiru onna* is a commedia that grants hope. Even here, however, Tsushima will not compromise her unrelenting honesty. Takiko, the heroine (whose name ironically means "many pleasures"), longs for the body of the man (who is called "divine wood"), but the two are never to consummate their attraction. Takiko has sex with an old friend who at least satisfies her lust, and she knows there is little more that she can desire and obtain. When Takiko meets her man again, however, she feels for a moment that she is standing at the height of a hill (p. 330). That is where Tsushima's most hopeful tale comes to a close.

Tsushima's fictional territory seems nearly always circumscribed by the life she has lived. The events of that life—while still in her infancy, her writer-father's double suicide with his mistress;[34] her lonely childhood with her widowed mother, an older sister, and a retarded older brother; her deep love for this language-less brother and his sudden death while they are both still small; her troubled adolescence; her pregnancy and marriage, and divorce soon thereafter; her young motherhood with two children; her difficulties with grown-ups; her children's growth and her need for her own space; her guilt and her struggle with it; her children's distancing themselves from her; her son's death in an accident—such a series of losses and bereavements as well as growths and maturations constitutes the stuff of her imaginary space. It has been an eventful life indeed, often darkened by tragic shadows. Tsushima's is a critical spirit nevertheless, and in her numerous fictional works she examines and reexamines specific events, from all possible angles of recollections and reconstructions, lost options and escaped alternatives. Fantasies and reveries, too, are recaptured and reassessed. Not a lament or mourning for personal grief, her narrative is always a rigorous scrutiny, transforming personal matters into a reflection of general conditions. *Child of Fortune* (*Choji,* 1978) is such a laboratory to test a woman's regrets, desires, and fortitude.

Child of Fortune opens with the heroine's dream of genesis, a still "unhomogenized"—that is, unintegrated and discrete[35]—cosmos. This image also suggests a woman's body before impregnation. Koko, the heroine, has a daughter who lives separately with her aunt, the heroine's well-to-do sister. As the girl is about to enter high school, the mother feels that the daughter already has her own life and belongs more with her sister than with her. Koko is a typical Tsushima woman—independent, uncompromising, untamed, but vulnerable. She has her own small condominium where she lives as she pleases. The men she has loved in the past all tried to force her into a preconceived mold. While she is glad to be rid of them, she misses the days when she lived with them. Likewise, she wants to be with her daughter, although she is also content to be alone. While she of course feels guilty to be less than a "good mother," she also enjoys the pleasure of being by herself. She once wanted her men to love her daughter, and her daughter to love them, but then she also appreciates a solitary life without anyone. Ambivalence persists.

Koko throughout has a strong sexual drive: "Sex always gave her a healthy appetite."[36] What propels her desire for a man, however, is ultimately not sex. She feels a man's body "unbearably dear to her" (p. 47), and yet "she couldn't relate the pleasure that she felt to the physical desire between a man and a woman. Whatever it was she wanted from [her lover], if anything, it was not sex" (p. 48). Men are incapable of understanding this unnamed desire, and she is humiliated with the thought that men see her as simply "highly sexed" (p. 49). Still, she also feels that if she was "born this way, what's the use in trying to change now": she is "in the grip of instincts that [have] no place in the rational scheme of things" (p. 110). Sex makes her feel alive. She loves her freedom, "a fine estate," but she is also afraid of having no one around who would disagree with her (p. 76). The only consolation is the certainty that "she had never betrayed the small child she'd once been" (p. 78).

During this period of vacillation and uncertainty, she finds herself pregnant. As she watches herself grow bigger, however, she is quite certain that she will not abort the baby this time. Against all social pressure and despite her past reservations about maternity, she is resolute:

> She was proud of her resolve. The only way she could escape the molten lava of her own sexuality had been to conceive and have the baby. And when she remembered the looks she'd had from [her former lover] and her sister, and [another lover] and [her divorced husband] before them, it was with anger this time. Giving birth to this baby was the only way to show [the former lover] why she wouldn't become pregnant during her time with him, and how badly she had wanted to escape the power of sex. To [the lover] her body must have seemed as safe as mud. (p. 112)

As she decides on giving birth to the baby, however, Koko discovers that the pregnancy is imaginary. There is the final contradiction and irresolution she still has to confront:

> The doctors, however, had said that unlike ordinary illnesses this one was a case of self-delusion, pure and simple. It would never have happened if she hadn't thought it was happening. . . . Most bewildering of all, these two things had both been real, and *both at the same time*. Neither was a figment, nor a fleeting image. She'd believed, in spending her time the way she did, that this reality was the only one there was; simultaneously, this same Koko had been pumping air into her belly, wishing her way to pregnancy. . . . But when had she split into two? She didn't know. And how was she going to piece her two selves back together again? She didn't know. (p. 130)

Koko has no doubt what to do when the moment of decision arrives. Firmly turning from her former husband and lover, who between them scheme to take responsible action on her behalf, she walks away. Pregnancy, which would ordinarily bind a woman to the order of patriarchy, is in Koko's mind unrelated to the presence of a man. She was alone in the act of "conception"; and she can be alone without the baby. She succeeds in freeing herself from the function of re-production.

In the last scene, Koko is seen playing with a small boy, pretending she is a creature from outer space. It is her return to the opening scene of the primeval world where beings are still separate, unhomogenized. The boy doesn't respond, and she is left alone. The beginning and the ending of *Child of Fortune* seem to suggest the character's recognition of her unalterable situation. In between the narrative describes the process of a life, which largely consists of Koko's severe criticism of herself as well as of others. At any rate, the die has been cast. Although her future course is hardly mapped out, Koko has to walk into the unknown, just like the other women of Japan who are learning to find their own space and gather their voices for their own future.

Conversation and Conference: Forms of Discourse

Industrial nations are increasingly finding themselves faced with some kind of crisis in written culture. Long persuaded that civilization progresses from orality to literacy,[1] cultural theorists are now hard put to explain the connection between a reputed glut of images and a universal indifference to reading and writing. Visual media cannot be the principal culprit since in fact it is widely acknowledged that there has been a recent decline in the production of serious or even popular films and TV programs. Nor can resistance to written culture be hastily dismissed as a temporary derangement of youth or as a decay of humanistic values. Instead, this phenomenon is likely complicit with the dominant consumerism and mass manipulation that characterize late-stage capitalism. It is perfectly possible, however, that should manipulation and pressure on popular culture cease, there would still be a pervasive indifference to reading and writing and a profound orality. In the United States at least, populist anti-literatism may well evince a distrust of proponents of literate culture so fundamental as to make any such hypothesis extremely difficult to prove.

In Japan, the symptoms of this unconcern with writing are quite different from those in the United States. Schooling seems successful enough, if by success is meant a virtually universal attain-

ment of literacy and acquisition of the skills that enable citizens to
participate usefully in the process of production. Students do regularly attend schools; their mathematical proficiency is high; and they
are so efficiently socialized that the crime rate as well as the number
of incidents of school violence generally remain low, despite perhaps
exaggerated reactions to a few occasional events. (Japan's crimes
seem to be largely confined to the rich and powerful and the *yakuza,*
the shadowy doubles of the "legitimate" criminals.)[2] And yet such
training and indoctrination of citizens as effective workers is not
necessarily conducive to a vigorous cultivation of critical, articulate,
and diverse views and opinions. People seem content with the immediate circumference of daily life. Of late their desultory silence is
generally shared by the cultural leaders and managers. Ooka Shohei,
one of the most respected Japanese writers, recently addressed
himself precisely to these issues in a talk titled "The Development
of Entertainment in Relation to the Abandonment of Books" ("En-
tateinmento eno tenkai: shoseki banare to no kanren ni oite").[3]

Ooka's rambling essay is not at all easy to summarize, but he
seems preoccupied with the ominous changes that have taken place
since the immediate postwar years, when intellectual criticism was
still very much alive. The disappearance of "pure literature" *(jun
bungaku),* surplus production, intensified consumption, the popular-
ization of general culture, leisure activities, the replacement of
books by comics and TV, the noticeable rejection of TV in recent
years, and the rise of "postmodernism" (which he leaves undefined)
are among his topics as he describes the transformation of literature
into performance and entertainment. Stylishly up to date, Ooka
refers to many translated theorists such as Lyotard, Jauss, Derrida,
and Eagleton in addition to a good number of today's active Japanese writers, although their roles in his argument are sometimes
not discernible. What is utterly convincing about the piece, however,
is Ooka's bewilderment and perplexity over the decline of written
culture in Japan and its political and economic significance.

Of course, Ooka's voice may not be representative of Japanese
intellectuals. Younger writers, for example, maintain that Japan's
recent status as an economic superpower calls for a more serious
treatment by European and American intellectuals, that Japan is
ahead in some ongoing race for intellectual status.[4] It is perfectly

reasonable to expect more attention from Western intellectuals, if Japan's intellectual production is as appealing and useful to the targeted buyers as, say, the productions of Sony, Toyota, or Nikon. In fact, if they could voice their views from an oppositionist position, these Japanese intellectuals might receive a careful hearing from the rest of the world, and if still ignored, they would then have a legitimate ground for demanding attention. There seems to be a serious ambivalence among these writers, however, as to whether they are speaking from the position of First World or Third World intellectuals. This disorientation is reflected in their tone of voice, which is neither dominant nor resistant. Very much like intellectuals in a colonized society, many of them sound alternatively strident, chauvinistic, sophisticated, cosmopolitan, or dourly defensive.[5] In any case, the reciprocity that Japanese intellectuals ask from their Western colleagues has so far not materialized.[6]

A far less conspicuous but probably more important aspect of Japanese intellectual life is the increasing replacement of written discourse by spoken words. I mean by this the ubiquitous publication of interviews *(intabyu),* dialogues *(taidan),* panel discussions before an audience *(toron),* and roundtable talks *(zadankai),* all of which might be subsumed under the heading of conversation. To open a magazine or scholarly periodical is to come across at least one of these conversational forms of exchange. (For example, the August 1990 issue of *Sekai,* one of the few remaining journals of opinion, contains four *zadankai,* four interviews, and one *taidan.)* There is hardly any "writer" who does not practice this form of group talk-think. In fact, more and more books now being published in Japan are merely collections of transcribed conversations, usually packaged under some imaginative or even provocative title. I want to explore the likely connection between the prevalence of these spoken forms and a corresponding crowding out of written expositions on the one hand and, on the other hand, the growing debility of critical discourse in Japan.[7]

To begin with, the conversational forms are by definition interpersonal and social, whereas writing takes place in isolation. As an individual faces a blank sheet—or increasingly a blank screen—he or she has to imagine a respondent. The respondent can be an identifiable person but is usually a generalized auditor whose imagined response propels the writing to the next stage. How does a writer shape his or her respondent? Is the relationship one of hostility, intimacy, condescension, respect, or equality? How extensive is the respondent's frame of reference, or horizon of knowledge, imagined to be? How fast should the exposition progress? How concentrated or digressive should it be? All such questions must be formed, understood, answered, and integrated into the tone, style, and structure of writing. Throughout, as the writer pursues his or her discourse in loneliness, the final audience, too, must be imagined. Is there a specific readership? Which one? The marvel and terror of writing are in this confrontation with solitude and void, one's encounter with one's own shadow.

The conversational forms are sharply different. There is, of course, no "writer," nor is there a "speaker." Everyone is a *participant*. All the participants, even the person being interviewed, are encased in a common space with at least one other person. In the most typical situation the participants know each other and share an interest, practice, experience, expertise, or social position. They are usually placed in a comfortable space and in a tolerably relaxing atmosphere, with the aid of several accommodating editors and assistants, who not only operate the indispensable audio-visual recorder but also perform service functions that range from filling glasses and cups to intervening with strategic questions. There is a distinct sense of the inside, and of insiders; the participants occupy a secluded space apart from the world of daily life inhabited by ordinary people. The awareness of the presence of other participants is of the utmost importance: they are together in this exclusive, insider's space. One does not think alone, or rather one does not think so much as circulate suggestions. There is no need to invent a respondent, since another person in the room will actually respond, and one's counterresponse keeps the conversation going. If anyone gropes for words and ideas, someone else will interpose; if someone looks for an answer to a question, he or she can remain silent, knowing the silence will be broken by the ever helpful others. Silence in this conversational arena is not the same as absence or a vacuum; it is an invitation to share, an appeal for a loan. Likewise, one can repeat another's remark without seeming repetitious, since repetition functions here as assent or elaboration. Speculation seems to happen passively.

The frame of reference and horizon of knowledge, the two requisites that a writer must negotiate, emerge as the group cooperates in the enterprise. Even when there is disagreement, the group consciousness is all-powerful. The art of conversation consists of sensitivity to the flow of the group's inclination and mood. Ignorance and error do not matter much; they simply provide a blank for others to fill in as a gesture of grace and cooperation. Both *taidan* and *zadankai* are occasions to display social grace and group dynamics as a form of learning. If there is warmth in the group, it can stand in for intellectual rigor. Or rather, if the level of discourse happens to be low, the participants can work together to increase the warmth, thereby turning the conversation into a pleasurable performance. In its practice of the art of modulation and fluctuation, *zadankai* is a laid-back postmodern version of *renga,* group-composed linked poetry.

The difference between written discourse and conversation of this kind is finally cognate, though not identical, with the difference between literacy and orality. It may not be too useful to discuss here—or anywhere else—the relative privileges of orality and literacy as we compare "group think-talk" and "individual think-write." However, when the two discursive modes are paired, they share numerous features with the orality/literacy pairing. A brief review here might suggest the general outline.[8] To put it simply, orality is characterized by short memory, homeostasis in memory, the speaker and listener's sharing a site, hence shared tribalism, transience of textuality, poor transmission, intimacy, direct social control, paratactic and noncumulative narrativity, adjectival description, and types as narrative personae. Literacy, on the other hand, is marked by physical textual permanence, longer memory, spatial freedom in textual dissemination, isolation and alienation, individualist liberation, syntactic and cumulative narrativity, and introspective analysis.

Before going further, a warning is in order. This kind of binarism can at any time degenerate into a racist theory of the great divide between the literate and the nonliterate, between the civilized and the savage, between the Western and the non-Western. It can deteriorate into an essentialist and bigoted operation that merely muddies the issue, as it sometimes has among Western ethnocentric culturalists and writers from Karl Marx to Matthew Arnold, from

Charles Darwin to Thomas Mann, not to mention most Western academics to this day. Derrida's attack on Rousseau and Lévi-Strauss is right, at least in his contention that the line, between oral and literate societies hardly exists. Nevertheless, the rejection of a facile distinction between the West and the non-West on the basis of writing and speech does not mean that the latter two are indistinguishable. Indeed, the difference between individual think-write and group think-talk, between written speculation and spoken conversation, is crucial to any consideration of the health of Japan's critical discourse.

What I call group think-talk can of course be valuable—especially when the participants are serious practitioners of other arts and activities. Writers and artists, thinkers and politicians, can clarify and adumbrate their programs and priorities; they can relate their publicly available works to their speaking voices. The conversational context softens and diffuses the differences that might otherwise be too sharply enunciated, linking the participants with each other in unexpected ways. More important, conversation can send the listener back as a reader to the primary works of the participants.

Discussions among like-minded people who are at the same time adversarial on a number of crucial issues can be stunningly illuminating. There have been many such exchanges among Maruyama Masao, Otsuka Hisao, and others, on the urgent issues of "going beyond modernity" (kindai no chokoku) and "subjectivity/autonomy" (shutaisei ron). There was, for another example, an uncompromising argument between Oe Kenzaburo and Eto Jun in the sixties about the future of postwar literature as they saw it. In these transcribed conversations, the previously published works of the participants are very much in evidence, enabling the listener who also reads to interweave whatever is revealed in the talks into a wider context of the writers and the problematical issues they face. The frozen written texts are retrieved from isolation and animated. Written words share time and space with spoken words. Such contextualization at least promises to build a site and structure of discourse. Whether such an ideological edifice still stands unassaulted is hardly relevant. It has left a site and structure one can contest even now, which as I take it is what is meant by intellectual exchange.

These are conversations we wish we could have joined. But there are fewer and fewer such occasions; cultural consumerism seems to be erasing systematic and structured analysis and speculation, and along with this the conversations of Japan's cultural leaders have begun to deteriorate. Instead of a gathering of minds, their public conversations are occasions for bartering associations and impressions, for exchanging pleasantries or for staging altercations.[9] At best, they are a depository of information from sundry sources; at worst, they are an opportunity to drop names. Either way, they are likely to be shapeless, unstructured, elusive, and—to borrow Ooka's term again—for entertainment only.

The *taidan* or *zadankai* alone, without close reference to the participants' own written words, are unlikely to help build any impressive discursive structure. Unlike the speculation of a single writer, sustained over the course of numerous occasions, a conversational exchange is intermittent and dispersed. From one *zadankai* to another there is hardly any continuity. The list of participants seldom remains identical. Topics and themes, not to say resolutions and conclusions, remain changeable and mobile. Participants cannot resume their discourse when they enter a new session. Topics and arguments almost always start afresh, which means continuity between one *zadankai* and another is scarcely possible. Because statements are made orally, documentation is neither expected nor given, and thus references to any external evidence are disjointed or absent. Quotations are by and large approximate, although sometimes a notation of exact wording is added to the printed *zadankai*. The end result is opaqueness, imprecision, and often obfuscation.[10]

There are more serious pitfalls. The textuality of transcribed conversations is vulnerable to various modes of adulteration. I cannot of course detail how participants treat the subsequent written transcriptions, but I imagine it would be very hard to resist improving one's performance through editing, when there is no risk at all of being caught in the act. Perhaps this presents no problem in most cases because *zadankai* does not pretend to reproduce the actual oral exchange, but occasionally authenticity may be involved. As long as the taped recording is not transcribed, translated, and edited by a third party, the sole source of information is the participants and editors. When a writer interviews a foreign scholar who speaks no Japanese, for instance, there is little likelihood of the inter-viewee's gaining access to the published version in Japanese. Hence, the interviewer is more or less free to revise, if not invent, at least some parts of the text. After all, a Derrida, an Eco, or a Chomsky is unlikely to inspect a Japanese transcript.[11]

The group format allows several other possible licenses. As long as it is not openly rejected, a statement made in the presence of others appears to have the consent and authority of these co-partic-ipants. Therefore, every statement unchallenged in the text seems to bear the imprimatur of the group. And since most *zadankai* are populated by experts and authorities in a given field, a *zadankai* tends to turn into an occasion for mutual promotion. Literary Critic A shows off her knowledge of Witold Gombrowicz; Critic B inter-rupts her with his insight into Bakhtin; at this point Writer C inter-jects his admiration for Formalists; after a few exchanges like this they settle on a feature or two of the "Slavic mind." The end result of this *zadankai* might be a joint certification of all participants as experts in Slavism.

Editors and publishers seem by now quite used to and attached to this format. It is relatively effortlessly produced. All writers are accustomed to the invitations and need little inducement, much less coercion to perform. As long as the participants have a chance to edit and revise their speeches before printing, they are not likely to fuss overly much. For periodical editors in particular, the *zadankai* format is vitally attractive. Though the amount paid as an hono-rarium is rising, production costs can be held to a pretty modest sum. In this way editors can involve a big-time writer who might otherwise be reluctant to contribute a fresh essay. The planning is easy enough: a rough outline and a few topics are all that is needed; the rest can be arranged by the invited participants. Instant planning, instant production. Few editorial gimmicks come easier or cheaper.

The advantage of the format to the writer is equally apparent. Even the most careless writer would have to spend time moving a pen or "processing" words, if not composing and revising. Some would even have to read, think, and choose words before beginning to write. The group think-talk form eliminates these and many such bothers of thinking and writing. Open a book or two, think for a few minutes on the way to the meeting place in a taxi or subway—that is usually enough. Sober reading in preparation for extended expositions might prove too showy for other participants, and thus undesirable. Everyone's cooperation is more or less guaranteed so that all may shine. And then there are always assurances that corrections can be made.

Financial considerations obviously count. In addition to paying honoraria for periodical publication, the *taidan* are frequently collected and published in book form later on. If the sales are not phenomenal, there is at least a core of dedicated readers who are willing to rehear and overhear the conversations of the greats. The monetary rewards at least partly account for the amazing productivity of writers such as Yoshimoto Takaaki or Yamaguchi Masao. The predominance of collected *taidan* is remarkable in Japan's publishing world today—with no trifling effect on the intellectual health of the nation.

How about the reader-buyers? Why do they wish to read published conversations? There are truly devoted followers, always attracted to their heroes' performances in various situations, around different topics, and on new panels. For many more casual readers, however, the lure is not any specific writer but rather the topic. One wants to know about, say, poststructuralism or Showa militarism, and if the choice is between monographs or collections of *zadankai* on such topics, the latter are much less intimidating, more casual, and readily accessible. Their looseness of reference and tendency toward generalization provide the reader with a relaxed engagement that a written exposition seldom allows. The reader is continually reassured by the experienced editors and participants, who do not fail to season the performance with regularly spaced humor, regardless of the topic—a feature not often available in analytic essays in Japan. Although more serious readers might protest against the predominance of this loosened form, there are always enough buyer-readers who keep the industry going.

Conversationalism—as by now I might be allowed to call this whole drift toward oralization—has come to infect the general style and substance of written discourse. The fragmented and paratactic nature of the conversational form has become a feature of current cultural conditions in general. A person who habitually participates in *zadankai* thinks in a similar fashion when he or she must write.

Japanese writing style has been undergoing a radical change lately, and whether the change is a cause or an effect, conversationalism is the dominant mode. Writers feel free to make assertions without much attempt to back them up with hard evidence. As in a conversation, they assume a pervasive consent and approval. If faced with disagreement, they can always apologize or forget. Thus the colloquial formulaic disclaimers—"I am not an expert on this, but . . ." or "I don't have enough time now, but . . ." or "I await your guidance and correction, should I prove to be in egregious error"— are unselfconsciously utilized as if such rhetorical alibis were sufficient excuses for nonarguments or substitutes for arguments. Views and opinions tend to be no more than random thoughts (*sunpyo,* or "inch-long comments"; *danso,* or "fragmentary ideas"), respectable only because they emanate from respectable masters. There are usually no intrinsic merits in such statements, except that they reassure and comfort those who are implicated in the hierarchic system of authority. Consensus of opinion and overall agreement seem to be the presiding genius of Japanese society at the present time. Discussion and criticism imply dissent and protest, which most people seem eager to avoid. Unity and homogeneity are felt to be a key to that cosmology and epistemology that Japanese cultural leaders have agreed to mythologize.

The economy and ecology of conversationalism constitute an important factor in social control, lest conversation prove to be contestational rather than consensual. The policy of social control can be seen to operate over conversation itself. Let me take an instance of space and its relation to the site or place for talk. Japan's shortage of space, worsening every year around the megalopolis of Tokyo, is habitually presented as a catch-all explanation of the low quality of life in Japan. Japan is small, and much of its area is both unarable and uninhabitable, hence the nearly unbearable but inevitable congestion around Tokyo (involving a major portion of the Japanese people). Such a routine explanation should not automatically be accepted as valid or even plausible. Japan does have enough space should it choose to disperse its concentrated population. Even if Tanaka Kakuei's *Retto kaikaku ron (Restructuring the Japanese Archipelago)* was a self-serving enterprise (which it certainly was), the proposal nonetheless merits serious consideration.[12] Japan can

and should be radically decentralized, beginning with the diversi-
fication of metropolitan functions. In other words, before resorting
to the economic colonialism of "Silver Columbia" (the 1986 proposal
for the construction of a city in Australia for the retired Japanese)
or the even more bizarre "Multifunctionpolis," both dreamed up by
the MITI bureaucrats for the purpose of acquiring expansive—and
cheap—Australian land, Japan ought to look inward to reflect on the
cultural and political meaning of its spatial policy.[13]

Spatial restrictions that reduce the effects of Japan's great wealth
to quite an amazing extent can only be regarded at this point as part
of a deliberate plan by Japan's central policy makers.[14] The populace
has been carefully deprived of public space and therefore of sites
for gathering and talk, the sort of activity that could easily be
transformed into programs for oppositional action. At the present
time, Japan has carefully erased from the metropolitan centers all
space for assembly and demonstration. It may be hard to believe for
anyone who has not been to Tokyo, but that great city contains not
a square foot where its citizens can stand without admission or rent.
There are few parks and squares, and what few public places remain
(Hibiya Park, Shinjuku Garden, Ueno Park, Palace Garden, railway
and station plazas) are all guarded and controlled.[15] This ensures
safety against criminal violence, as Americans would be acutely
aware, but at the price of having political freedom quietly restricted
in Japanese daily life. Outside their workplace, there is simply no
place for citizens to assemble.

As further evidence of the effects of consensual conversationalism
on daily life, newly built colleges and universities deliberately omit
facilities for free assembly such as a large auditorium or plaza.[16]
Neither faculty nor students are apparently upset by such a policy.
Both teachers and students have better things to do: the former dash
off to teach or work at a second or third institution; the latter are
increasingly inclined to think of education merely as a vocational
prerequisite. Far worse, however, is the fact that by night Tokyo
has a virtual curfew, and nobody seems ever to protest: public
transportation service ends before midnight, and since most
people—including writers and intellectuals—live in far-flung sub-
urbs, they usually go home before they have to hire costly taxis.
Their time for private conversation is thus kept to a minimum after

a long day's work. People do not often entertain friends or colleagues at home because homes are too far apart, or too small for guests, even one at a time.[17] Restaurants, coffee shops, and bars might be expected to offer a respite, but they are also small, too crowded, and too noisy (thanks to ear-splitting music played constantly to keep customer turnover commercially profitable). Unless a publisher or some other institution arranges a formal conversation, people in Japan seldom have a chance to talk or freely exchange views and opinions. Isolation and alienation are acute for those who have nonetheless managed to keep their wits together to think about such things. They do grieve for the loss of time, space, and talk, and yet the general conditions of monetary reward and collective planning make it virtually impossible to contest the situation on behalf of genuine conversation.

The *zadankai* form, then, is best understood as purchased talk. Talk—an activity that is part of civilized life in most other places—is now marked off as contracted labor for sale. Cultural leaders and managers talk together so that they may earn money from it. Or rather, they no longer think and write, or learn and speculate, in isolation. They don't talk unless they are paid, just as there is no space unless it is rented. As economy directly intervenes in space, it also suffuses all aspects of human intercourse.

This bleak situation is of course not limited to Japan. Oralization and visualization of culture, expanding through electronic technologies, is widely perceived as a major cultural problem by Americans as well. As Guy Debord puts it, "the image is the last stage of commodity reification."[18] In the United States conditions are in many ways quite different from those in Japan, however, and although the matter properly requires another essay in another book, it might be well just to suggest the barest outline of the differences. Though conversationalism is increasingly conspicuous in the United States, interviews, debates, roundtable discussions, and "talk shows" are only infrequently transcribed and printed in journals and books. They are still limited mostly to radio and television programs.[19] What is notable on the recent U.S. intellectual scene is the proliferation of conferences. Among academics especially, the workshop and symposium as well as conference seem to attract participants, both students and faculty, in large numbers. Scholars of any standing are regularly invited to these, all expenses paid, with increasingly large honoraria. Among the academic establishments and counterestablishments, people talk openly about acute cases of conference burnout or of workshop junkies. But could these gatherings be called "group think-talks"? Not quite. What is fascinating about the American version of conversationalism is that in many of these meetings, conversations simply fail to take place. The participants behave almost in opposition to their Japanese counterparts: they adhere to their written texts, hardly ever deviating from prepared lectures. In fact, even in cases where the texts are distributed in advance among the participants and the audiences so as to allow time for discussion, the speakers by and large insist on reading the manuscripts aloud without deviation from the text, and then avoiding as much as possible informal talk or discussion of it.

As always, there are numerous exceptions, but it is not an overstatement to say that the scholarly gathering in the United States is deeply embedded in the individual think-write mode, as against the possibility of working or thinking in groups. This is an equally disturbing trend, because the workshop, symposium, or conference whose objective is the contextualization of opinions, perspectives, and methodologies does not often in fact provide that; the participants remain as disparate as when they came. I am not sure what all this adds up to, but it seems to me symptomatic of a loss of trust that prevails among American intellectuals, a loss of trust not only in the group of which they are members but finally in themselves. They have a defensive isolationist resistance against exchange and intercourse; they need their own brilliance to be left unquestioned. At any rate, if I am right in my assumptions about the different attitudes toward orality and literacy in Japanese and American societies, the different uses of written texts must be deemed one of the clearest manifestations, and the situation in both cases is indeed dismal.

All the talk of crisis surrounding the orality/literacy modes (including this book) can finally be linked to the variable and unstable relationship between the (speaking/writing) subject and his or her utterance. In the Japanese conversational model, the subject is nearly incorporated into the text and context of utterance. Speech is virtually composed by the conversing group of which a speaker is a member. The disembodied and disenfranchised self seems to occupy a highly abstract communal space, in which another exchange, that of commodities, is also being carried on. In this country of *purinto banare* (abandonment of printed materials) cultural leaders and managers share this commodification of speech with the masses. Critics and scholars accept the role of commentators, then celebrities, and finally entertainers. In this sense, intellectuals are not perceived as constituting a class of patricians detached and aloof from the people. But what an exorbitant price they pay for the mythology of homogeneity and collectivity.

The American model of written speculation, on the other hand, seems to exact the high price of isolation and alienation. There is no feeling in America that its elite culture suffers from discursive laxness; there is indeed an unchallengeable confidence—bordering on arrogance—among intellectual elites that theirs is the mind of humanity that thinks for all. The intertextual discourse into which every writer professedly inserts idiosyncrasy is continually being revised with greater precision, sophistication, and elaboration. Such complication and refinement have begun to exclude even educated people, cutting off any meaningful interaction between the intellectual elite and the public. The severance, however, is even more extensive. The same complication and sophistication are now separating the speakers from their very voices, their voices from their spoken words. A text is so meticulously devised that it is hardly recoverable even for the speaker without constant recourse to it. The process of formulation is so demanding of exactitude that the text becomes almost independent of its writer. One does not know one's text; the text does not claim its writer. Taken much further, this could result in a total and disastrous separation of belief and praxis, which together presumably integrate the speaker, the voice, and the spoken words.

There is no easy solution to the problems raised here. But intervene we must. Where is our task to begin? If the *zadankai* format is a problem, the American conference is hardly the solution. These forms, conversational or speculative, are deeply grounded in the historical moments of the two societies. Japanese intellectuals might return to their separate studies to write in isolation, so as to restore the voice of criticism and opposition. American intellectuals might seek seriously to be understood by more of their own people. Reform in both societies is radically needed to change the present relations among the speaker, the voice, and the words, between the speaking/writing subject and his or her utterance—so that ultimately intellectuals may regain the lost habit of praxis and return to the world.

Epilogue

Criticism and opposition, which were briefly vital in Japan's postwar years, have now become thoroughly vitiated. In today's Japan, ideas like culture, tradition, and literature are already suspect by themselves. Culture, as the idea is deployed, is a byproduct of culturalism, a project planned and executed consensually. Whether such accord is centrally dictated or generally spontaneous, the culture is unbreakably circumscriptive. Literature, on the other hand, has run its course by now: invented as a part of the nation-building program, the discourse was long kept esoteric and uncontaminated ("pure" literature [*jun bungaku*] they call it, to make sure that it remains aloof). Such a literature, a self-conscious modernist enterprise, was from the beginning an imported construct, but it has been dispersed and denatured by now. As we have seen throughout this book, it has been mixed and adulterated with all forms of social expressions and exchanges. The transformation itself is a matter neither to be commended nor deplored. The vanishing of criticism is quite otherwise.

Three strands of residual literature are evident in this post-1970 era. One is the works of writers acutely aware of the boredom and sterility of managed society, which they carefully nurture so that they may plausibly postulate style and snobbery as a cure. These descendents of Mishima Yukio are now represented by Murakami Haruki. The second is a bastardized line running parallel to the first, from Tanaka Yasuo's *Somehow Crystal* to Yoshimoto Banana's books. The last is the product of the rear-guard group of modernist writers who trace their lineage from the postwar *shutaisei* intellectuals to Oe Kenzaburo.

To begin with the first, Mishima and Murakami are both stylists in the sense that they believe snobbish style alone would rescue them from boredom. Neither is intellectually immersed; they dabble in a blasé, offhand fashion. Unlike Murakami, Mishima read a lot and used his knowledge in forging a style. His ideas were ultimately subsumed, however, by gesture and pose. After their initial successes, both wrote for export. Mishima was very good at it—better than any other Japanese writer so far; Murakami is about to begin his campaign. For this purpose, they both custom-tailor their goods to their clients abroad: Mishima displayed an exotic Japan, its nationalist side; Murakami is also exhibiting an exotic Japan, its international version. Both, however, are preoccupied with the idea of Japan, or to put it more precisely, with what they imagine the foreign buyers like to see in it.

Murakami parodies Mishima and Oe, and entertains those who are in the know with clever jokes. His tales are remarkably fragmented. Adorned with well-placed aphorisms, however, they are "pick-uppable" on any page, and that means an entirely easy read—a smooth, popular item of consumption. For those who want to play a symbol-deciphering game, on the other hand, he provides a sheep, a pinball machine, and a rat. Readers are best advised not to take this too far—they might soon reach the limits. Besides, only a very few would be silly enough to get interested in deep reading. Murakami's poise—always cool, never ruffled—is the selling point. In fact, even his sex scenes are stylish; their copulating couples remain collected, observant, and uninvolved as they pace themselves through orgasms. Their breathing remains normal, their pulse does not quicken, nor, of course, do they interact emotionally. Murakami's wit and humor consist of irrelevant comments, which break tension and sustain poise. Everyday trivia are smoothed over and prettied up, and all the players come off cool and clean.

His *Pinball, 1973* (*1973 nen no pin booru,* 1980) is a pastiche of Oe Kenzaburo's *Football in the First Year of the Era of Manen [1860]* (*Manen gannen no futtoboru;* trans. as *The Silent Cry*), as Karatani Kojin has detected.[1] But it is hardly clear what is being substituted for Oe's passionate inquiry. *Hear the Wind Sing* (*Kaze no uta o kike,* 1979), *Pinball, 1973,* and *A Wild Sheep Chase* (*Hitsuji o meguru boken,* 1982; trans. 1989) are all sophisticated stylizations of trivia, flying over the boredom and irritation of everyday life. They are story-less stories of nameless characters. The breezy style discourages any attempt to figure out the plot or ponder the characters; as a matter of fact, even the sequence of events and the relations among characters are hard to remember. The most attractive feature is Murakami's prose, which is consistently affected, at times effectively funny, and carries along the reader to the very end.[2] After these tales Murakami wrote one story with named characters and a memorable plot-line. Called *Norwegian Wood* (*Noruwei no mori,* 1987), it arguably tries to simulate the mood of the Beatles song—at least, it erases history, converting the 1960s to a mood, a sentiment, and a style. As a love story, it is even more vacuous than Erich Segal's *Love Story,* being hopelessly sentimental and disembodiedly erotic. Its inanity must have been unapparent, however, to the more than four million people who bought the book, which came packaged in a glossy red dust jacket with green lettering (vol. 1) and a glossy green dust jacket with red lettering (vol. 2), complete with a gold foil wraparound, and was published shortly before Christmas 1987. Murakami is a careful writer, to specify such design details on behalf of his mainly "college girl"[3] readers' aesthetic.

Murakami is the poet laureate of Japan in the 1980s and 1990s. He sells well and plans to expand his market to the United States. He has had his first three books translated into English, and is scheduling to release one every year in the United States. Herbert Mitgang of the *New York Times* is apparently impressed with Murakami's artistic and intellectual accomplishment: he wrote two uninformed and misguided reviews for his paper, as if his assignment were to follow the U.S. administration's open-door policy in the book market.[4] It will be an interesting test of the U.S. readership when the literary market distributes the Murakami productions, although I have my own reasons to doubt that they will ever find as many buyers here as do Honda automobiles or Sony camcorders.

Murakami's work looks learned and profound alongside Yoshimoto Banana's books. Her output is entirely couched in baby talk, uninterrupted by humor, emotion, idea, not to say irony or intelligence. No one could summarize any of these books, for they have even less plot and character than Murakami's unplotted and characterless works. There is no style, no poise, no imagery. I have read, or think I have read, all the books she has published, but I don't remember. Reopening my copy of *Kitchen*,[5] I find these passages marked:

> The other day, lo and behold, my grandmother died. I was surprised. (p. 8)

> I placed the bedding in a quiet well-lit kitchen, drawing silently soft sleepiness that comes with saturated sadness not relieved by tears. I fell asleep wrapped up in a blanket like Linus [of *Peanuts*]. (p. 9)

> Yuichi said with great pleasure, "I bought a word processor!" (p. 44)

> "Listen, I bought a juicer!" Eriko said with great pleasure, pulling out a big box from a paper bag. . . . There emerged a splendid juicer that would turn everything into juice. (p. 50)

> I opened it and found a pretty glass with a picture of bananas. . . . My precious, precious glass. (p. 51)

Most of her books have been selling by the millions (give or take a few thousand).

These two writers, one believed to be highbrow and the other, amazingly enough, also considered a literary figure, are still not the most eccentric.[6] I discovered an essay called "*The Leica of Love and Sadness* and Its World" in a periodical which was once one of the most respected journals of opinion in Japan. The article, written by a published author, describes his new work. He explains that the book is meant to help the Japanese shed their provincialism at this moment of internationalization. He laments the insular boorishness of his countrymen who have not yet acquired the cosmopolitan taste for elegance. He finds that the top-ranking brand-name goods that the Japanese love to talk about in daily life are not sufficiently introduced into their fictional world. The Japanese must understand how important these objects are as international status symbols. Thus his book presents ten short stories set in ten metropolitan cities like Milan, Honolulu, Shanghai, and New York, each constructed around luxury consumer objects such as a Dunhill lighter, a Rolex watch, a Leica camera, Cuban cigars, etc. Serving as an advertisement of his own new book, the unashamed "essay" is devoid of self-irony.[7]

These instances suggest the general setting against which the surviving writers and critics of the third category, who prefer to think, observe, and criticize, will have to persist. Their ranks are thinning year by year, with no sizeable reinforcement expected from younger generations. The prospect is indeed bleak. People read fewer books, and those few journals that have somehow survived publish shorter and shorter pieces as if the general reader's—and writer's—concentration lasted a maximum of ten pages. Even moviegoers are vanishing: in 1989 an audience a mere 13 percent of the peak year 1958 audience visited Japan's movie houses.[8] Brief impressions and unsubstantiated rumors take the place of criticism and argument. A huge number of periodicals appear every year only to disappear the next—after generating sufficient initial profits, tax write-offs, and advertising revenues for the publishers.

Against all such odds, certain people hang on: Oe Kenzaburo, Furui Yukichi, Inoue Hisashi, Nakagami Kenji, Kono Taeko, Tomioka Taeko, Tsushima Yuko among writers, and Kato Shuichi, Sakamoto Yoshikazu, Fujita Shozo, Oda Makoto, Karatani Kojin among critics. And there are their readers, too, though incomparably fewer than Yoshimoto's and Murakami's. They are the bearers of light into the 1990s and beyond. But these writers' difficulties are immense: even though they continue to write and receive respect, admiration, and prizes, there are very few critics who respond to them with detailed critiques. They are marginalized in such a way that no one really engages them in serious conversations. Awed and overwhelmed, the reader and critic stand at distance, leaving the isolated writers alone. Their writing is thus monologic, a specular dialogue of the mind with itself, endlessly turning inward and introspective. And yet they must keep their eyes open to the outside, and speak up to the unlistening world. To be concerned and to live in history is nearly an impossible dream.

If there is anyone now in Japan whose work deserves full-scale studies, it is Oe Kenzaburo, who at the same time cannot free himself from this isolation. Without doubt Oe's awesome learning, frightening memory, complex ideas, unbridled imagination, resilient political will, and indiscriminate modesty tempered by absolute self-assurance make him the most formidable figure in the literary world of Japan now. Nobody dares challenge him, leaving him apart from anybody else. This might be an overstatement, since there have been monographs in English and Japanese in addition to numerous articles discussing his work. We are also aware that he is the only serious writer with a sizeable readership in Japan, and that he continues to receive honors and awards from foreign and domestic sources. And yet one feels that Oe has not received the proper feedback. Readers and critics stand off with timidity verging on fear. The studies so far published do little justice to one of the most intricate minds in the world today. Admiration for Oe is ironically the very impediment to his intercourse with the world. And no one can survive for long the intellectual isolation Oe has been enduring. It is indeed unfortunate that the Western critics have repeated the myth of Oe as a difficult stylist whose Japanese resists attempts at translation. His writing is often hilarious, with a whimsical and grotesque humor that breaks out unexpectedly from among the dense speculations and tormented examinations.

Oe's topos is in the margins. He constructs a mountain village inhabited by a group of eccentric rustics who appear and reappear among his works. He sets up a synchronic view of the center-periphery paradigm, à la Lévi-Strauss, Victor Turner, and their Japanese facilitator, Yamaguchi Masao, among others. Liminality enables Oe to compensate for dominant metropolitan centralism, releasing him from the sterile hegemonism of today's Japanese intellectuals. His structuralist perspective, however, is implicated in a conservatism that would approve and maintain the marginal as complementary and subordinate to the center. Centrality is not eschewed, nor is the holism of concentric communality. In Oe's world there is often a patriarchy organized around the father/god, who seems saturated with moral intelligence. The godhead is problematically powerful, though always scrutinized. Family and community are always suspect ideologically, because they are finally instrumental to an ulterior end, no matter how it is concealed by their portrayal as transcendental values. Similarly, synchronic balance between the center and periphery also guarantees the stability of "pure literature" in remaining elitist and exclusive. Such will to excellence and authority contradict Oe's political sympathy with the wretched of the earth. While it is undeniable that this contradiction generates fracture, which activates and intensifies the involution of meaning, Oe is surprisingly nostalgic in his critical works, where flattening of language is both unavoidable and required. Abstractions such as "humanism," "culture," "pure literature," "village," "author," and "family" are invested with privilege and authority.

From *The Silent Cry* to *Doojidai geem* (*A Contemporary Game*, 1979), *Ame no ki o kiku onnatachi* (*Women Listening to the Rain-Trees*, 1982), *Atarashii hito yo mezameyo* (*Rouse Up, O, Young Men of a New Age*, 1983), *Kaba ni kamareru* (*Bitten by a Hippo*, 1985), *M/T to mori no fushigina monogatari* (*A Curious Tale of M/T and the Wood*, 1986), *Natsukashii toshi e no tegami* (*Letters to the Bygone Years*, 1987), *Jinsei no shinseki* (*Life-Relatives*, 1989), to *Shizukana seikatsu* (*A Quiet Life*, 1990), every work is a meticulous execution of form and a bold actualization of ideas.

The Silent Cry rigorously probes into the nature of storytelling.[9] As it gathers together gossip and rumors, myths and legends, letters and documents, into fiction and history, that is, into a form, *The Silent Cry* retraces the way an event is told, disputed, revised, verified, retried, and retold. Oe's story is kept open to anyone who would reread and revise it, as it emerges from two brothers' search in the 1960s for their family roots and their relationships to them. *The Silent Cry*, whose Japanese title translates as *Football in the First Year of the Era of Manen*, highlights the year of 1860, when Japan's first official embassy was sent abroad to commence its intercourse with the outside world.[10] It was also the year of an insurrection in which the brothers' great-grandfather and his brother were deeply implicated.

As the 1860 riot involved a pair of brothers with opposed views on authority, the brother-heroes of the main story, the great-grand-sons of the 1860 brothers are embroiled in the 1960 student move-ment. Oe reexamines the options available in 1960, between action and speculation, between participation and standing by. The older brother, called Mitsusaburo (meaning "honey-third son"), and Takashi (meaning "falcon-fourth son") are obviously ideological doubles, just like their great-grandfather and his brother. The con-templative older brother, who shares with Oe a part of his given name ("-saburo"), receives a heavier share of the authorial burden, but he is not allowed to represent him. Although it looks like an I-fiction, *The Silent Cry* in fact refuses to surrender itself to an authorial voice. Continually shifting the narrative perspective from a call for action and presentation to an appeal to contemplation and representation, it is relentlessly critical toward both the terror of unspeculative commitment and the horror of paralyzed observation. Honesty and deception constantly intersect with accuracy and error, lucidity and insanity. The protagonists' bodies are recalled in their exact physical details, disallowing heroic falsification and nostalgic commodification, unlike in Mishima's fiction. When one "tells the truth" in this work, one hears only a cry in silence. And even such a desperate enunciation is not romanticized, as in the suicide's bizarre hanging corpse. (A comparison with Mishima's glamorized and narcissistic *seppuku* scenes will illuminate the difference be-tween Oe and Mishima, despite their seemingly similar topical pre-occupations.) The escape into a pit to assume a fetal position ends with a milkman's rude intrusion; many heads are bashed in in this tale—only to reveal utter nothing as the crushed skulls spill out their bloody contents.

As the heroic aura is mercilessly removed, a meditative calm is starkly exposed. A villain may turn out to be a hero, but then a hero is likely to be a coward. History is collected in bits and pieces, and yet the outcome always seems to await further revisions. Thus the author is nearly an editor, and his voice is audible only through numerous quotations.

The impact of Japan's discovery of and exposure to the outside world in 1860 marks the entire narrative. The great turmoil of 1960, in fact a mere aftershock of Japan's surrender in 1945, is likewise registered in every character's everyday sufferings and difficulties. The main event of *The Silent Cry* is a battle over retail business, between a "large-scale store" operated by the Korean "Emperor of the Supermarkets" and the indigenous villagers' small shops. Here, the story subtly evolves around the fair-minded Korean and the bigoted Japanese, but the gradual disappearance of a village community is unmistakably recorded (reminding us of the trade negotiations discussed in Chapter 3). Oe insists here on situating the domestic and familial romance in the context of social and public history. The power of *The Silent Cry*, however, finally rests in Oe's tireless cumulation of layers and layers of truths that persistently revise themselves, and in the density of his details that connect and contest among themselves with the minutest descriptions charged with precise meanings. *The Silent Cry* closes with the revelation of a concealed cellar that contains the secret history of the great-grandfather's brother's life. It opens the possibility of finding another secret that might require still another revision. Oe's work demands such an endless probing, always further complicating the senses of seeing and doing, believing and revising.[11]

In *Rouse Up, O, Young Men of a New Age*[12] Oe's accustomed patriarchic narrative identity is overshadowed by the retarded son's simple sentences. The young persona speaks through the authorial narrative web and joins William Blake's lines. Instead of being dependent on a European canonic poet's mythic authority, a marginal youngster's piercing lucidity nearly shines through it. Together with Oe's more recent experiment in voicing a female character in *Jinsei no shinseki* and *Shizukana seikatsu*, this work points to a future that has not yet been mapped or traversed. Is the idea of diversity increasingly weighing in his mind, has the voice of the Other been haunting him? One looks forward to a new phase that seems to be opening up in his uninterrupted career of probing and retrial.

Oe's isolation seems to suggest that the only hope of Japan is, paradoxically, in the ills of prosperity. Long touted as unprecedentedly leveling and equalizing, Japan's economic success is no longer class-blind, but once again is splitting people into the super-rich and the poor. At the moment, real estate is the divider. There is another possible source of division. As the European Community has Africa, and North America has Central and South America, Japan and the Asian NIEs have the Asian have-nots. Japan's experience in exploiting the Other will be radically challenged in the coming years as it tries to accommodate the new situation. The Japanese want cheap labor as well as the market; the Southeast Asians need jobs and capital. Are they going to create a tolerable relationship, or are they going to fail again, thereby precipitating a crisis with great risks for all? The Japanese may never eagerly rejoin Asia, but they will be forced to, if they are to survive into the next century and beyond.

The labor migration and ethnic commingling in other economic regions, too, will be an inducement. The interracial diversity of the United States, frequently derided by Japanese officials and businessmen, will yet someday prove to be a source of its strength. There is already clear sign of a large number of Americans who will not be silenced by the ignorant cries of discriminatory demagoguery. Though things are generally dismal in Europe, at least in Britain, the imported Commonwealth laborers have by now become sufficiently rooted to produce a group of "foreign native" writers such as Salman Rushdie, Timothy Mo, Hanif Kureishi, V. S. Naipaul, Kazuo Ishiguro, Ngũgĩ Wa Thiong'o, and many others. These writers are bound to produce an effect on the Japanese, who are always eager to learn—from the West. The Other may have to be made visible through the mediation of the West, once again.

Faced with such emergence of the Other, the accustomed perception of difference in Japan might be challenged. And if justifications cease to be acceptable and explanations are no longer satisfying, the agreement might at long last begin to unravel. In the search for an operable narrative, criticism might be reborn and resistance might be reinstituted. As of now, no prediction is meaningful one way or the other. It is clear, however, that the Japanese will have to break out of the myth of homogeneity and harmony. A life without thought, analysis, comparison, criticism, and exchange may have been the necessary price for rapid expansion at a certain stage, but it cannot possibly last for long. Between the past domination by the First World and the present deprivation of the Third, Japan will have to chart its own future, and it needs to know its destination. It requires conversation, argument, and disagreement before making a decision. Most writers and critics who have been integrated into corporate Japan are not likely to offer Japan or the world a meaningful alternative in these turbulent future years. Are the staunch critics of the world, who have so far resisted the lures for easeful surrender, willing to help write the future of humanity, together with those unable to rise from the never-ending suffering? Is their solidarity to be with the hurt and the unheard?

Can dissent and opposition awaken Japan from its untroubled somnambulance to a world without a center?

Notes

Introduction

1. There were several unexpected responses to the title. One reviewer complained the title was confusing. Rutgers University borrowed the title—without asking me for permission, incidentally—for a historical exhibition of Commodore Perry memorabilia that lasted from December 6, 1980, to March 15, 1981. The exhibition curators, however, interpreted the title to mean "as the Westerners interpreted the Japanese." Apparently some scholars hate irony and ambiguity. (See the handsome catalogue and poster for the exhibition prepared by Clark L. Beck and Ardath W. Burks.)

2. Berkeley: University of California Press, 1974.

3. Berkeley: University of California Press, 1979.

4. Ethnic consciousness and pride are understood to be vital and indispensable instruments only until the day of decolonization, autonomy, and equality—and not a single day longer.

1. Against the Native Grain

1. Japan is by now an economic superpower that cannot possibly be placed among Third World nations. (In 1990, Japan's foreign aid exceeded that of the United States, leading all industrial nations, to take just one example.) There is, however, an immense gap between the economic statistics and the cultural perception of a nation. Although it is more than conceivable that Japan will eventually gain "cultural hegemony" as it has achieved economic and industrial hegemony, the Japanese intellectuals'

self-perception—as well as the perceptions of the intellectuals outside—at this point hardly locate Japan in the "First World." European intellectuals, and even the more Asia-conscious Americans, seldom think about Japanese philosophers, theorists, or writers when they talk about philosophy, theory, or literature. When Japanese critics complain that they are not being treated seriously in the West, they are both wistful and plaintive—so much so that one could even wish that they would embrace Third World oppositionism to First World "universalism," rather than coveting an honorary membership in the West.

Merely three decades ago, Japan was one of the twenty-nine participants in the Bandung Conference, and the past is not eraseable—at least not that fast. The West, which has been nearly euphoric since the "collapse" of the East, is not about to alter its overall scheme regardless of Japan's economic success. In so many respects, Japan remains utterly exotic to the First World.

To the use of the totalizing terms "First World" and "Third World"—especially in view of the uncertain future of the "Second World"—a number of serious challenges can admittedly be made. These are no single regional entities but are both assemblies of complexly diversified and differentiated nations and societies. Nevertheless, in terms of social and cultural development as well as economic and military domination throughout history and at present, there is some context in which these terms are still useful—albeit they must be deployed with pliancy and elasticity.

2. Christopher Hope's term in his talk titled "Foreign Natives: Some Contemporary British Novelists," delivered on June 12, 1990, at the Wheatland Conference on Literature in San Francisco.

3. Most writers from former colonies are forced by historical circumstances to write in the language of their former oppressors. This creates complex problems regarding the relationship between language and substance. See for example Ngũgĩ Wa Thiong'o's recent decision to use not English but his native Gikuyu. This, however, is at best a partial measure, leaving out the whole question of non-Gikuyu readership.

4. Perhaps it is common sense that translation is a far more serious need in a society that feels itself less dominant. The Japanese were fanatic translators: the presence of several editions of canonic Western writers and philosophers, the speed and simultaneity in translation, and the sheer range of translated works and authors are some of the indications of their devotion to a plan to "catch up." The recent decline in the sales of translated materials in Japan only reinforces this correlation between translation and "advanced-nation" consciousness.

5. See John W. Dower's "E. H. Norman, Japan, and the Uses of History," in his edition of *Origins of the Modern Japanese State: Selected Writings of E. H. Norman* (New York: Pantheon Books, 1975), pp. 3–101, especially p. 31. For the remoter history of American-Japanese exchange, see my *As We Saw Them: The First Japanese Embassy to the United States (1860)* (Berkeley: University of California Press, 1979).

6. Obviously there are a number of exceptions, as is always the case with any generalization. One need not list here the names of those scholars with serious intellectual commitment in the field, although their presence is of particular significance in the context of "Japanology."

7. See Chapter 3.

8. I have received, and ignored, a few dubious proposals to organize a conference for the purpose of establishing a "closer friendship" between Japan and the United States. To take just one example, Sasakawa Ryoichi's several organizations are offering millions of dollars to various scholarly institutions. They are legitimate, as far as law is concerned. In view of Mr. Sasakawa's wartime records and his current capacities as the head of a speed-boat gambling operation and alleged illicit enterprises in developing countries, as well as his publicly acknowledged personal craving for a Nobel Peace Prize, the acceptance of his munificence is at least unsavory, if not outright irresponsible. And yet the list of the recipient institutions include numerous leading academies of the world. See Pat Choate, *Agents of Influence: How Japan's Lobbyists in the United States Manipulate America's Political and Economic System* (New York: Alfred A. Knopf, 1990).

9. Letter to a student from Helen C. McCullough, Professor of Oriental Languages, University of California, Berkeley. Though she wrote the letter as a semi-personal, semi-official one, she released it, together with the rest of her correspondence with the student, to the campus newspaper for publication.

10. Ihab Hassan, "The Burden of Mutual Perceptions: Japan and the United States," *Salmagundi*, No. 85–86 (Winter–Spring 1990), pp. 71–86. The essay is a reprint from the *International House of Japan Bulletin*, Vol. 10, No. 1 (Winter 1990), which transcribes Hassan's speech at the I-House on May 15, 1989.

11. The conferees include Kobayashi Hideo, Nishitani Keiji, Kawakami Tetsutaro, Kamei Katsuichiro, and Nakamura Mitsuo. See H. D. Harootunian, "Visible Discourse/Invisible Ideologies," *Postmodernism and Japan*, ed. Masao Miyoshi and H. D. Harootunian (Durham and London: Duke University Press, 1989), pp. 63–92. See also Matsumoto Kenichi, ed., *Kindai no Chokoku* (Fuzanbo Hyakka Bunko, 1979).

12. *Asahi Janaru*, Vol. 26, No. 22 (May 25, 1984).

13. For the recent debate on "modern" Japan in the country itself, see Fujita Shozo, *Seishin teki kosatsu* (Miraisha, 1982) and Takabatake Michitoshi, *Toron: Sengo Nihon no seiji shiso* (Sanichi Shobo, 1977). On postmodernism and Japan, see Miyoshi and Harootunian, *Postmodernism and Japan*. A vast number of books in the so-called *Nihon-jin ron* field (studies in the Japanese people) more or less touch some aspects of modernity, although most are likely to be essentialist manifestos.

14. Lucien Goldmann, "The Revolt of Arts and Letters in Advanced Civilization," in *Cultural Creation*, trans. Bart Grahl (Saint Louis: Telos Press, 1976), p. 52.

15. Daniel Lloyd Spencer, "Japan's Pre-Perry Preparation for Economic Growth," *American Journal of Economics and Sociology,* Vol. 17, No. 2 (January 1958), p. 197. See also Charles David Sheldon, *The Rise of the Merchant Class in Tokugawa Japan* (Locust Valley, N.Y.: J. J. Augustin, 1958); Nobutaka Ike, *The Beginnings of Political Democracy in Japan* (Baltimore: Johns Hopkins University Press, 1950); and Sumiya Mikio and Taira Koji, eds., *The Outline of Japanese Economic History, 1603–1946: Major Works and Research Findings* (Tokyo University Press, 1979).

16. See Konda Yoichi, *Edo no honya-san,* 2 vols. (Iwanami Shoten, 1977).

17. Roland Barthes, *Writing Degree Zero,* trans. Annette Lavers and Colin Smith (New York: Hill and Wang, 1968), p. 30.

18. See Hayden White, "The Value of Narrativity in the Representation of Reality," *Critical Inquiry,* Vol. 7, No. 1 (Autumn 1980), pp. 5–27.

19. Serialization, the standard form for novel publishing in the nineteenth-century West, is still prevalent in Japan, and most *shosetsu* are published in that form. For an extreme example, Kojima Nobuo completed a work in 1981 that had been serialized for fourteen years. Toward its end, the work makes many references to contemporary events, radically altering what the novel had been in its earlier sections.

20. See Yamazaki Masakazu, *Yawarakai kojin shugi no jidai* (Chuo Koronsha, 1984).

21. See Chapter 9.

22. I owe this information to Ryusawa Takeshi, editor-in-chief of Heibonsha, one of the most well-established publishing companies in Japan.

23. There have been numerous discussions of literary prizes and awards in recent years. By now they are one of the most effective promotional means and have little to do with serious evaluation. Yet the prizes grow both in monetary amount and number. Earlier, Domeki Kyosaburo deplored the degradation of the award system in the *Asahi* newspaper (March 3 and 5, 1981), and Honda Katsuichi attacked the prizes offered by Bungei Shunju Publishing Company in "Bunshun-kei hankaku bungakusha tachi no oshie o kou," *Ushio,* November 1982, pp. 148–151, and elsewhere. Such controversies continue unabated. One should remember, however, that such disputes are often intricately and inextricably involved in the partisan-political affiliations of publishing companies and their editors.

24. Boredom with printed media is, of course, a perennial topic in Japan, as in any other industrial nation. See for just one example a statistical survey published in the *Mainichi* newspaper, October 27, 1981. As for the general decline in magazine readership, see, among many others, Odagiri Hideo, "Bungaku gaikan," *Bungei nenkan,* 1980, pp. 58–62, and Matsuura Sozo, "Sogo zasshi wa saisei shiuruka," *Shuppan nyusu,* mid-March 1981. Kida Junichiro has written a number of informative books on the subject, one of which is *Dokusho senso* (Sanichi Shinsho, 1978). Its first chapter is called "Reading, This Perishing Activity" ("Dokusho, kono horobiyuku mono").

25. Of course, such interdependence in the literary enterprise is evident

in any society. Power coagulates, everywhere. The Japanese mutual security agreement, however, is quite extreme. One never sees in Japan, for example, an equivalent of the devastating review by Benjamin De Mott of Norman Mailer's *Ancient Evenings* (published by Little, Brown) that appeared in the *New York Times Book Review* (April 10, 1983).

26. Tsutsumi Shunsuke and Inoue Hisashi, "Kirikirikoku wa dokoni aruka," *Umi,* March 1982, p. 165. This dialogue (pp. 140–146) is one of the most informative documents for reading Inoue's masterpiece.

27. Northrop Frye, *Anatomy of Criticism* (Princeton: Princeton University Press, 1957), p. 250.

28. This description applies more appropriately to the *mugen* (ghostly type), the more dominant of the two major Noh types.

29. Roland Barthes, "Lesson in Writing," *Image-Music-Text,* trans. Stephen Heath (New York: Hill and Wang, 1977), p. 172.

30. Bertolt Brecht, "Alienation Effects in Chinese Acting," *Brecht on Theatre,* trans. John Willet (New York: Hill and Wang, 1978), pp. 91–99.

31. By "performative form" I do not mean any sort of formalistic notion. The Noh was established by Shogun Ashikaga Yoshimitsu, who devised the form of dramatic presentation in order to control rival warlords. He assigned them various roles to play in public performance, thus dexterously placing them in his paradigm of power. The mode of training, performing, and seating—which are strictly formalized and enforced—was a calculated political design developed by the shogun who acutely felt the absence of a politically discursive forum in contemporary Japan. It is thus possible to consider the Noh form as a theater of Japan's early political discourse. I owe this insight to a chapter in an unpublished doctoral dissertation in history by K. Anthony Namkung at the University of California, Berkeley.

2. The "Great Divide" Once Again

1. See S. F. Cook and W. W. Borah, *The Indian Population of Central Mexico, 1531–1610* (Berkeley: University of California Press, 1960).

2. An excellent analysis of the intellectual situation of the time is offered by Johannes Fabian in *Time and the Other* (New York: Columbia University Press, 1983).

3. The Tokugawa officials and the early Meiji rulers were absorbing all they could as they faced the Western diplomats and administrators. See my *As We Saw Them: The First Japanese Embassy to the United States (1860)* (Berkeley: University of California Press, 1979), especially chaps. 1 and 4.

4. "Third World" is a triadic term, but "Second World" is—was?—not in much use. Does this mean that binarism is always an irresistible epistemological compulsion, or that the author(s) of the terms believed the geopolitical situation required a triad, and yet considered the relationship between the rich and the poor, or the colonizers and the colonized, for various reasons to be more crucial than the relationship between the Eastern and

the Western blocs? Is there going to be a change in the use of the term after the end of the Cold War? Is the Second World going to be absorbed into the Third? For an interesting discussion of this binarism in the earlier years, see Carl E. Pletsch, "The Three Worlds, or the Division of Social Scientific Labor, Circa 1950–1975," *Comparative Studies in Society and History,* Vol. 23, No. 1 (October 1981), pp. 565–590. For the most incisive discussion of the post–Cold War situation regarding the First World and the Third, see Noam Chomsky, "The Third World in the 'New World Order,'" in *Blätter für deutsche und internationale Politik,* forthcoming.

5. See the last chapter of Brian S. Turner, *Marxism and the End of Orientalism* (London: George Allen and Unwin, 1978).

6. Most studies of Chinese fiction as of now are conventionally thematic ones. More theoretical works are by Andrew H. Plaks, *Archetype and Allegory in the Dream of the Red Chamber* (Princeton: Princeton University Press, 1976) and *The Four Masterworks of the Ming Novel* (Princeton: Princeton University Press, 1987); and Marston Anderson, *The Limits of Realism: Chinese Fiction in the Revolutionary Period* (Berkeley: University of California Press, 1990). See also E. Perry Link, *Mandarin Ducks and Butterflies* (Berkeley: University of California Press, 1981). Fredric Jameson, "Third World Literature in the Era of Multinational Capitalism," *Social Text: Theory/Culture/Ideology,* No. 15 (1986), pp. 65–88, offers a number of shrewd insights. As a First World writer, Jameson is not free from a universalistic impulse, and his critical terms are inevitably cosmopolitan. Still, his argument is for "the importance and interest of non-canonical forms of literature," and as such it deserves a careful reading.

7. Mary N. Layoun, *Travels of a Genre: The Modern Novel and Ideology* (Princeton: Princeton University Press, 1990) is one of the few inclusive studies of the "novel" form, dealing with Greek, Egyptian, Palestinian, and Japanese cases. Her discussion of Arab novelists is, as far as I am aware, exceptionally profitable.

8. See, for instance, Jean Franco, *Society and the Artist: The Modern Culture of Latin America* (London: Pall Mall, 1967) and *An Introduction to Spanish American Literature* (Cambridge: Cambridge University Press, 1971); and Gerald Martin, *Journeys through the Labyrinth: Latin American Fiction in the Twentieth Century* (London: Verso, 1989).

9. To take an example, *The Norton Anthology of World Masterpieces,* 2 vols. 5th ed. (New York: W. W. Norton and Company, 1985), a textbook widely used in junior colleges and in lower-division literature courses, devotes about 100 pages altogether to Third World writers—Borges (10 pp.), Narayan (14 pp.), Mishima (26 pp.), García Márquez (12 pp.), and Soyinka (54 pp.)—out of the 4210 pages of the two volumes.

10. The assaults from feminist and ethnic minority critics and scholars are too many and too well known to be listed here. The challenges from the Third World are, predictably, little known among "general" readers. To take a few examples, George Lamming's *The Pleasures of Exile* (London and

New York: Allison and Busby, 1960) and Ngũgĩ Wa Thiong'o's *Decolonizing the Mind: The Politics of Language in African Literature* (London: James Currey, 1986) are indispensable to the correct understanding of the Third World writers' struggle.

11. Futabatei Shimei's *Ukigumo* (1989)—written increasingly in a "translation style" as its composition progressed—has been called Japan's first modern novel. Japan had had earlier encounters with dominant civilizations such as China, India, and Portugal/Spain. These experiences had taught the Japanese the technique of accommodation. Japan's confusion and "contamination" in sequel to its encounter with the West are both familiar and unfamiliar. The Japanese have long coexisted with Confucianism and Buddhism, and they are likely to live with Western capitalism, the Enlightenment, "humanism," and modernism, although their future course is of course far from unclouded.

12. There are of course writers and critics acutely aware of the predicament: earlier, Natsume Soseki is one; later, Oe Kenzaburo is another, as I have argued in Chapter 1 and in *Accomplices of Silence: The Modern Japanese Novel* (Berkeley: University of California Press, 1974). There are numerous writers and theorists on similar experiences in the "decolonized" regions. See, for example, Third World writers like Ngũgĩ, Lamming, Sembene, Achebe, Rushdie, and García Márquez as well as Frantz Fanon, Edward Said, and other theorists in colonialism/minorities discourse.

13. See Maeda Ai, *Bakumatsu, ishinki no bungaku* (Hosei Daigaku Shuppankyoku, 1972) and *Kindai dokusha no seiritsdu* (Yuseido, 1973).

14. Kenneth Burke, *A Grammar of Motives* (New York: Prentice-Hall, 1954).

15. The *shosetsu* is typically published in serial form in either a monthly or a daily, and either regularly or irregularly. When installed regularly in one periodical, a *shosetsu* resembles a Victorian novel, at times it is even as carefully planned. A *shosetsu,* however, is very writerly and often published in several different periodicals at random intervals at the author's whim. It often reads like a series of strung-together short stories. The mode of publication can be either a cause or an effect of the narrative form, but either way, it suggests an inclination against centralized and structured control, while the author's personal freedom is jealously guarded. As to the more recent dispersal/disintegration of prose fiction as "high art," see Part 3.

16. Kuki Shuzo's discussion of *iki, Iki no kozo* (1930), has not yet been translated into English. Kuki constructs an aesthetic model to define the "essence" of Japanese culture. It is understandable that Kuki felt the need to discover some role for his own culture that was totally ignored by European philosophy and aesthetics, as he studied them with Husserl, Heidegger, and Sartre in the 1920s. However, his is finally an attempt to create a counteruniversal model for the Japanese nation, and as such it is inevitably hegemonic. See Leslie Pincus, "In a Labyrinth of Western Desire:

Kuki Shuzo and the Discovery of Japanese Being," in *Boundary 2*, forthcoming.

17. Zeami's esoteric text on the Noh, *Kadensho*, refers to the principle but offers no explanation, as is usually the case with the theoretical attempts. The mode of Japanese learning in arts and crafts has been predominantly through repeated practice rather than verbal explanation, although of course the mode is rapidly changing. See Yamazaki Masakazu, *On the Art of the No Drama: The Major Treatises of Zeami*, trans. J. Thomas Rimer (Princeton: Princeton University Press, 1984).

18. The 1985 edition, published by Princeton University Press, has a new introduction by C. Scott Littleton, who justifies Lévy-Bruhl as a relativist.

19. "The Consequences of Literacy," reprinted in *Literacy in Traditional Societies*, ed. Jack Goody (Cambridge: Cambridge University Press, 1968), pp. 27–68.

20. Kathleen Goff, however, disagrees with the two on several important points. Writing is for her an enabling factor but not a sufficient reason for various cognitive changes as described by Goody and Watt. She also firmly corrects Goody and Watt's over-enthusiasm for Western civilization—without explicitly discussing it. "Implications of Literacy in Traditional China and India" and "Literacy in Kerala," in Goody, *Literacy in Traditional Societies*, pp. 69–84 and 132–160.

21. Watt's comments on *Heart of Darkness*, a novel of disturbed alterity par excellence, are as follows: "But *Heart of Darkness* is not essentially a political work; Conrad mainly followed his own direct imaginative perceptions; and insofar as he treated the Africans at all, it was essentially as human beings seen from the inward and subjective point of view which characterizes *Heart of Darkness* as a whole." *Conrad in the Nineteenth Century* (Berkeley: University of California Press, 1979), p. 160. Watt's book is an attempt to recuperate Conrad the "artist" from the mires of colonial discourse.

22. "A Writing Lesson," *Tristes Tropiques*, trans. John Russell (New York: Atheneum, 1972), p. 292.

23. Some of them—like Ong and McLuhan—are also interested in the impact of literacy and printing within European history. There are many others, such as Elizabeth L. Eisenstein, François Furet, and Jacques Ozouf, who have also made significant contributions to the ongoing literacy/orality discourse.

24. Trans. Gayatri Chakravorty Spivak (Baltimore: Johns Hopkins University Press, 1976), p. 120.

25. Street's attack on Jack Goody constitutes one of the central chapters of the monograph (Cambridge: Cambridge University Press, 1984), pp. 44–65.

26. Trans. Lydia G. Lochrane (Princeton: Princeton University Press, 1987), p. 343.

27. One of the clearest expositions concerning the relationship between writing and speech is in Roland Barthes' *Writing Degree Zero*, trans. Annette Lavers and Colin Smith (New York: Hill and Wang, 1967).

28. See Roland Barthes, "The Great Family of Man," *Mythologies*, trans. Annette Lavers (New York: Hill and Wang, 1972), pp. 100–102.

29. See Anne McClintock's and Rob Nixon's response in *Critical Inquiry*, Vol. 13 , No. 1 (Autumn 1986), pp. 140–154, to Derrida's "Racism's Last Word," in *Critical Inquiry*, Vol. 12, No. 1 (Autumn 1985), pp. 290–299, and Derrida's response to the two. Derrida edited a volume of homages to Nelson Mandela, *For Nelson Mandela,* with Mustapha Tlili (New York: Henry Holt and Company, 1987), in which he includes his own essay "The Laws of Reflection: Nelson Mandela, in Admiration," trans. Mary Ann Caws and Isabelle Lorenz, pp. 11–42.

30. Derrida, for example, is not denying the tie between literacy and colonialism. "Yet once again, I do not profess that writing may not and does not in fact play this role [of suppression], but from that to attribute to writing the specificity of this role and to conclude that speech is exempt from it, is an abyss that one must not leap over so lightly" (*Of Grammatology,* p. 133).

31. Although *The Tempest* is a drama and not a novel, it requires some comment here because of its thematic importance and its critical history. *The Tempest* proposes a site of the European domination over the "barbarians." And yet the play has not been so read until very recent days. The Romantics—Coleridge and Hazlitt, for instance—saw a "noble being" and "classical dignity" in Caliban, but such praise for the creature was still placed in the general frame of "'the liberty of wit' and 'the law' of understanding." For Shakespearean scholars since, *The Tempest* has been a pastoral drama whose main concern is with the opposition between "Prospero's Art" and "Caliban's Nature." This reading of the play, by Frank Kermode and most other scholars, thus subscribes to the scheme of degree and hierarchy and reaffirms its modern version—Eurocentricity, class elitism, and patriarchy—as if they were unrelated to historical development. In his introduction to the Arden *Tempest,* Kermode insists "there is nothing in *The Tempest* fundamental to its structure of ideas which could not have existed had America remained undiscovered, and the Bermuda voyage never taken place" (Cambridge, Mass.: Harvard University Press, 1954). It is hardly surprising that a more historical reading of the play should arise in the context of post–World War II decolonization outside the conventional literary exercise: Dominique Octave Mannoni's *Prospero and Caliban: The Psychology of Colonization* (1950), Frantz Fanon's *Black Skin, White Masks* (1952), Aimé Césaire's *Discourse on Colonialism* (1955) and *Une Tempête* (1969), and George Lamming's *The Pleasure of Exile* (1960), among others.

The conventional reading of the play still persists in the West, however. (See, for example, Stephen Orgel's introduction to the Oxford Edition [1987].) And although there are some politicized readings of the play within the context of colonialism among Anglo-American scholars (e.g., Paul Brown, Francis Baker and Peter Hulme, Stephen J. Greenblatt), they all seem determined to rescue the bard from complicity in colonialism: Paul Brown sees in the play "not simply a reflection of colonialist practices but an intervention in an ambivalent and even contradictory discourse" ("'This thing of Darkness I acknowledge mine': *The Tempest* and the Discourse of Colonialism," *Political Shakespeare: New Essays in Cultural Materialism,* ed. Jonathan Dollimore and Alan Sinfield [Ithaca and London: Cornell University Press, 1985], p. 48). Where did this interventionary will originate? In post-colonial hindsight? Does the critic mean that Shakespeare somehow knew the conditions of colonialism and projected the aporia into Prospero's rhetoric of power and conquest? Isn't this strategy finally directed to a project of recuperating Shakespeare so that the bard can survive as the national monument, in postcolonial garb?

Three observations must be made here. First, the history of *Tempest* criticism was for long complicit with the dominant ideology of Eurocentricity and the discourse of colonialism in particular. Even Blake and Shelley were unable to discover in Caliban what they could readily detect in Milton's Satan. If *Tempest* criticism did not actively use the play for promoting expansionism (although some critics did—like G. Wilson Knight, who asserted in 1947 that the play celebrates England's will "to raise savage peoples from superstition, taboos, and witchcraft . . . to a more enlightened existence"; *The Crown of Life,* rept. ed. [New York: Barnes and Noble, 1966], p. 255), it did nothing to intervene in the colonial practice by rereading the play—until Third World writers began to voice their alternative readings. Second, the revisionists' rereadings are timid and defensive, as if their real objective is to establish their own interpretive authority by rescuing the national monument. As far as I know, there is only one instance of direct critical involvement with *The Tempest* itself: Thomas Cartelli's "Prospero in Africa: *The Tempest* as colonialist text and pretext" in *Shakespeare Reproduced: The Text in History and Ideology,* ed. Jean E. Howard and Marion F. O'Connor (London: Methuen, 1987), pp. 99–115. Third, our own reading of the play participates in the ongoing formation of the textuality of *The Tempest.* Our acquiescence to the play's "indeterminacy"—our inclination to listen to Prospero's voice that drowns out Caliban's—in turn serves to lengthen the moment of domination.

In 1987 there was a stage production of *The Tempest* in Tokyo that fused the Noh masks and music with the Shakespearean stage. According to its director, Ninakawa Yukio, the new production, which was suggested by "Princess Diana, who visited Japan in May [1986]," is a study of aging: "Love and hatred, joy and suffering—as one gets older one can see all these things of life in their entirety and still accept them" (*Yomiuri* newspaper, satellite ed., April 1987). Ninakawa directed a film version of *The Tempest* that was released in England in the summer of 1988. I have not had the chance to see it, but according to a number of reviews in Britain, the conventional Eurocentric ("yellow skin, white masks") interpretation seems to prevail.

32. "Of [Crusoe's] prayers," remarks Karl Marx, "we take no account, since they are a source of pleasure to him, and he looks on them as so much recreation." *Capital: A Critique of Political Economy*, 3 vols. (Chicago: Charles H. Kerr, 1906), vol. 1, p. 88.

33. References to colonies are simply everywhere, in novels by Jane Austen, the Brontës, Dickens, Thackeray, Gaskell, George Eliot, Hardy, Balzac, Flaubert, Lermontov, etc., etc. The departure for a colony closes many novels—Dickens' *Dombey and Son, David Copperfield,* and *Great Expectations,* Elizabeth Gaskell's *North and South,* George Eliot's *Daniel Deronda,* to name only a few at random.

34. See Brian V. Street, *The Savage in Literature: Representations of Primitive Society in English Fiction 1858–1920* (London and Boston: Routledge and Kegan Paul, 1975), Hugh Ridley, *Images of Imperial Rule* (London and Canberra: Croom Helm, 1983), and Martin Green, *Dreams of Adventure, Deeds of Empire* (New York: Basic Books, 1979).

35. Fish's "affectivism" is one of the shortest-lived liberation movements in literary criticism. It thawed textuality from the New Criticism freeze and then refroze it in the professor's proclaimed expertise and control. See *Is There a Text in This Class?* (Cambridge, Mass.: Harvard University Press, 1980).

3. Bashers and Bashing in the World

1. These facts are in Daniel Burstein, *Yen! Japan's New Financial Empire and Its Threat to America* (New York: Simon and Schuster, 1988).

2. The MITI officials are perhaps right: the news of the Japanese buying up one of the most important New York landmarks had a stunning effect on many Americans. A 1990 television commercial for Pontiac dealers exploits the situation: "Imagine a few years from now. It's December, and the whole family is going to see the big Christmas tree at Hirohito Center. Go on, keep buying Japanese cars." *New York Times,* July 11, 1990.

3. Clyde V. Prestowitz, Jr., *Trading Places: How We Allowed Japan to Take the Lead* (New York: Basic Books, 1988), p. 312. Of course, this is a meaningless statement: the market value of Japanese land will nose-dive once selling in exchange for American land begins in earnest.

4. *Shin-Sekai o yomu kii waado,* special issue of *Sekai,* No. 530 (Iwanami Shoten, July 1989), pp. 204 and 206.

5. Prestowitz, *Trading Places,* p. 308. The July 31, 1990, *New York Times* reports Fujitsu Ltd.'s purchase of 80 percent of ICL, P.L.C., Britain's only manufacturer of mainframe computers. If the deal is approved without

government intervention, Fujitsu will be the second largest computer company behind IBM.

6. Prestowitz, *Trading Places*, p. 308, and Bill Emmott, *The Sun Also Sets: The Limits to Japan's Economic Power* (New York: Times Books, 1989), pp. 21 and 239.

7. Emmott's *The Sun Also Sets* is a calm analysis of Japan's likely economic life expectancy. Clearly and attractively written, the book nonetheless is not very persuasive.

8. For a brief discussion of the Japanese quality of life, see "Feeling the Quality," in Emmott, *The Sun Also Sets,* pp. 52–57.

9. David Brock, "The Theory and Practice of Japan-Bashing," *The National Interest* (Fall 1989), pp. 29–40. See also Chapter 9 below (especially note 16).

10. There are numerous books now being published on the subject in Japan. Some are by nervous and insecure writers worried about their unaccustomed wealth, while others are by serious economists and writers. See Uzawa Hirofumi, *Yutakana shakai no mazushisa* (Iwanami Shoten, 1990), Teruoka Itsuko, *Yutakasa to wa nanika* (Iwanami Shoten, 1989), Watanabe Osamu, *Yutakana shakai Nihon no kozo* (Rodo Jumposha, 1990), and Honda Katsuichi, *Hinkon naru seishin, A–D* (Asahi Bunko, 1971–1990).

11. Ivan P. Hall, in the *Wall Street Journal,* July 6, 1987, portrays the Japanologists as a whole as too committed to the defense of Japan: "Yesterday's American Japanologist often becomes today's 'Japanapologist.'" His observation, however, is at best a half-truth. While the Japanologist no doubt has a propensity to become an apologist, a negative critic is not necessarily a better—not to say "neutral" or "objective"—judge.

12. July 11, 1988, quoted by David Brock, p. 31. The April 28–May 4, 1989, issue (No. 4,491) of the *Times Literary Supplement* has several articles on the subject of bashing. The most negative toward Japan among them is by Ian Buruma, a journalist (see below), while the review of Karel van Wolferen's book by J. A. A. Stockwin is a distinct apologia for Japan's trading performance. I note, incidentally, that Professor Stockwin holds a chair at Oxford endowed by Nissan. Sasakawa Ryoichi, a determined seeker of a Nobel Peace Prize, has been donating millions of dollars to Scandinavian, British, and U.S. educational institutions through the three foundations he has established. Though perfectly legal, his contributions are less than impeccably ethical. For his unsavory background and wartime history, see articles in *Insight* (April 1978); *New York Times,* July 2, 1974, and May 28, 1981; *Los Angeles Times,* March 30, 1984; *Business Week,* July 28, 1986; and David E. Kaplan and Alec Dubro, *Yakuza: The Explosive Account of Japan's Criminal Underworld* (New York: Collier Books, 1986). See also Pat Choate, *Agents of Influence: How Japan's Lobbyists in the United States Manipulate America's Political and Economic System* (New York: Alfred A. Knopf, 1990).

13. This is "the most generous host-nation support agreement the U.S. enjoys anywhere in the world." Brock, "The Money and Practice of Japan-Bashing," p. 39.

14. "Article 9. Aspiring sincerely to an international peace based on justice and order, the Japanese people forever renounce war as a sovereign right of the nation and the threat or use of force as a means of settling international disputes.

"(2) In order to accomplish the aim of the preceding paragraph, land, sea, and air forces, as well as other war potential, will never be maintained. The right of belligerency of the state will not be recognized."

15. Japan's response to the U.S. pressure in relation to the Persian Gulf situation seems to endorse this view. People's resistance was so overwhelming that the LDP cabinet had to abandon its plan to dispatch "troops," even if unarmed and noncombatant. See *Sekai*, No. 548 (December 1990), devoted to the question of the Japanese Constitution and Prime Minister Kaifu's (President Bush's?) proposal for "cooperation with the U.N. resolution."

16. Prestowitz, *Trading Places*, p. 327.

17. Ibid., p. 77. See also my *As We Saw Them*.

18. Burstein, *Yen!*, p. 66.

19. *Atlantic Monthly* (May 1989).

20. Boston: Houghton Mifflin, 1989.

21. SII was launched by President Bush and then Prime Minister Uno in July 1989 with the aim of identifying and solving structural problems in both countries that stand as impediments to reciprocal trade. The Working Group, consisting of delegations from each country, is to meet at regular intervals to discuss the progress of the measures discussed and agreed on. The first reports—"United States Report on U.S. Initiatives Pursuant to S.I.I. Discussions" and "Final Japan Structural Impediments Initiative report, Pursuant to June 1990 Talks"—were issued in June 1990. I have obtained the official texts by the courtesy of the Consulate General of Japan, Los Angeles.

22. I owe Chalmers Johnson for this discussion of the Large-Scale Retail Store Law. See his "Trade, Revisionism, and the Future of Japanese-American Relations," *Japan's Economic Structure: Should It Change?*, ed. Kozo Yamamura (Seattle: Society for Japanese Studies, 1990), pp. 105–136. Chalmers Johnson has been a generous colleague in sharing his work with me over the last several years. My criticism of his work in this chapter is in fact an expression of my appreciation of his scholarly perfectionism and scrupulousness. Whatever errors I make in the course of my discussion are, of course, my own.

23. Lewis Mumford, *The City in History: Its Origins, Its Transformations, and Its Prospects* (New York: Harcourt Brace Jovanovich, 1961), especially chap. 14, "Commercial Expansion and Urban Dissolution," pp. 410–445;

Jane Jacobs, *The Economy of Cities* (New York: Vintage Books, 1970);
Maeda Ai, *Toshi kukan no nakano bungaku* (Chikuma Shobo, 1982).

24. The March 27, 1990, issue of the *New York Times* quotes Kuroda
Makoto, a former high official of MITI, as calling the U.S. suggestions "a
bunch of very crazy ideas." He goes on to say, "But as long as you gave
us your crazy ideas, we thought we would give you a few of ours." The
editorial of the following day comments, "By and large, they [the crazy ideas
from both sides] make sense—and they don't stand a chance of being
adopted." Kuroda had published a book earlier describing his trade-negoti-
ation experience, *Nichi-Bei kankei no kangaekata: boeki masatsu o ikite*
(*How to Think about Japan-U.S. Trade Relationships: Living through Trade
Frictions;* Yuhikaku, 1989).

One is tempted to suspect at this point that the U.S. administration is
quite half-hearted about SII. Reasons for this less-than-all-out confrontational gesture might be: (1) the administration represents an interest group
that stands to gain from Japan's trade hegemonism; (2) the administration
at the same time needs to pacify revisionists such as Congressman Gephardt
and Senator Danforth, and populists advocating retaliatory protectionist
measures; (3) SII may thus prove to be no more than a smoke screen to
cover its pro–multinational corporation position.

25. See Ishihara Shintaro, "Kozo kyogi towa nani nanoka?" *Chuo koron*
(June 1990), pp. 328–338, where Ishihara argues that the SII was an *American* initiative, but Japan should have taken advantage of the opportunity
to express its views of American structural impediments seriously and
honestly.

26. A *New York Times* article, "Japanese Give in Grudgingly on a New
Way of Shopping," by David E. Sanger, on November 12, 1990, reports that
this U.S.-instigated plan to expand large stores is not resulting in the expansion of U.S. retail outlets, but in the rush of Japanese shopkeepers taking
advantage of the changed law. Although chain stores are definitely growing,
"what remains unclear is whether all this change is achieving the goal the
United States had in mind."

27. A special issue of *Sekai, Shin sekai o yomu kii waado* (Iwanami
Shoten, July 1989), p. 230.

28. Walter LaFeber, *The American Age: United States Foreign Policy at
Home and Abroad Since 1750* (New York: W. W. Norton and Company,
1989), p. 458.

29. Ian Buruma, "From Hirohito to *Heimat*," *New York Review of Books,*
October 26, 1989.

30. *Times Literary Supplement,* No. 4,491 (April 28–May 4, 1989), pp. 454
and 458.

31. See Chapter 9 for a criticism of this form of discourse.

32. Peter N. Dale, *The Myth of Japanese Uniqueness* (New York: St.
Martin's Press, 1986).

33. Valéry, "The Crisis of the Mind," trans. Denise Folliot and Jackson

Matthews, *History and Politics, The Collected Works in English,* vol. 10 (New York: Bollingen Foundations, 1962), pp. 23–36. Husserl, trans. Quentin Lauer, *Phenomenology and the Crisis of Philosophy* (New York: Harper Torchbooks, 1965), pp. 149–192.

34. *"Nyozetsuroku," Tanizaki Junichiro zenshu,* vol. 20 (Chuo Koronsha, 1982), pp. 88–89. See also Donald Keene's similar contention about the same point on Tanizaki in *Dawn to the West* (New York: Holt, Rinehart and Winston, 1984), p. 756.

35. Kosaka Jun, *Nihon ideorogii ron: gendai Nihon ni okeru Nihon shugi, fasshizumu, jiyu shugi, shiso no hihan, Tosaka Jun zenshu,* vol. 2 (Keiso Shobo, 1985), pp. 223–438.

36. Geertz feels "a bit shaken as he wonders how valid it is for some humans to study others, and whether, in the end, he may have been looking at others all along far more through the uncertain prism of himself than he could have realized. . . . he said that he had lost confidence in some generally accepted notions of anthropology." May 11, 1988.

37. Shimomura Mitsuko, *Asahi shimbun,* March 20, 1990.

38. Van Wolferen, *The Enigma of Japanese Power,* p. 272.

39. Quoted from an unidentified copy received from an identified sender. Apparently there are several variant texts, since my pagination does not seem to coincide with other citations. Thus I give both English and Japanese citations (J., pp. 14–15; Eng., p. 3) The published English-language version of the book differs substantially from the earlier circulating copies: it lists Ishihara as the sole author, omits many of the controversial passages, and adds a lengthy new section that is different in both substance and tone. Shintaro Ishihara, *The Japan That Can Say No,* trans. Frank Baldwin (New York: Simon & Schuster, 1991).

40. If the Self-Defense Force was established to defend Japan from an invading army, its expenditures on heavy tanks (which have no possible use in Japanese terrain) make no sense. Similarly, Japan's plan to build its own defensive fighter planes has validity—as long as Japan is to have unconstitutional armed forces. The U.S. disapproval of Japan's plan is nothing but another expression of its wish to keep military domination over Japan. See James E. Auer, "FSX kosho wa koshite ketchaku shita," trans. Imoo Sakutao, *Chuo koron* (June 1990), pp. 156–171.

41. "A Sovereign Nation Can Say No," *Los Angeles Times,* January 17, 1990.

42. Ishihara's interview with Karatani Kojin, "Changing Paradigm: Toward Radicalism" ("Henyo suru yoshiki: rajikaru ni mukatte"), *Subaru* (October 1989), pp. 176–193. There are several other publications by Ishihara, which ought to be carefully attended to. Especially the sequel to the Morita-Ishihara book, called *Soredemo "No" to ieru Nihon* (Kobunsha, 1990), is more pernicious, as a whole, than the original. Watanabe Shoichi, who contributes to this volume, is inordinately irresponsible and incendiary. He reiterates the theme of Japanese supremacy in Asia, now denying its

sordid record in China—the 1937 rape of Nanjing, for instance. Watanabe's successful presence in Japan's media today raises interesting issues which few of his compatriots seem willing to confront. And Ishihara's approval of Watanabe is quite ominous.

43. *Gaiko Foramu,* No. 13 (October 1989), p. 18. The journal is a semi-official publication of the Ministry of Foreign Affairs.

44. See Earl Miner, "Toward a New Approach to Classical Japanese Poetics," *Studies on Japanese Culture,* 2 vols. (Tokyo, 1973), vol. 1, pp. 99–113, and "That Literature Is a Kind of Knowledge," *Critical Inquiry,* vol. 2, no. 3 (Spring 1976), pp. 487–518.

45. See Chantal Mouffe, "Radical Democracy: Modern or Postmodern?" in Andrew Ross, ed. *Universal Abandon?: The Politics of Postmodernism* (Minneapolis: University of Minnesota Press, 1988), pp. 31–45.

4. Who Decides, and Who Speaks?

1. Around the University of Kyoto, there were numerous ideologues and philosophers who before and during World War II worked to formulate and articulate the position of Japan as a political and mythical polity. Names like Nishida Kitaro, Nishitani Keijiro, Tanabe Hajime, and Watsuji Tetsuro were among the most conspicuous.

2. *New Japanese-English Dictionary,* ed. Masuda Koh, 4th ed. (1974). Shogakkan's *Nihon Kokugo Daijiten,* ed. Ichiko Sadaji et al. (1981) has a long entry that reads: "A modern philosophical term. Being an individual agent that works on the surrounding situations ethically and practically as well as being ontologically an existence in possession of a consciousness and a body. The condition of truly realizing one's own self as one acts on one's own will. Being and existence. Generally, being self-conscious in action, on the basis of one's own will and judgment. Also, such an attitude and character" (my translation).

3. The best evidence is the records of the negotiation between the Japanese and the Americans concerning Constitutional revisions. At the final confrontation between Foreign Minister Yoshida Shigeru, Minister of State Matsumoto Joji and General Courtney Whitney, in February 1946, the Japanese hope for the status quo was completely demolished. See Yoshida Shigeru, *Kaiso Junen* (Shinchosha, 1957), vol. 4, pp. 170–190; also Mark Gayn, *Japan Diary* (New York: William Sloan Associates, 1948), pp. 125–131.

4. See the abbreviated but clear references to such efforts in the *Asahi* newspaper as early as the first half of 1945.

5. See the Miyamoto Yuriko section in Chapter 8.

6. *The Japan Reader: Postwar Japan, 1945 to the Present,* ed. John Livingston et al. (New York: Pantheon, 1973), p. 7.

7. *Memoirs, 1925–1950* (New York: Pantheon, 1967), p. 382. See also John Curtis Perry, *Beneath the Eagle's Wings: Americans in Occupied Japan* (New York: Dodd, Mead, 1980), p. 47.

8. See, for example, William Appleman Williams, *The Strategy of American Diplomacy,* 2nd ed. (New York: Dell, 1972), p. 207. See also John Lewis Gaddis, *The United States and the Origin of the Cold War, 1941–1947* (New York and London: Columbia University Press, 1972); D. F. Fleming, *The Cold War and Its Origins, 1917–1960,* 2 vols. (New York: Doubleday, 1961); and Gabriel Kolko, *The Politics of War: The World and the United States Foreign Policy, 1943–45* (New York: Random House, 1968).

9. State Department Policy Planning Study 23, February 24, 1948, quoted by Noam Chomsky in *On Power and Ideology: The Managua Lectures* (Boston: South End Press, 1987), pp. 15–16.

10. William Manchester, *American Caesar: Douglas MacArthur, 1880–1964* (Boston: Little, Brown, 1978), pp. 184 and 441.

11. *The Japan Reader,* pp. 116–119, and the NSC report, October 7, 1948.

12. Yoshida's own memoirs provide interesting materials. See *Kaiso Junen,* vol. 1 (Shinchosha, 1957), pp. 80–121; *Gekido no hyakunen shi* (Shirakawa Shoin, 1978), p. 154; and *Oiso Seidan* (Bungei Shunju Shinsha, 1956), pp. 138–139.

13. Richard Nixon, *Leaders* (New York: Warner Books, 1982), "Douglas MacArthur and Shigeru Yoshida," pp. 81–132.

14. The most comprehensive Japanese study of Occupation censorship is Matsuura Sozo, *Senryoka no genron danatsu* (Gendai Janarizumu Shuppankai, 1969), but this book is neither systematic nor coherent. Jay Rubin, "From Wholesomeness to Decadence: The Censorship of Literature under the Allied Occupation," *Journal of Japanese Studies,* Vol. 11, No. 1 (Winter 1985), pp. 71–103, is excellent in disputing Eto Jun's determined misrepresentation of the subject and in covering the Prange Collection of occupation materials at the University of Maryland's McKeldin Library. His approach, however, is largely taxonomical, failing to analyze the objectives, methods, and capabilities of the censors involved. Their inability to understand Japanese, for instance, is a significant factor that requires further study, so that the censors' incompetence—rather than malice—may be fully comprehended.

15. See the report of Higashikuni's press interview, *Asahi,* August 30, 1945. He repeated the plea in his speech to the Diet on September 5, 1945.

16. Vol. 1, No. 3 (March 1946), p. 24 (my translation).

17. "In Egoistos," originally published in *Kindai bungaku,* July 1947, reprinted in *Sengo bungaku ronso,* ed. Usui Yoshimi, vol. 1 (Bancho Shobo, 1972), pp. 243–247.

18. Originally in *Shin-Nihon bungaku,* May–June 1946, reprinted in *Sengo bungaku ronso,* pp. 72–82.

19. *Sekai,* vol. 1 (May 1946), pp. 2–15.

20. "Cho kokka shugi no ronri to shinri," p. 13.

21. *Koei no ichi kara* (Miraisha, 1982), p. 114.

22. The contemporary journals do contain articles analyzing the Cold War situation (for instance, the May 1948 issue of *Chuo koron*). They do not seem to have been widely read, however. See, for instance, a 1968 *zadankai*

discussing the circumstances of intellectual communities in Japan in 1948, published for the first time in *Sekai,* Special Issue, July 1985, pp. 2–53.

23. Noam Chomsky, "The Revolutionary Pacifism of A. J. Muste," *American Power and the New Mandarins* (New York: Pantheon Books, 1967), p. 183.

24. "Kindai no chokoku," published originally in November 1959, reprinted in *Nihon gendai bungaku zenshu,* 93 (Kodansha, 1968), pp. 360–388, is one of the few serious discussions of Japan's aggression in the context of Western hegemonism. An example of the increasingly more visible reactionary revisionist publications is *Dai-Toa senso kotei ron,* reprinted in *Hayashi Fusao chosakushu,* 1 (Tsubasa Shoin, 1977).

25. *Shigaku,* November 1955. Reprinted in *Sengo bungaku ronso,* pp. 129–139.

26. *The Tokyo War Crimes Trial,* ed. R. John Pritchard and Sonia Magbanua Zaide, vol. 21: *Separate Opinions* (New York and London: Garland Publishing, 1981), pp. 983–984.

27. For further discussion of Tanizaki, see Chapter 5.

28. See my discussion of Kawabata in *Accomplices of Silence: The Modern Japanese Novel* (Berkeley: University of California Press, 1974), chap. 4.

29. *Noma Hiroshi shu, Chikuma gendai bungaku taikei,* 65 (Chikuma Shobo, 1975), p. 324.

30. *Shiina Rinzo shu, Chikuma gendai bungaku taikei,* 66 (Chikuma Shobo, 1976), p. 362.

31. *Kitahara Takeo, Inoue Tomoichiro, Tamura Taijun shu, Nihon gendai bungaku zenshu,* 94 (Kodansha, 1968), p. 332.

32. Nishikawa Nagao's recent book, *Nihon no sengo shosetsu: haikyo no hikari* (Iwanami Shoten, 1988) discusses these postwar writers and lists their references to Christ. Nishikawa is both literal and unanalytic, and his critical comments contain few interesting observations. See pp. 246–250 and 273–274.

33. For further discussion, see *Accomplices,* chap. 5.

34. *Sakaguchi Ango shu, Chikuma gendai bungaku taikei,* 58 (Chikuma Shobo, 1975), p. 452.

35. Ibid., p. 191.

36. Ibid., p. 327.

37. Fredric Jameson, "Postmodernism, or the Cultural Logic of Late Capitalism," *New Left Review,* No. 146 (July–August 1984), pp. 53–92.

5. The Lure of the "West"

1. See Eric Hobsbawm and Terence Ranger, ed., *The Invention of Tradition* (Cambridge: Cambridge University Press, 1983).

2. *Seven Japanese Tales,* trans. Howard Hibbett (New York: Berkley, 1965), p. 111. The original appears in *Tanizaki Junichiro Zenshu* (hereafter *TJZ*), 30 vols. (Chuo Koron Sha, 1982–83), vol. 1, p. 67.

3. Actually, it was many years earlier that Tanizaki first thought about writing a tale of an upper-class Osaka household as seen from the servants' point of view. In one of those amazing letters he wrote to his third wife—in which he begs her to treat him as her menial houseboy (*genan*) in a startlingly self-demeaning style—he explains the idea as her contribution. Letter 154 (July 6, 1935), *TJZ*, vol. 25, pp. 164–165.

4. The writer closest to Tanizaki in temperament at this stage is Nagai Kafu, who was one of the earliest discoverers of Tanizaki's talent. After returning from the United States and France, Nagai saw Japan as hatefully dull, barren, and backward. His strategy was to invent a "downtown Tokyo" in which the Edo tradition, as he saw it, survived. He filled this imagined community with the features of the Other and lived for the rest of his life without paying much heed to the historical Japan. Tanizaki's admiration for Nagai needs no explanation. As the war intensified later, Nagai—who lost his home twice to air raids—moved in with the Tanizakis briefly.

5. Not that Tanizaki did not have his share of self-doubt. He was full of anxieties, as most young writers are in a rapidly changing society, and his works were often not only awkward and inarticulate but incoherent and fragmentary. Such confusion is evident even in the titles: "Until I Was Abandoned" ("Suterareru made"), "Wordy Jack" ("Jotaro"), "Lonely Search" ("Dokutan"), "Prodigy" ("Sindo"), "The Era of Terror" ("Kyofu jidai"), "A Heretic's Desolation" ("Itansha no kanashimi"), "A Boy's Blackmail" ("Shonen no kyohaku"), and "Ex-Convict" ("Zenkasha"). In a way, his later works are his efforts to find a path out of such murky self-probings.

6. Naomi's entry in the tale is very much like Lolita's in Nabokov's work years later—linguistic. "I learned that her real name was *Naomi,* written with three Chinese characters. The name excited my curiosity. A splendid name, I thought; written in Roman letters, it could be a Western name." *Naomi,* trans. Anthony H. Chambers (New York: Alfred A. Knopf, 1985), p. 4. "Lo-lee-ta: the tip of the tongue taking a trip of three steps down the palate to tap, at three, on the teeth. Lo. Lee. Ta." (New York: Berkley, 1966), p. 11.

7. *Seven Japanese Tales,* p. 126; *TJZ,* vol. 8, p. 229.

8. Surprising as it might seem to the non-Japanese reader, Tanizaki's dramatic monologues are usually read by the Japanese as personal confessions. The irony that seems obvious to American readers is unrecognized by many in Japan. While Tanizaki's own sense of irony is irrefutable, as I see it, his intended effect on what must have been his predictable reader is not quite clear. For an example of the straitlaced reading, see Okuno Takeo's analysis in *Tanizaki Junichiro kenkyu* (Yagi Shoten, 1972), pp. 146–153. Even the otherwise exceedingly intelligent *Tanizaki Junichiro ron* by Noguchi Takehiko (Chuo Koronsha, 1971) sees no irony (and is also quite unguardedly sexist). A recent American reading is offered by Jacqueline Austin in "By Love Possessed," *Village Voice,* January 7, 1986.

9. See, for instance, "Watashi no mita Osaka oyobi Osaka-jin," *TJZ,* vol. 20, pp. 360–366.

10. "Tokyo o omou" ("Reflections on Tokyo"), *TJZ*, vol. 21, p. 49.

11. "Kansai no onna o kataru" ("Reflections on the Kansai women"), *TJZ*, vol. 22, pp. 240–243.

12. Kono Taeko, *Tanizaki bungaku to kotei no yokubo* (*Tanizaki's Fiction and Desire for Affirmation;* Chuo Bunko, 1980), is remarkably sensitive and informed. Her discussion of sexuality and Kansai, especially its dialect, in Tanizaki is quite distinguished.

13. See essays like "Watashi no mita Osaka oyobi Osaka-jin" ("Osaka and Osaka people as I Saw Them"), *TJZ*, vol. 20, pp. 347–397, and "Tokyo o omou" ("Reflections on Tokyo"), *TJZ*, vol. 21, pp. 1–76, among many others.

14. There is an earlier version of *Some Prefer Nettles* based on the same triangular relations of Tanizaki, his wife, and Sato Haruo: "Kami to hito tono aida" ("Between God and Man," 1923). In a way, Tanizaki thinks through various options of life as he plots out his fiction. The relationship of this mode of fiction to the I-novel convention, the confession-after-the-event form, might prove interesting.

15. See, for instance, his letters to Matsuko in *TJZ*, nos. 129, 132, 134, 135, 140, 148, 154, 157, and 172; and Matsuko's memoir, *Ishoan no yume* (Chuo Koronsha, 1967). He even asked her to call him by the more menial-sounding "Junichi" (written in appropriate characters) and to instruct other servants to treat him as one of them. Tanizaki married Matsuko in January 1935.

16. For an acute study of Tanizaki's "exoticism" in relation to his sexuality, Noguchi Takehiko's *Tanizaki Junichiro ron* is excellent. Chapter 4, "Kokyo to shiteno ikyo" ("The Foreign Country as Homeland"), is especially full of helpful insights, to which I am gratefully indebted.

17. "Shanghai kenbun roku" and "Shanghai koyu ki" appear in *TJZ*, vol. 10, pp. 553–559 and 561–598; see especially pp. 577–580. Tanizaki briefly relates his move to Kansai, his second trip to Shanghai, and his gradual disenchantment with the "Western style" (*yofu*) in "Tokyo o omou," *TJZ*, vol. 21, pp. 23–26.

18. Jay Rubin, *Injurious to Public Morals: Writers and the Meiji State* (Seattle and London: University of Washington Press, 1984), pp. 277–278. The complete translation of this brief story appears on p. 278, the last page of the book. It is not clear why Rubin chose this piece rather than the Singapore speech.

19. "Shingapooru no kanraku ni saishite" ("On the Occasion of the Fall of Singapore"), *TJZ*, vol. 22, p. 348; my translation.

20. See note 30. Tanizaki's relationship with Watsuji Tetsuro, one of the leading Kyoto philosophers, who contributed significantly to the construction of war ideologies and, after the war, to the reconstruction of emperorism as well as *Nihonjin-ron* (Japanism), needs to be further studied. The two were classmates at the University of Tokyo, but before long they drifted apart, as Tanizaki did not win Watsuji's moral approval.

21. See Noguchi Takehiko's brilliant reading of the *Ashikari* landscape, which resembles a female body; the reed bush where the two meet is the womb. Further, the location is known to be the site of ancient palaces and quarters where many forms of "play" have taken place. See *Tanizaki Junichiro ron,* pp. 198–200.

22. *Ashikari,* trans. Roy Humpherson and Hajime Okita (Westport, Conn.: Greenwood Press, 1970), p. 67.

23. Undoubtedly, Tanizaki's aestheticization of women is repugnant to a critically aware reader today. Although Tanizaki is far more attentive to the problems of feminism than most male Japanese writers—such as, say, Soseki or Kawabata—he is finally, like nearly all other male writers of the time, guilty of sexist biases.

24. *In Praise of Shadows,* trans. Thomas J. Harper and Edward G. Seidensticker (New Haven: Leete's Island Books, 1977), pp. 31–32.

25. In *In Praise of Shadows* Tanizaki quotes from the president of a publishing company a foolish remark concerning Albert Einstein. Although Tanizaki does not rebut the statement, he clearly dissociates himself from it; see pp. 35–36.

26. Thomas J. Harper, afterword, *In Praise of Shadows,* p. 48.

27. Its first portions were serialized in the periodical *Chuo koron* in January and March 1943 before publication was halted at the protest of the military information office. In 1944 Tanizaki published 200 copies of the first part of *Silent Snow* on his own and distributed them among his friends. He was prohibited from publishing the second part, although it had been completed by December 1944. It was not until June 1946 that he was able to publish the first part in book form. The second part was published in February 1947 and the third part was serialized from March to October 1947. See "The Reminiscence on *Silent Snow*" ("*Sasameyuki* kaiko"), *TJZ,* vol. 22, pp. 362–366.

28. See "When I Wrote *Silent Snow*" ("*Sasameyuki* o kaita koro"), *TJZ,* vol. 23, pp. 364–365, and "A Chat on *Silent Snow*" ("*Sasameyuki* sadan"), vol. 23, pp. 237–240.

29. "The Reminiscence on *Silent Snow,*" *TJZ,* vol. 22, p. 364. See also "A Chat on *Silent Snow,*" pp. 237–240.

30. Jay Rubin points out that Tanizaki accepted advice from Yamada Yoshio, a right-wing ideologue, when he was translating *The Tale of Genji* for the first time. Furthermore, he deleted several key episodes in translation following Yamada's recommendation without explicitly stating the editorial changes in the text. Tanizaki's accommodations are of course reprehensible, but from a man who spoke about the fall of Singapore with such exhilaration, this editorial decision is at least not as surprising as Rubin finds it. In a similar vein, Peter N. Dale wrongheadedly takes Tanizaki to task for his assertion in *Bunsho tokuhon* (*Manual of Composition*) of the uniqueness of the Japanese language, in *The Myth of Japanese Uniqueness* (New York: St. Martin's Press, 1986). See Chapter 3 above.

31. Tanizaki was not free from the Allied General Headquarters censorship, however. His "Letters from Mrs. A" ("A-Fujin no tegami") was banned in the fall of 1946. Only fragments published in *Chuo koron* in 1950 have survived. The published portions describe an upper-class housewife's fantasies about the pilot of a fighter plane that flies over her house. The published parts contain Tanizaki's own drawings for illustrations, but they do not promise a great story. I am not sure what the intentions of the GHQ censors were, but the idea of Tanizaki writing a love story involving an imperial fighter pilot during the Occupation years is rather intriguing.

32. There are several diaries written between 1944 and 1947, all published in *TJZ,* vol. 16. The extent of editing is uncertain, although some omission is suggested in a few passages. Records of his daily responses to the war situation as well as everyday activities, the diaries are of considerable interest. According to them, Tanizaki seems to have remained rather aloof through the critical years. One should remember that the diaries were published in the immediate postwar years when American censorship was nearly as strenuous as the Japanese militarists'—at least in the minds of writers and publishers.

33. *Odd Obsession,* directed by Ichikawa Kon.

34. *The Key,* trans. Howard Hibbett (New York: G. P. Putnam's Sons, 1981), p. 182.

35. *The Diary of a Mad Old Man,* trans. Howard Hibbett (New York: Alfred A. Knopf, 1965), p. 101.

6. Stepping beyond History

1. Edward Said's favorite term. See *The World, the Text, and the Critic* (Cambridge, Mass.: Harvard University Press, 1983).

2. In the recent Wheatland Conference on Literature, in San Francisco, on June 10–16, 1990, Pierre Mertens, a Belgian writer, indignantly replied to Oe Kenzaburo's and my statements at the conference that Mishima was not a serious writer: "The Japanese don't own Yukio Mishima." I heartily agree with Mertens. I only hope that he will be consistent when he talks next time about Maeterlinck and other Belgian, French, and European writers with critics from the outside world.

3. Earl Jackson's militantly gay explanation of Mishima's appeal to the First World in "Queering Japan" (unpublished) contains several interesting observations.

4. "The Novelist in Today's World: A Conversation between Kazuo Ishiguro and Oe Kenzaburo," *The Japan Foundation Newsletter,* vol. 17, no. 4 (1990), pp. 8–14.

5. There is a huge quantity of literature on the sixties in Japan. One of the most recent and incisive papers is Takabatake Michitoshi's "'60 nen anpo' no seishin shi," *Sengo Nihon no seishin shi,* ed. Tetsuo Najita, Maeda Ai, and Kamishima Jiro (Tokyo: Iwanami Shoten, 1988), pp. 70–91. It has

an excellent selective bibliography. See also Masumi Junnosuke, *Nihon seiji shi, 4, Senryo kaikaku: Jiyuto shihai* (Tokyo: Tokyo Daigaku Shuppankai, 1988). For materials in English, see George R. Packard, *Protest in Tokyo* (Princeton: Princeton University Press, 1966); Robert A. Scalapino and Masumi Junnosuke, *Parties and Politics in Contemporary Japan* (Berkeley: University of California Press, 1962), chap. 5; Harada Hisato, "The Anti-Ampo Struggle," *Zengakuren: Japan's Revolutionary Students*, ed. Stuart Dowsey (Berkeley: The Ishi Press, 1970); and Ellis S. Krauss, *Japanese Radicals Revisited: Student Protest in Postwar Japan* (Berkeley: University of California Press, 1974).

6. Mishima's only work in which he seriously tried to grapple with the personal problems of his persona is *Confessions of a Mask* (*Kamen no kokuhaku*, 1949). And even there Mishima is a poseur in so many "scenes": only occasionally does the acute sense of loneliness break through without sentimentalization or gesticulation. As for his later works, Mishima seems bored with them most of the time.

7. See the Chronology ("Nempu"), in *Mishima Yukio Zenshu*, Supplement 1 (Tokyo: Shinchosha, 1976), p. 747.

8. Actually, the third volume, *The Temple of Dawn*, is divided into two parts, the first of which is set in the years preceding and during the Pacific War. This tale is the weakest of a weak tetralogy, in the sense that the Thai episode has little relevance to the main story. In addition, its voyeurism and lesbianism, supposedly depraved acts in the context of the work, are as tediously daring as they are pointless.

9. The text of *Hamamatsu chunagon monogatari* that Mishima read is the Iwanami *Nihon koten bungaku taikei* edition, 77, published in 1964. This edition has a long introduction by Matsuo Satoshi, its editor. In it Matsuo explains that there was only one manuscript of *Hamamatsu chunagon monogatari*, in four volumes, for several centuries, and that in 1930 he found a manuscript with an additional concluding volume. The present five-volume text reproduced in the Iwanami edition, however, is still incomplete. Its Vols. 1 through 5 are actually Vols. 2 through 6 of the original text. Matsuo then gives a reconstructed plot summary of the missing Volume 1 in three pages. It is this plot outline (in modern Japanese) of the missing first volume that corresponds to the story of Mishima's *Spring Snow*. In other words, the existing *Hamamatsu chunagon monogatari* has hardly anything to do with either *Spring Snow* (despite Mishima's explicit claim at its end) or the entire tetralogy (despite critics' frequent assertions). Mishima's use of tradition is in fact neither recovery nor reproduction, but a pure act of simulation, or even deception.

10. The best analysis of Mishima's idea of emperorism is in Noguchi Takehiko, *Mishima Yukio to Kita Ikki* (Fukumura Shuppan, 1985).

11. See Suzuki Kojin, *Boryoku no kagami: Hangyaku to zen-ei no kozo* (Tairyusha, 1983).

12. *Spring Snow* and *Runaway Horses*, serialized in *Shincho* September

1965–January 1967 and February 1967–August 1968 respectively, were published in book form in January 1969. *The Temple of Dawn* was serialized in the same magazine between September 1968 and April 1970 and was published as a book in July 1970. *The Decay of the Angel* was similarly serialized from July 1970 to January 1971, a few months after Mishima's suicide. This means that he had seen three parts of the tetralogy in print before his death. The absence of critical response, not to say acclaim, from the literary world of Japan apparently depressed, if not exactly shocked, the author.

13. Mishima's tetralogy could best be compared with the classical four-frame comic form observed from *Blondie* to *Bloom County,* from *Tokyo Puck* to *Kobo-chan.* Four panels are seen as if they contained a sequential, progressive narrative, each displaying a semi-autonomous story. Most often, however, the first three frames are merely repetitious. Only in the last picture, somewhat as in Shakespeare's sonnets, is the preceding narrative switched around or turned over. The punch line endows the earlier pictures with a new meaning. Mishima's last work is very much like this comic serial. Is there a suggestion of Mishima's life itself as he saw it in his nihilistic last moments?

The last volume of *The Sea of Fertility* is prophetic in another sense. According to an editor of Kodansha Publishing Company's *Shonen Magazine,* the novel as a publication form was replaced by comic books (*Manga*) around 1970 (when Mishima's completion of the tetralogy and his death took place "simultaneously"). One of the reasons for this replacement is that the length of time needed to read a 320-page comic magazine is merely twenty minutes (at the rate of 3.75 seconds a page) as against several hours for a novel, much too long for busy future producers of Japanese goods. Henceforth, the *shosetsu* writer must compete with the *manga* artist in mass-manufacturing increasingly more commodified and unresisting tales and romances. See Frederik L. Schodt, *Manga! Manga!: The World of Japanese Comics* (New York: Kodansha International, 1983).

14. See Chapter 7.

7. Out of Agreement

1. Take, for example, Clifford Geertz's latest book, *Works and Lives: The Anthropologist as Author* (Stanford: Stanford University Press, 1988), where Geertz insists that ethnographic descriptions are "homemade"— "they are describers' descriptions, not those of the described" (p. 145). His recommendation to the ethnographer is not "being there" but "being here." He is no exception, however, in such a view of the discipline. Many of the "critical anthropologists" who have been engaged in self-examination are likewise preoccupied with their own perception rather than with the Other out there. Are we to interpret this as an improvement in self-criticism, or a return to isolationism? Do we see a similar self-preoccupation among literary critics?

2. Because of the nature of emperorism, there was hardly any discussion of the system before 1945. Minobe Tatsukichi's famous "theory on the function of the emperor" *(tenno kikan setsu),* for example, was condemned, seriously affecting the direction of constitutional scholarship before the war. After 1945, emperorism was an object of sustained study, and a number of useful books and articles appeared, by Maruyama Masao, Kamishima Jiro, Takeda Kiyoko, Toyama Shigeki, Inoue Kiyoshi, and Shimoyama Saburo, among many others. Most recently, two collections of essays were published: Toyama Shigeki, ed., *Kindai tenno-sei no seiritsu* (Tokyo: Iwanami Shoten, 1987) and Toyama Shigeki, ed., *Kindai tenno-sei no tenkai* (Tokyo: Iwanami Shoten, 1988). The consensus among social scientists and legal scholars was highly critical of the anti-democratic features of the Meiji polity, until the recent surge of apologists. There have been countless signs of interest since Hirohito's illness and death, and a good number of works seem to be efforts at apology and justification rather than analysis and criticism. See Yamaguchi Masao's functionalist *Tenno sei no bunka jinruigaku* (1989) and Yoshimoto Takaaki's religionist "Tenno oyobi tenno sei ni tsuite," *Yoshimoto Takaaki zenshu sen 5: Shukyo* (1987), for instance. A brief bibliographical guide in Washida Koyata, *Tenno ron* (1989), is helpful. There are numerous journalistic books and essays as well, but few are worth close attention. Examinations of the medieval emperor system by Kuroda Toshio and Amino Yoshihiko are excellent exceptions. Although a huge number of documents—diaries and memoirs by Hirohito's chamberlains, interpreters, and other functionaries—were published in 1990, they await further studies and analyses. Thoroughgoing historical and theoretical interpretations of the modern emperor system are yet to be attempted.

3. See Chapter 4.

4. *Genten: Nihon kempo shiryo shu,* ed. Matsumoto Shoetsu (Soseisha, 1988), p. 823.

5. Kenneth Burke, *A Grammar of Motives* (New York: Prentice-Hall, 1954), pp. 430–440.

6. For a recent restatement of the doctrine of Japan as a family structure, see Murakami Yasusuke, Kimibumi Shumpei, and Sato Seizaburo, *Bunmei to shite no ie shakai* (Chuo Koronsha, 1988). This book has nothing to say about the wartime ideology, asserting a "continuity" between the prewar and postwar periods (p. 466).

7. See Matthew Arnold's *Culture and Anarchy,* especially chap. 2, "Doing as One Likes," and the conclusion. The most convenient edition is by J. Dover Wilson (Cambridge: Cambridge University Press, 1961), p. 94 and p. 204, in particular.

8. *Sekai,* March 1989, pp. 125–126.

9. According to *Asahi,* October 31, 1988, there was a marked increase in the number of letters to the editors, most of which expressed bewilderment or dissatisfaction with the coercive atmosphere.

10. *Asahi*, February 8, 1989.

11. See Chapter 9 for a general discussion of *zadankai*, which is proving to be a dominant discursive form in Japan today.

12. There were, for instance, two collections of papers from symposiums that were quickly organized on college campuses: *Hosei Heiwa Daigaku marason koza: tenno mondai o kangaeru* [Seminar at Hosei Peace University: On the Emperor Issues] (Orijin Shuppan Senta, 1989) and *Dokyumento, Meiji Gakuin Daigaku: Gakumon no jiyu to tennosei* [Document, Meiji Gakuin University: Freedom of Learning and the Emperor System] (Iwanami Shoten, 1989). The authors are admirable in their display of courage and commitment, though the substance of these short papers is unfortunately negligible.

13. "Nagasaki shicho wa sampo o yameta; 10 kiro yaseta" (The Mayor of Nagasaki Quit Strolls, Lost 10 kg); *Asahi,* April 30, 1989. These letters were published as *Nagasaki Shicho e no 7300 tsu no tegami,* ed. Kei Shobo (Kei Shobo, 1989).

14. Oda Makoto and Irokawa Daikichi organized a march after the demonstration that ultimately attracted 370 people. *Asahi shimbun,* January 22, 1990.

15. See "Kiku no tabu ka: o katta '*tokumei kibo,*'" (Many Requests for Anonymity: A Chrysanthemum Taboo?), *Mainichi shimbun,* February 9, 1989. Kumon Tatsuo, its writer, comments that during the several months around the emperor's death, over a hundred readers wrote on various issues concerning emperorism to the editors of the Kyoto edition, out of whom the overwhelming majority requested—in fear of possible retaliation—that they be left unidentified. He concludes by deploring the absence of free speech in today's Japan.

16. March 1989, pp. 125–130.

17. There were a good number of journalistic contributions by the Western experts, who were by and large laudatory of the emperor's wartime activities. As to the Japanese press's sensitivity to the outside responses, see "Uchi naru soto kara: Japanorojisuto no me" (From the Outsiders Inside: The Eyes of Foreign Japanologists), which collected opinions of the foreign scholars staying in Japan at the time of the emperor's death (*Asahi,* March 6–9, 1989). See also *Asahi,* October 19, 1988, which reported on the coverage by foreign news reporters such as Dan Rather of the "restraint." Foreign responses to the event were collected and published as *Kaigai shi ni miru tenno hodo (The News about the Emperor in the Foreign News Media),* ed. Ajia Minshu Hotei Junbi Kai (Gaifusha, 1989). See also "The Emperor and His Times," *The Japan Times,* January 9, 1989; Richard Bowring, "Hirohito," *London Review of Books,* February 2, 1989; and "Japanese Power," *London Review of Books,* June 14, 1990; and Norma Field's letter to the *New York Times* on the U.S. experts' responses to Edward Behr's BBC documentary on Hirohito, February 23, 1989.

18. Japanese periodicals advertise the detailed contents of their new issues in major daily newspapers. Thus by keeping track of the ads in *Asahi* (the Los Angeles satellite edition in my case), one can assess the general

trend of popular topics. Around the beginning of May 1989, the papers began to publish imperial news once again, though not of course to the extent of the end-of-Showa days.

19. Alexander Kojeve, *Introduction to the Reading of Hegel,* trans. James H. Nichols, Jr. (New York: Basic Books, 1969), p. 160.

20. There are a few books on the migrant workers, mostly published by small publishers, but they do not seem to interest the discursive mainstream. Utsumi Aiko and Matsui Yayori, ed., *Ajiya kara kita dekasegi rodosha tachi* (Akashi Shoten, 1988) is an example of a good but marginalized publication.

21. Julia Kristeva, *Etrangères a nous-mêmes* (Paris: Fayard, 1988) and Tzvetan Todorov, *Nous et les autres: La réflexion française sur la diversité humaine* (Paris: Edition du Seuil, 1989).

22. This need for "pressure from outside" is also mentioned by James Fallows in his "Containing Japan," *The Atlantic,* May 1989, p. 52. Fallows makes a number of good observations of today's Japan, although his historical analysis of Japanese culture must be seriously challenged, as I have discussed in Chapter 3.

23. As I looked for a film made by the Chinese or other Asians about a Japanese prison camp, I found that in 1989 a PRC–Hong Kong joint company produced a film titled *The Black Sun: Unit 731.* It is based on the notorious "Unit 731," an actual Japanese army division organized specifically to conduct biological "experimentations" on human subjects— mostly captured enemy soldiers and civilians—during the Fifteen-Year War. The film depicts the brutalities and atrocities in such sensational detail that at least this viewer was unable to sit through it. The acts of inhuman violence by the medical unit are historically "accurate," and the Chinese filmmakers' hatred is perfectly understandable. But unless the film was made for the purpose of revenge directed solely at a Japanese audience, its effect is sheer exploitation. The Japanese soldiers in the film are nothing more than sadistic brutes.

24. John Wakeman, ed., *World Authors: 1950–1970* (New York: Wilson, 1975).

25. Sato Tadao, *Oshima Nagisa no sekai* (Tokyo: Asahi Bunko, 1987), p. 409.

26. Oshima Nagisa, *Kotaeru!* (*I Answer!*) (Tokyo: Dagereo Shuppan, 1983), p. 8.

27. Laurens Van der Post, *The Seed and the Sower* (New York: William Morrow and Company, 1963).

28. Published first in 1954, it was incorporated into *The Seed and the Sower* in 1963. It was reissued as a book by The Hogarth Press in 1972.

29. See his ponderous and banal *The Prisoner and the Bomb* (New York: William Morrow, 1971), published in Britain under the title of *The Night of the New Moon.* Van der Post equates Japanese brutality in the treatment of prisoners of war with the American devastation by atomic bombs. But the problem of the book is not so much its wrong ideas as its self-important air.

30. I do not mean that *Merry Christmas* is as pregnant with possibilities

as *Lord Jim*. But Van der Post has, it seems to me, obviously read Conrad. Aside from the novels' locations, the two share a great deal in form. Marlowe, *Lord Jim*'s narrator, receives a bundle of papers by and about Jim after he returns to London, for instance. Even the last scene, in which Jim walks up to face his death, is not unlike Celliers' fully conscious act of self-destruction. Lord Jim's spotless snow-white dress and Jacques Celliers' pure white-blond appearance have a great deal in common, too, in their colonialist "difference" from the Asian natives. I suspect that it is precisely what attracted Oshima Nagisa.

31. In a special issue of *Wide Angle* devoted to Oshima Nagisa (Vol. 9, No. 2, 1987), Adam Knee argues that Celliers is a "Christ figure" (p. 58). There is nothing wrong with the idea, since I suppose Christ is meant to stand for—and died for—everyone. But Knee might have thought a little bit more about why Oshima wanted to introduce Jesus into his film. See note 33, Chapter 4.

32. Van der Post asserts repeatedly that the Korean members of the Japanese army were more brutal and fanatic (*The Seed and the Sower*, p. 140; *The Prisoner and the Bomb*, p. 138, e.g.) without any further explanation. This is likely to be Van der Post's adoption of general anti-Korean feelings from the Japanese. Oshima's addition of this episode, where the Dutch victim does not complain and even goes to the extent of killing himself after the Korean's execution, seems to suggest Oshima's sympathy with the Koreans in general. The "rape" here is a consensual relationship comparable to the principal liaisons of Yonoi and Celliers, Hara and Lawrence.

33. Van der Post seems more interested in the two brothers, one spiritual and the other physical, both beautiful in different ways, than in the two officers, one white and the other yellow, both beautiful, getting together somehow in the battlefield. The theme of betrayal and redemption is more conspicuous in *The Seed and the Sower* than in the film. Oshima seems to be more interested in reading it as a story of cross-cultural and interracial encounter.

34. *Kotaeru!*, pp. 26–27.

35. Interview with Sato Tadao, *Oshima Nagisa*, p. 416.

36. Oshima published a number of books explaining his films and the problems he faced in them. Among them are *Sengo eiga: Hakai to sozo* (Tokyo: Sanichi Shobo, 1963), *Ma to zankoku no hasso* (Tokyo: Haga Shoten, 1966), and *Taiken teki sengo eizo ron* (Tokyo: Asahi Sensho, 1975).

37. The quotation is Oshima's addition; it is not in Van der Post's text.

38. In an article called "Nihon eiga no tembo" ("The Prospect of the Japanese Film") that concludes an eight-volume study of the Japanese film, *Nihon no eiga* (Tokyo: Iwanami Shoten, 1985–88), Oshima Nagisa declares the end of the Japanese film. As for the future, he proposes "internationalization." "A society or a race can maintain homogeneity until the wind of modernization begins to blow. Modernization is at the same time internationalization" (Vol. 8, 1988, p. 318). Are *Max, mon amour* as well as *Merry*

Christmas his models for this internationalization? (*Nihon no eiga* was co-edited by Imamura Shohei, Sato Tadao, Shindo Kanehito, Tsurumi Shunsuke, and Yamada Yoji.)

39. The budget for the film was six million dollars (*Kotaeru!*, p. 37), while his earlier films cost far less. The famed *Ceremony* (*Gishiki,* 1971), for instance, was the most expensive movie Oshima had made, but its budget was 20 million yen ($50,000). His *Town of Love and Hope* (*Ai to kibo no machi,* 1959), according to Oshima, cost 10 million yen ($30,000 at the exchange rate of the time). *Taiken teki sengo eizo ron* (Tokyo: Asahi Sensho, 1975), p. 292.

40. "On Ethnographic Allegory," *Writing Culture: The Poetics and Politics of Ethnography,* ed. James Clifford and George E. Marcus (Berkeley and Los Angeles: University of California Press, 1986), p. 116.

41. See Stephen Heath's reading of *Death by Hanging* in his *Questions of Cinema* (Bloomington: Indiana University Press, 1981), pp. 64–69.

8. Gathering Voices

1. See Chapter 2.

2. There are numerous studies of the early days in the civil rights movement in the sixties, among which are: John J. Ansbro, *Martin Luther King, Jr.: The Making of a Mind* (New York: Orbis Books, 1982); Taylor Branch, *Parting the Waters: America in the King Years 1954–63* (New York: Simon and Schuster, 1988); George Breitman, ed. *Malcolm X Speaks* (New York: Grove Press, 1966); Clayborne Carson, *In Struggle: SNCC and the Black Awakening of the 1960s* (Cambridge, Mass.: Harvard University Press, 1981); Council of Federal Organizations, *Mississippi Black Power* (New York: Random House, 1965); James Farmer, *Freedom—When?* (New York: Random House, 1965); James H. Meredith, *Three Years in Mississippi* (Bloomington: Indiana University Press, 1966); and Aldon D. Morris, *The Origins of the Civil Rights Movements* (New York: Free Press, 1984).

3. In the United States and elsewhere, abolitionism generated a discourse concerned with race issues. Anti-slavery nevertheless had a historically discrete trajectory from the later anti-racism, when not only legal and political rights but a broader range of historical, cultural, genetic, economic, and other aspects of equality were raised.

4. For nearly a decade after the publication of Said's *Orientalism,* there were numerous conferences held to discuss the impact of the book. The Association of Asian Studies, the Association of Anthropological Studies, not to say the Modern Language Association and the Middle Eastern Studies Association, sponsored meetings and symposia. There were of course countless workshops and discussions on university and college campuses.

5. See, for instance, Laurie Bebbington, "The Mexico International Women's Year Conference," *Meanjin Quarterly* (Summer 1975), pp. 373–

379, and Hanna Papanek, "The Work of Women: Postscript from Mexico City," *Signs: Journal of Women in Culture and Society,* (Autumn 1975), pp. 215–226.

6. See *Off Our Backs,* vol. 15 (October 1985). See also Angela Y. Davis, "Finishing the Agenda: Reflections on Forum '85, Nairobi, Kenya" and "Women in Egypt: A Personal View," *Women, Culture, and Politics* (New York: Random House, 1989), pp. 109–154.

7. At the time of World War II, forty women were enrolled in imperial universities, compared with 29,600 men, and there was not a single female student at the Imperial Universities of Tokyo and Kyoto. Joy Paulson, "Evolution of the Feminine Ideal," *Women in Changing Japan,* ed. Joyce Lebra, Joy Paulson, and Elizabeth Powers (Stanford: Stanford University Press, 1976), p. 16.

8. See Takamure Itsue, *Josei no rekishi* (Kodansha, 1972), Vol. 2, Chap. 4, Sect. 2, "Ryosai kembo kyoiku," pp. 79–92. Takamure's book is perhaps the most authoritative and comprehensive treatment of the history of Japanese women. It is a remarkable achievement in the presentation of facts and resources. Her Eurocentric notion of "progress" as well as her embrace of aspects of wartime ideologies, however, distort her interpretations of numerous Japanese events and situations. I believe that Takamure's judgment regarding the source of the "good wife, wise mother" ideology is correct, but her characterization of it as a "pre-bourgeois residue of [Western] medievalism" is quite askew.

9. Takamure, *Josei no rekishi,* Vol. 2, Chap. 5, Sect. 2, "Senkusha Hiratsuka Raicho," pp. 268–314.

10. See John David Morley's *Pictures from the Water Trade: Adventures of a Westerner in Japan* (New York: Harper & Row, 1985) for an amusing, though essentialized and distorted, view of the sex and entertainment industry today.

11. For studies of earlier "rebel women," see Mikiso Hane, *Reflections on the Way to the Gallows: Rebel Women in Prewar Japan* (Berkeley: University of California Press and Pantheon Books, 1988) and Sharon L. Sievers, *Flowers in Salt: The Beginnings of Feminist Consciousness in Modern Japan* (Stanford: Stanford University Press, 1983). Miriam Silverberg describes the idea of "modern women" in the 1920s and 1930s in "The Modern Girl as Militant," *Recreating the Japanese Woman,* ed. Gail Bernstein (Berkeley: University of California Press, 1991). See also Silverberg's *Changing Song: The Marxist Manifestos of Nakano Shigeharu* (Princeton: Princeton University Press, 1990).

12. The Minister of Agriculture in Prime Minister Uno's cabinet asked "Can women be useful in the world of politics?" on July 7, 1989, and made the situation worse afterward by refusing to apologize ("I have said nothing wrong"). The Vice–Prime Minister of the conservative party had said in January that "Mrs. Thatcher is married [so she is a capable politician], but Miss Doi [the head of the Socialist Party] has no man [in her life]. She

doesn't know men. . . . ." Such statements, together with the revelation of Prime Minister Uno's sex scandal, contributed a great deal to the serious crisis in the Liberal Democratic Party. All the turmoil, at the same time, was overshadowed by the immense scale of the political bribe and donation scandals that involved practically every senior member of the party.

13. *Asahi,* satellite edition, August 1989. Miura is a novelist and critic, married to a well-known writer, Sono Ayako.

14. Ihara Saikaku's *A Life of an Amorous Man* (*Koshoku ichidai otoko,* 1682) and Ryutei Tanehiko's *The False Murasaki's Rustic Genji* (*Nise Murasaki inaka Genji,* 1825) are both parodies of *The Tale of Genji.* Aside from such full-scale literary works, *Genji* is seen in many unexpected places, such as an illustration of a comic tale, *Capricious Eels Broiled in Edo* (*Edo mumare uwaki no kabayaki,* 1785), by Santo Kyoden.

15. See *Two Gardens* (*Futatsu no niwa*), for instance. Discussing Miyamoto's debt to Shiga Naoya, Honda Shugo points to the firm self-affirmation ("ganko na jiga kotei") that is a common feature of the two writers' work. Honda is too imprecise in his terminology to see a sharp difference between them. Honda Shugo, "Kaisetsu," *Nihon no bungaku,* 45, *Miyamoto Yuriko* (Tokyo: Chuo Koronsha, 1969), pp. 525–526. Miyamoto herself is quite clear about the difference between Shiga's literary strategy and his self-indulgence. See her conversation with a number of critics in "Konnichi no bungaku: Miyamoto Yuriko o kakonde," *Zenshu,* vol. 27, pp. 346–357.

16. Itagaki Naoko, *Fujin sakka hyoden* (Tokyo: Nihon Tosho Senta, 1987), p. 242. A so-called Dutch-scholar (*rangakusha*) in the mid-nineteenth century, Nishimura Shigeki published a number of books on Western history and education. He later tutored Emperor Meiji on Western ideas. Despite such exposure to Western culture, he remained an uncompromising Confucian. He also wrote a book on women's education and ethics called *A Mirror for Women* (*Fujo kagami*). See William R. Braisted, trans., *Meiroku Zasshi: Journal of the Japanese Enlightenment* (Cambridge, Mass.: Harvard University Press, 1976), and Donald H. Shively, "Nishimura Shigeki: A Confucian View of Modernization," in Marius B. Jansen, ed., *Changing Japanese Attitudes Toward Modernization* (Princeton: Princeton University Press, 1965).

17. According to Yuasa, she herself was a lesbian, and their relationship was indeed an intimate one. As to their close relationship, Miyamoto's letters to Yuasa that constitute vol. 26 of *Zenshu* (564 pp.) are the best reference. See also Hirosawa Yumi's interview with Yuasa, Special Edition, *Takarajima,* 64, *Onna o aisuru onnatachi no monogatari* (May 1987), pp. 67–73. (According to Ehara Yumiko, this special *Takarajima* issue is "the first document that discusses lesbianism in Japan." See "Feminizumu no 70 nendai to 80 nendai," *Feminizumu ronso: 70 nendai kara 90 nendai e,* ed. Ehara Yumiko [Keiso Shobo, 1990], p. 43.) There is a rough outline of Miyamoto's life with Yuasa in Itagaki Naoko's *Fujin Sakka Hyoden*

(Tokyo, 1987), especially pp. 272 and 275–276, and in Miyamoto Kenji, *Yuriko Tsuiso* (Daisan Shobo, 1951), p. 37.

18. See Chapter 4.

19. There was an attempt to unseat him by the younger members of the party in June 1990 ("Miyamoto taisei e no fuman: Kyosa kabu toin ra," *Asahi*, satellite edition, June 15, 1990); later *Asahi* articles in July indicate, however, that he successfully fought back the challenge.

20. In spite of the general neglect of Miyamoto Yuriko and her work in the United States, there are a few studies, all published in the *Bulletin of Concerned Asian Scholars*. Noriko Mizuta Lippit, "Literature, Ideology, and Women's Happiness: The Autobiographical Novels of Miyamoto Yuriko," *BCAS*, Vol. 10, No. 2 (April–June 1978); Brett de Bary, "After the War: Translations from Miyamoto Yuriko," *BCAS*, Vol. 16, No. 2 (April–June 1984); and Susan Phillips, "Beyond Borders: Class Struggle and Feminist Humanism in *Banshu heiya*," *BCAS*, Vol. 19, No. 1 (January–March 1987).

21. *Miyamoto Yuriko zenshu*, 26 (Shin Nihon Shuppansha, 1981), pp. 56–64, especially pp. 61–63.

22. According to a recently published bibliographical guide to books on women's studies (*Josei gaku gaido bukku*, ed. Joseigaku Kenkyujo [Shibundo, 1988]), the category called "The Woman's Mind and Body: Body, Psychology, Life-Cycle, Sex, and Prostitution" lists about 160 items, of which those that discuss sexuality in general terms—rather than specific topics such as childbirth or prostitution—are rather few, and most among them seem to be popular and elementary introductions to sexuality. What is interesting is that of those books that directly deal with sexuality, a vast majority are translations from Western books, and the books by Japanese authors are mostly by men. In short, still relatively few Japanese women write about female—or any other—sexuality. As for the representations of male violence against the female body in Japanese comics, there are unpublished articles by Ann Allison and Sandra Buckley that suggest that the male fantasies in the comics are not at all simple escape or diversion but instruments of control and domination over the female.

23. Earl Jackson's unpublished article, "Queering Japan," explains the West's feminization of Japan in terms of homoeroticism and Orientalist hegemonism.

24. *To Live and to Write: Selections by Japanese Women Writers*, ed. Yukiko Tanaka (Seattle: The Seal Press, 1987) has a few excerpts and brief explanatory notes on Miyamoto, Hirabayashi, and Sata, among others. More of Enchi's work has been translated in recent years than work by others.

25. Of course, this does not mean that the three were preoccupied with their material betterment alone. After the war, Sata joined the Japan Communist Party and belonged until she was expelled in 1951. She was aware of interracial issues, as can be seen in *Juei* (*The Shadows of Trees*, 1970–

1972), which describes a friendship between a Chinese and a Japanese painter. One of her most recent works, incidentally, is a biography of Miyamoto Yuriko.

26. Enchi Fumiko, *The Waiting Years,* trans. John Bester (Tokyo, New York, and San Francisco: Kodansha International, 1971), p. 202.

27. There is one exception: a daughter-in-law whose sensuality apparently matches her father-in-law's. The two engage in an illicit liaison with no regard for the other woman, or even for the adulteress's husband, the master's son.

28. One of the most fascinating documents concerning the ongoing employment discrimination between the sexes is the annual publication in the *Asahi* newspaper of the breakdown of available positions among Japan's leading corporations. The list is divided for four-year college, two-year college, and high school graduates, executive career positions and "general" (meaning clerical) positions, administrative vs. engineering jobs, and, more important, between male and female positions. As can be easily surmised, the executive positions are mostly for male college graduates, and in many companies no positions at all are open to female college graduates. To take a few examples: Shimizu Construction Company (75 open for men, 0 for women), Kanebuchi Chemical Industry (25 men, 0 women), Mitsubushi Metallurgy (25 men, 0 women), Toyota (150 men, 0 women). Among more progressive companies are Asahi Beer (100 men, 150 women), Toshiba (300 men, 50 women), Fujitsu (250 men, 100 women; in the engineering category, 750 men, 250 women), Nintendo (10 men, 10 women). Many companies announce that they will hire men or women without preference, but the actual records show that men are overwhelmingly chosen (Sumitomo Trust Bank announced in 1990 that it has no sexual preference, but in 1989 it hired 155 men and 13 women; likewise, in 1989 Nikko Security hired 356 men and 24 women). Finally, the positions open to men are all potentially executive training jobs, while those open to women are clearly divided between executive career jobs (few) and general clerical jobs (many). *Asahi,* July 2, 1990.

29. See Iwao Sumiko and Hara Hiroko, *Joseigaku koto hajime* (Kodansha, 1979). See also Ueno Chizuko, ed., *Shufu ronso o yomu,* 2 vols. (Keiso Shobo, 1982); Aoki Yayoi, *Josei: Sono sei no shinwa* (Orijin Shuppan Senta, 1982); Dorothy Robbins-Mowry, *The Hidden Sun: Women of Modern Japan* (Boulder, Colo.: Westview Press, 1983); Esashi Akiko, "Shufu no za," Kodo Seicho and Kangaeru Kai, eds., *Kodo seicho to Nihon-jin,* Part 2: *Kazoku no seikatsu no monogatari* (Nihon Edita Skuru Shuppanbu, 1985), pp. 197–225; Sandra Buckley and Vera Mackie, "Women in the New Japanese State," *Democracy in Contemporary Japan,* ed. Gavan McCormack and Yoshio Sugimoto (Armonk, N. Y.: M. E. Sharpe, 1986), pp. 173–185; Anne E. Imamura, *Urban Japanese Housewives: At Home and in the Community* (Honolulu: University of Hawaii Press, 1987); and Vera Mackie, "Feminist Politics in Japan," *New Left Review.* No. 167 (1988), pp. 53–76.

Ehara Yumiko, ed., *Feminizumu ronso: 70 nendai kara 90 nendai e* (Keiso Shobo, 1990) is helpful in locating various theoretical gender issues in Japan now. A markedly cultural-essentialist view of Japanese women is expressed by Merry White in "The Virtue of Japanese Mothers: Cultural Definitions of Women's Lives," *Daedalus,* Vol. 116, No. 3 (Summer 1987), pp. 149–204.

30. *Shufu ronso o yomu,* ed. Ueno Chizuko, 2 vols. (Keiso Shobo, 1982), collects documents going back to the 1950s that deal with the issue of the housewife. The place occupied by the wife in a family is a principal—though not central—issue, and as such the book offers significant information concerning the postwar history of the women's movement in Japan. At the same time, as the editor acknowledges, "the conditions around the housewife have not fundamentally changed since [1955]." See also *Kodo seicho to Nihon-jin,* Part I, *Tanjo kara shi made no monogatari;* Part II, *Kazoku no seikatsu no monogatari,* ed. Kodo Seichoki and Kangaeru Kai (Nihon Editaa Sukuuuru Shuppanbu, 1985), and Ehara, *Feminizumu ronso.*

Three more items might be mentioned here: (1) Although more women attend college than men, they overwhelmingly choose two-year colleges over four-year universities, majoring in subjects such as education and home economics. See annual government reports such as *Kokumin seikatsu hakusho* or *Wagakuni no kyoiku suijun.* (2) An interesting development is the establishment of a women's bookstore, Kyokado, in Kyoto, which serves as a networking center for feminist activities, publishing books and planning events and projects. (3) Centers for women's studies are gradually multiplying among women's colleges, such as Ochanomizu Women's College. It is quite possible that this institutionalization might accelerate the feminist movement in Japan.

31. Trans. Geraldine Harcourt (New York: Pantheon, 1991).

32. A grammatical category of adjectives and adverbs that is hard to define. A word of this category usually consists of a duplication of a two-syllable phrase *(hira-hira, kari-kari, musha-musha)* that supposedly describes "phonetically" the manner of an act or a condition. A master in the use of *gitaigo,* subtly generating comic, ironic, or sentimental effects, is Dazai Osamu, Tsushima's father. One who avoids its use, as does Tsushima, is Mishima Yukio.

33. *Yama o hashiru onna* (Kodansha, 1984), p. 251.

34. For comments on Dazai Osamu, Tsushima's father, see my *Accomplices of Silence: The Modern Japanese Novel* (Berkeley: University of California Press, 1974), chap. 5.

35. The word comes from a milk carton Koko happens to have seen before going to sleep. Thus the "sharply peaked mountain of ice," which continues in her cosmogenic dream, is obviously phallic but is still frozen and unconjunctive. It is a fitting opening for the story of a woman's rigorously isolated identity, although the prose is quite dense, as if the character—and author?—is unwilling to read her own dream too precisely.

36. *Child of Fortune,* trans. Geraldine Harcourt (Kodansha International Ltd., 1983), p. 60.

9. Conversation and Conference

1. See Chapter 2.

2. Chalmers Johnson, "Rethinking Japanese Politics: A Godfather Reports," *Freedom at Issue,* November–December 1989, p. 8.

3. *Sekai* (August 1988), pp. 201–215.

4. In his lecture at the Center for East Asian Studies at the University of Chicago in 1986, Kurimoto Shinichiro expressed this judgment, although according to those who were present he did not provide reasons for it. There are numerous expressions of this kind in unrestrainedly chauvinistic magazines such as *Shokun, Seiron,* or the popular weeklies.

5. Frantz Fanon's description of the colonial situation in *Black Skin, White Masks,* trans. Lam Markmann (New York: Grove Press, 1967), is surprisingly applicable to some aspects of Japan's intellectual scene. As for the ambivalence in question, see a *zadankai* called "Sengo bungaku was sakoku no nakade tsukurareta" ("Postwar Literature Was Produced in a State of National Isolation"), *Bungakkai,* June 1985, pp. 206–232, among Karatani Kojin, Aono Satoshi, Sakamoto Ryuichi, and Nakagami Kenji.

6. Japanese cultural managers and planners such as the Ministry of Education and leading newspaper and book publishers as well as research universities have been organizing a great number of international conferences inviting prominent artists, writers, and scholars from all over the world. This does not mean, however, that genuine exchanges are in fact taking place: for one thing, the mannerisms of Japanese scholars at such meetings—polite, formal, and self-enclosed—seem to persist; for another, visiting scholars—except for the experts on Japan—tend to remain uninterested and uninvolved in Japanese cultural problematics.

7. I am mainly concerned here with the conversational forms that find their way into print. There is of course another mode, the televised conversation, which shares many traits with them.

8. See Chapter 2 for a more extensive discussion of orality and literacy.

9. There was a *zadankai* a few years ago that ended with the most senior of the participants calling his opponent speaker "bakayaro," an equivalent of "damned bastard." The event is memorable for its unusual surliness and uncivility. Quite entertaining as a cross-generational squabble, the discussion yielded few insightful observations. "Sengo bungaku no naibu to gaibu" ("The Interiors and Exteriors of Postwar Literature"), *Bungakkai,* August 1985, pp. 182–215.

10. Careful documentation of references is not a general practice even in written discourse in Japan. I don't know the exact nature of the relationship between this reluctance to cite and the orality of discourse, but either way the outcome seems to be a marked disjuncture and isolation among studies,

as if everyone were always starting his or her speculation from scratch. In a more generalized context, Maruyama Masao sees a similar unwillingness to structure and integrate ideas into a public syntax. His *Nihon no shiso* (*Thoughts in Japan;* Iwanami Shoten, 1961) is full of such observations.

11. The situation may be quickly changing, however. Most Japanese long assumed that Westerners did not understand their language, and that whatever was written in Japanese would not reach Western eyes. Thus many remarks about the people they met or the experiences they had while visiting Europe or the United States would not have been published had they suspected the Westerners involved might have access to them. Of course, the acquisition of Japanese is rapidly spreading in the West now. In fact, if the speakers are of any academic or social consequence, it is hard to imagine that their comments could be successfully contained within Japan.

12. Translated into English by Saimaru International as *Building a New Japan: A Plan for Remodeling the Japanese Archipelago* (Saimaru International, 1973).

13. "A Multifunctionpolis Scheme for the 21st Century: Basic Concept," MFP Planning Committee, the Ministry of International Trade and Industry [MITI], Tokyo, September 30, 1987. Its Japanese text is dated September 17, 1987. There are reports of this project in Australian newspapers (*Sydney Morning Herald,* June 9, 1988) and in *Nihon Keizai Shinbun,* February 1988. As I understand it, the MFP project was accepted by the Australian government, but vigorous protests by its citizens have so far deterred its realization.

14. Whether any government is capable of designing such a plan, not to say enforcing it, is of course questionable. In "Eastern Economics," Eamonn Fingleton suggests exactly this possibility, although he attributes the maintenance of the "stratospheric land prices" to Japan's policy of keeping the country free of foreign business outlets. *The Atlantic,* October 1990, pp. 72–85.

15. The sole exception may be the famous Harajuku streets, where young men and women gather to show off their *outré* outfits and dance skills. The authorities are tolerant of the weekend performances, most probably because of their largely apolitical orientation—although their challenge to bourgeois decorum can lead to serious rebellion.

16. To take two examples: Tsukuba University and Yokohama National Engineering University.

17. Tokyo's difficult housing situation is too well known for a lengthy explanation here. In brief, the housing cost is truly exorbitant: as many Americans know by now, the real estate value of the whole of Japan—one twenty-fifth of the United States in area—is now estimated at least twice, some say five times, that of the entire United States. (Of course, these figures are meaningless: should there be mass sales and purchases in the two countries, the values would fall and rise, respectively, to reverse the balance. Still, the disproportionate rates prevail at the moment, enabling

Japanese investors to acquire choice properties in the United States.) Ordinary citizens without substantial inheritance cannot own their own homes in the city; they must travel a considerable distance from the city in search of affordable housing. They do have money to buy automobiles, but they are of little use, since there is no parking space in the inner city. Besides, the few highways are frequently at a standstill. Those who insist on living in the city and can afford it must get accustomed to an extremely small apartment or condominium. The class division that is slowly developing again seems to run along the line of real estate inheritance. The 1989 housing costs, according to the official 1989 *White Paper on People's Life* in Tokyo (*Kokumin seikatsu hakusho,* November 1989), are for an average residence, $558,000; for an average apartment, $375,000 ($ = 150 yen).

18. Quoted by Fredric Jameson in his foreword to Jean-François Lyotard, *The Post Modern Condition: A Report on Knowledge,* trans. Geoff Bennington and Brian Massumi (Minneapolis: University of Minnesota Press, 1979), p. xv.

19. The United States, too, has its share of *zadankai.* Perhaps related to the gradual increase in the use of the format on television, periodicals publish from time to time transcribed conversations as well as interviews. There is a publication called *Interview,* devoted (naturally) to interviews; interviews with individual writers are a staple of literary magazines such as *Paris Review* and *American Poetry Review;* there are even books that collect *zadankai* (e.g., Hal Foster, ed., *Discussions in Contemporary Culture,* Number One [Seattle: Bay Press, 1987]), but their number is still incomparably small. The December 22, 1988, issue of the *New York Review of Books* has a "symposium" on "The Election and the Future," but it is not so much a *zadankai* as a group of separate essays by nine writers.

Epilogue

1. "Murakami Haruki no fukei: 1973 nen no pin-booru," *Shuuen o megutte* (Fukutake Shoten, 1990), p. 75–113.

2. For some reason, Murakami seems to believe his prose resembles the actual language people speak. Many writers tend to hold this foolish idea, but a sophisticate like Murakami? Murakami repeats such a characterization of his writing in dialogues with Murakami Ryu, *Wooku, donto ran* (Kodansha, 1981). In another interview with an *Asahi* reporter, he uses the word *sunao* (naive, innocent, honest, pliant, straight) several times to describe his work and language.

3. "Onna no ko," "Bundan hokai no naka no 'bungei fukko,'" *Shukan Dokushojin* No. 1763 (December 19, 1988).

4. "Young, Slangy Mix of U.S. and Japan," October 21, 1989, and "Letter from Tokyo: Brando, the Stones and Banana Yoshimoto," June 1990.

5. *Kitchin* (Fukutake Shoten, 1988).

6. In fact, Yoshimoto has a supporter in Nakamura Shinichiro, a respected senior critic, who is quoted by Janice Fuhrman, "Japan's Literary Brat Pack Finding Their Place in the Sun," *Los Angeles Times,* September 15, 1989, as saying that Yoshimoto broke new ground by "totally ignoring traditional literary accomplishment and describing feelings and senses freely. I felt a new literature came from this defiant attitude of keeping these things on the page whether or not they fit the old rules of literature."

7. The writer's name is Baba Keiichi, *Chuo koron* (June 1990), pp. 38–39.

8. Karl Schoenberger, "Japanese Film: The Sinking Sun," *Los Angeles Times,* April 5, 1990.

9. *Manen gannen no futtoboru* (Kodansha, 1967); trans. John Bester (Kodansha International, 1974).

10. See my *As We Saw Them: The First Japanese Embassy to the United States (1860)* (Berkeley: University of California Press, 1979).

11. There is an excellent study of *The Silent Cry* by Mary N. Layoun, "Hunting Whales and Elephants, (Re)producing Narratives," *Travels of a Genre: The Modern Novel and Ideology* (Princeton: Princeton University Press, 1990), chap. 7, pp. 209–242. Her detection of Oe's inclination toward centralism is both shrewd and important.

12. *Atarashii hito yo mezameyo* (Kodansha, 1983). An English translation will be published by Kodansha International in the fall of 1991 under the title *Rouse Up, O, Young Men of a New Age,* a quotation from William Blake's *Milton.*

Acknowledgments

Earlier versions of several portions of this book have been published as separate articles. Because of the nature of the argument, some were first published in foreign countries or in translation. At every stage, revisions and alterations have been made, often quite extensively. I am grateful to the following journals for permission to reprint this material in this volume: *Report on International Conference on East Asian Literature* (Seoul, Korea) and *South Atlantic Quarterly* for "Against the Native Grain"; *Culture and History* (Copenhagen) for "The 'Great Divide' Once Again"; *Raritan* for "Thinking Aloud in Japan" (here revised and renamed "Conversation and Conference"), reprinted by permission from *Raritan: A Quarterly Review*, vol. 9, no. 2 (Fall 1989), copyright © 1989 by *Raritan*, 165 College Ave., New Brunswick, N.J. 08903. These and "Who Decides, and Who Speaks?" have been translated into Chinese, Japanese, and Korean, and I am grateful to the editors of the following journals for their interest: *Sege ni munhak* (Seoul, Korea); *Gendai shiso* (Tokyo); *Sengo Nihon no seishin shi* (Tokyo: Iwanami Shoten); *Herumesu* (Tokyo); *Shiso no kagaku* (Tokyo); and *Culture and Aesthetics* (Taiwan: Lien-ching Press).

Many people have read this book at different stages in various forms, and I am especially thankful for comments and encouragement from the following friends: Eqbal Ahmad, Martha L. Archibald, Nancy Armstrong, Chen Ying-Chen, Noam Chomsky, James Clifford, Brett De Bary, Arif Dirlik, John Dower, Ted Fowler, James Fujii, Carol Gluck, H. D. Harootunian, Fredric Jameson, Chalmers Johnson, Kim Uchang, S.-Y. Kuroda, Mary Layoun, Marianne McDonald, Earl Miner, Tetsuo Najita, Oe Kenzaburo, Richard Okada, Frances Rosenbluth, Naoki Sakai, Miriam Silverberg, John Solt, Leonard Tennenhouse, Christena Turner, Janet Walker, Rob Wilson, and Wai-lim Yip. Eiji Yutani, the head of the Japanese Collection of the Library at the University of California, San Diego, once again supplied needed materials under extremely difficult circumstances. I am thankful for his able and generous help. I owe a great deal to Jennifer Snodgrass of Harvard University Press, who gave a meticulous reading to the manuscript. I am also grateful to the following institutions for grants and fellowships: University of California, Berkeley; the Japan Foundation; the Joint Committee on Japanese Studies, American Council of Learned Societies and Social Science Research Council; the University of California Humanities Research Institute; and the Organized Research Projects in the Humanities, University of California, San Diego. I have presented portions of the book at numerous colleges and universities, and comments and responses have been gratefully—but at times, defiantly—incorporated into this present form.

Index